Halfway to Paradise

Also by Patsi Bale Cox

A Country Music Christmas
50 Years Down a Country Road
The View from Nashville
Jenny Jones: My Story
Nickel Dreams: My Life with Tanya Tucker
Still Woman Enough: A Memoir with Loretta Lynn

Halfway to Paradise

TONY ORLANDO
with Patsi Bale Cox

St. Martin's Press ♒ New York

For my family, my world—
Frannie, Jon, and Jenny Rose

Contents

Contents

Acknowledgments

As I finish this memoir, I'm back in Las Vegas, playing a three-month gig at the historic Golden Nugget. My wife, Frannie, and daughter, Jenny Rose, are with me. Mamma now lives in Las Vegas, so she comes to the casino. Frannie's mother, Rose, comes, as well. My son, Jon, flies in between his own gigs as a stand-up comic. I'm seeing a lot of old friends, and people seem to love the show. I just won Best All Around Celebrity Performer at the Best of Las Vegas Awards. Life is good.

I'm lucky to have been in the business this long. It never fails to amaze and thrill me that I can still fill a room and earn a living for my family and my band in a business that caters to a youthful image, an industry that is always looking for the next big thing. It's been an amazing journey. I've lost a lot of people along the way, and I almost lost myself during a couple of very bad years. But for the most part, it's all been good.

I like the fact that I've finally earned my stripes as an adult.

For most of my life, I felt like sixteen years old was just the other day. I never felt grown up. Now, at fifty-seven, I watch my son, Jon, succeed at his chosen career, my daughter, Jenny Rose, blossom into a beautiful, wise young lady, my wife, Frannie, remain my best friend—and I finally feel like I'm looking at life through adult eyes.

Just as our lives are the result of family, friends—relationships—careers are never the result of one person's talent. They come about through the efforts of a lot of people. In my case, I was lucky enough to find a mentor, a champion, at the beginning of what I refer to as each "chunk" of my life. I owe a great debt of gratitude to all of them.

First there was Donnie Kirshner, who gave me the chance to sing, to write, to interact with people of the caliber of Bobby Darin, Jack Keller, Carole King, Gerry Goffin, Barry Mann, and Cynthia Weil. Those people taught me to turn my love of songs into a lifetime occupation. Donnie must have been crazy to bank on that overweight kid who walked into his office back in 1960. Thank God for crazy people.

If you look at your life with bookends, then Donnie stands in the front half, and Norman Brokaw stands at the other. It was Norman who gave life to the second half of my career, when others wouldn't have given me a chance in hell. The interesting thing is these two men saw the same thing—a largely untapped soul singer.

In between those bookends came men like Dick Clark and Murray the K—the star-makers. I was but one of many. Those two men have given life to countless careers, have given more to the music industry than most, and are owed huge debts by the industry. Their styles were completely different. Dick was the even hand, the gentleman of the business. Murray was the flamboyant, often outrageous showman—the inventor of submarine racing. Yet the results were the same: creative opportunity for hundreds—thousands—of hopeful artists.

When Beatlemania sunk the teen idol ship, the song publishing industry threw out a life jacket. Wally Schuster, the king of the song pluggers, gave me the shot at Robbins, Feist & Miller. And when my work with him resulted in the call from Neal

Acknowledgments

Anderson at April Blackwood, Wally patted me on the back and said, "Go for it, kid." When Hank Medress and Dave Appell thought they could make me a pop star, one of the greatest record men of all, CBS chief Clive Davis, patted me on the back and said, "Go for it, kid."

Fred Silverman took the biggest chance of all. He gave Telma, Joyce, and I television show. Meeting all the guest stars throughout the show was something akin to following along behind my father, Leo Cassivitis, through the magical world of the garment district, where he was almost royalty. I felt I was walking through an impossible dream.

And that brings me back to that other bookend, William Morris chairman, Norman Brokaw. I have no illusions about what others saw before Norman brought my career back to life. They saw a has-been bubblegummer who'd wasted every good card he'd been dealt.

Norman demanded a re-deal.

Norman Brokaw's sons, David and Sandy, have become very important cogs in the wheel that turns my career. William Morris's Mel Berger is an example of the great impact the Brokaws have had in my life. It was to Mel that David and Sandy took their vision when they conceived of a book about a kid from Tar Beach. Mel took the concept to a lady who agreed that we had a story to tell—a sharp, patient, and determined St. Martin's editor, Elizabeth Beier. Someone once said that the job of an editor is both the hardest and most rewarding in the world. I hope the hard part is over and the rewarding part has begun for Elizabeth.

If you look up the definitions of loyalty, intelligent creativity, and friendship in the dictionary, you will find the name Rob Wilcox, who has worked with me on press relations for years. As he moves on to a new and exciting chapter in his own life, I thank him for being such a vital part of mine.

ICM agent Marty Beck is the definition of old school integrity and good agenting.

Acknowledgments

Finally, it became all the more clear while writing this book just how important Telma Hopkins and Joyce Vincent Wilson were to me on so many levels throughout the years. In the end, thirty years later, we still have pride in what we accomplished as a group. Most important, through the ups and downs of the years since 1970, we remain brother and sisters in the end.

Preface

About a year before I began work on this memoir, I went home to Tar Beach. It was the first time in several years that I had stood on those asphalt rooftops in New York City. I was filming a VH-1 special, *Behind the Music,* and the show's producers asked me to do some very difficult things—to take a look back at some of the worst times of my life, to relive failures, losses, and despair. But in many ways the filming turned out to be a godsend, because I went back in time to some of my happiest days in the old neighborhood.

On West Twenty-first Street everybody's business was everybody's business, and everybody liked it that way. There was Sam the grocer, who lived two buildings from my tenement, and the other Sam, who owned the candy store on the corner of Eighth Avenue and Twenty-first Street. We knew when things were good and things were bad with their businesses and their families. We knew who was having *pasteles* for dinner and who was having goulash. It was a time of stickball games in the street, of cooling off in the water spewing from fire hydrants.

When people ask me how I can live in Branson, Missouri—a small town in the Ozarks—I always tell them I grew up on West

Twenty-first Street between Seventh and Eighth, and *it* was a small town.

Over the years I've tried to get back to those streets as often as possible, to my old neighborhood, my touchstone. But at no time did I return with such a sense of self-awareness as when we filmed that special.

The tenement rooftops known as Tar Beach are where I first started dream-weaving my life. In the winter those rooftops became a mountaintop, where we could throw snowballs and hear our voices echo through the downtown canyons. Tar Beach was also my first stage. The fire escapes were my box seats and every stoop a front-row ticket. I'd stand there in the shadow of the Empire State Building, looking out over the Manhattan skyline, singing to imaginary crowds lining the stoops and fire escapes. The skyscrapers almost seemed like standing ovations. And I could almost believe I was a star. The most amazing part of my Tar Beach dream-weaving is that it came true.

My mother loved theater. She loved Broadway, movies, vaudeville. When I was still a kid of three or four Mamma started taking me to shows at Radio City, the Roxy, and the Rialto. It was always a big event for us. Mamma dressed to the nines, and she'd put me in my Sunday suit, sometimes even with a hat. We'd see a movie, and after the final curtain came down, a vaudeville act would perform in front of it. Mamma loved to see the stars, especially if they acted humble, or in a way that she considered "real." One of Mamma's biggest thrills happened when she and Leo, my father, went to see Jerry Lewis and he left the theater at the very same time they did. Jerry held the door open for my parents and endeared himself to them for life. Years later, when I hosted my own television variety show, Mamma would have another thrill, seeing so many of the people we used to watch perform onstage with her son.

I loved all of it. I loved the musicals, the westerns—everything. Seeing those shows remained a huge affair even when I

was older and going to the movies by myself. I'd leave the theater singing, dancing, and pretending I was Gene Kelly in
Singing in the Rain, or whoever I'd seen on the movie screen
that day. I'd top off the event of the day by stopping at a store on
my way home, the Wing & Fin, a pet shop on Twenty-third
Street. Between watching the store's owner feed the piranhas
and looking at the exotic birds and fish, the experience was
almost as exciting and mysterious as the world of movies. And
there was a doorway on Twenty-third Street that was another
mystery to me. It seemed to go nowhere, just a long dark flight
of stairs leading up to Tar Beach territory. Sometimes I thought I
could almost hear music coming from somewhere up those
stairs, but I was never sure.

I kept thinking about that place, so one day, when I was
around ten years old, I got up the courage to check it out. I
didn't have any idea where I'd end up. I got about halfway up
and called out, "Is anybody here?"

There was no answer so I continued on and finally came to a
door. I opened it and inside was this fantastic banquet room dec-
orated like somebody was going to have a party or a wedding.
The tables were all lined up around a beautiful maple or walnut
dance floor that glistened with wax so slick you could have
skated on it. At the end of the room was a stage, and there was a
stand with one of those fifties-style microphones you always see
in Elvis pictures.

Again I called out, "Is anybody here?"

I started walking across the room toward the stage. It was so
quiet that I could hear my heels on the dance floor, like a Gene
Kelly movie with the clicking of tap shoes. I climbed the stairs
and stood on a stage for the first time in my life. As I looked out
over the room from that elevated stage, I felt a surge of power,
some kind of a strength surrounding me. I reached out and
tapped the mike, and found that it was open.

I took the mike in my hand and sang one of my family's

favorite songs, Roy Hamilton's version of "You'll Never Walk Alone." I could hear my voice going out over the mike and it sounded great to me. "When you walk through a storm, keep your head up high . . ." But when I finished the song I suddenly felt embarrassed, like I'd bared too much of myself up there. I jumped off the stage and hurried back down the stairs. I'd made it about halfway when I heard a solitary *clap, clap, clap*. I turned around and there was a guy in blue maintenance coveralls standing in the stairwell. The name "Lou" was stitched above one pocket.

"That was pretty good, kid. You ought to try doing it for a living."

From that day on I knew I wanted to be in show business. Until I had that open mike in my hand I wasn't sure I had the nerve to try it.

I started thinking about that day when I decided to write this book. The truth is, you never get over that fear of baring too much of yourself, about feeling too exposed. I've been to the top of the stairs and back down many times through this career and I've met a hell of a lot of people along the way. I wondered how the truth might hurt. Then I realized that if Michael Cassivitis a.k.a. Tony Orlando, from Twenty-first Street was gonna tell his story, it had to be told from an open mike.

Another encounter affected the writing of this memoir. I'd been working on the book for almost a year, when I was asked to present a Patriot award to our secretary of state, Colin Powell, at the College of the Ozarks. I'd just read his autobiography and had been reminded all over again that our secretary of state is as eloquent on paper as he is in his speeches.

I'd been struck with the magnitude of this man's life. He's not just witnessed some of the extraordinary events in this nation's history, he's been an integral part of them. Reading his words left me inspired, and I asked him if he had any suggestions for a very uncertain novice writer. He said he'd pass along some thoughts that a media person had offered while he wrote his book. First, the guy had told him to avoid beginning the book with topics like Soviet leaders, Ronald Reagan, George Bush, or the Gulf War. He reminded General Powell that his story began with family, with his upbringing. Then the fellow said, "Don't write so much that you've got a doorstop instead of a memoir, and don't get to the point where you're saying, 'And then I had lunch with so-and-so.' "

"That was the best advice I received, *paisan*," Colin Powell said.

I walked away thinking about this great country, America, where a guy like me, a kid from Tar Beach, could know a secretary of state, and have such a great man consider me his *paisano*. But, I also realized that this remarkable man and I had something very important in common: We are both products of the streets of New York, men of ethnic heritage with strong family ties.

I certainly never came close to the stratosphere inhabited by the secretary of state. But I realized your life isn't completely defined by your successes, but rather by your solitary struggles and small triumphs, whether you are a world leader named Colin Powell, a singer named Tony, or a janitor named Lou. It's the journey, not the destination that writes your life.

It's a journey that doesn't end until you leave this world, too. That's why I decided to title this memoir *Halfway to Paradise*, after the first song I had released on Epic Records, way back in 1961. You never do quite make it to paradise in show business. You will always have to prove yourself, audition, and reinvent yourself. My life has been one long history of doing just that. So much so, that I'd feel wrong to end a memoir with "the end." As with any memoir, I think the final words should read "to be continued."

In many ways, this memoir, this look back, is a way to acknowledge some of the people who helped me along that journey. Some of those were mentioned in the acknowledgments, but there were many others. People like Jackie Wilson, Jackie Gleason, Jerry Lewis, Frankie Lyman, Muhammad Ali, and Freddie Prinze. Acknowledging your creative debts is important.

One of the best pieces of advice I ever got was about saying thank you. It was while I was on Epic Records, at the beginning of my career. I was in Los Angeles, staying at the Beverly Hills Hotel, when Groucho Marx walked into the lobby. I couldn't stop myself from approaching him, even though I had no idea how he'd react at the intrusion. I introduced myself, and mentioned that I was just starting out in show business. He seemed friendly, and even threw out a couple of funny, one-line "Grouchoisms." I've always asked people for advice, for their opinions, whether about careers or life in general. And since Groucho had proved approachable, I asked him if he had any tips. I think I expected a joke, but he turned serious.

"Never lose the ability to say 'thank you,' and never ever underestimate its power," he said.

I thought about that advice many times over the years. One of the reasons I could count on friends and associates during the hard times, is because I tried to be appreciative all through the good ones. Groucho was so right—the power of a "thank you" is remarkable.

It's been a roller-coaster ride, this musical trip I've been on since the days when I was singing doo-wop with the Five Gents on the streets of New York, dream-weaving on Tar Beach. The reason I've been able to hang on, and to wind up a happy and contented man in his fifties, is the people who make up the tapestry of my life, starting right there on the streets of New York City.

Halfway to Paradise

Chapter 1

On West Twenty-first Street

Long before I ever heard the word "star" I understood the concept. I recognized it the first moment I followed my father down Seventh Avenue through New York's garment district. The year was 1947 and I was three years old. The streets were crowded with men pushing long carts of dresses and suits and furs from design houses to storage facilities or from warehouses to trucks waiting to deliver New York's finest to stores across the country. While I only somewhat understood what the garment industry was about, I thoroughly understood that my father was one of its stars. His name was Leo Cassivitis, but in the garment district he was known as Label the Furrier.

It was a heavily ethnic business; the owners of most of the great furrier companies were Jewish and the workers were Greek. My father was Greek, but his foreman position at Stone Furs at 333 Seventh Avenue, made him an important man, important enough that the Jewish men who owned the company fondly called him "Label," their word for Leo.

He would walk tall and proud through the streets, dressed handsomely in a cashmere coat, expensive tie, leather belt, and the smart-looking sandals that were considered high toned at that time. My father was a handsome, charismatic man, a natty dresser. Rugged and manly, yet soulful. He looked like Omar Sharif in *Doctor Zhivago* long before anyone had seen the 1965 film.

"Label!" a cabbie would shout. "How are you today?"

My father would tip his hat with the air of royalty. "I'm very good, thank you, Manny," he would answer.

Or maybe it would be a fellow with a pushcart or a woman opening up a shop on the street. They all called to him as if he were very important, and he was. When he entered Stone Furs on Seventh Avenue, he was in complete control of all the Greeks who spent their days cutting the pelts, stitching them together, and producing fine fur coats for the wealthy women of New York's Park Avenue or Boston's Beacon Street. The people who worked for him loved and respected him. He was known to be a fair man. Strong, tough, a man of rules, but always fair. He saw to it that the product was impeccable and that his employers made money. Those two things made him not just important, but invaluable.

My father was a deeply complicated man. All that he was affected me then and even now. First, his star status dazzled me as a child. How could anyone ever live up to Label the Furrier, to whom the wondrous garment district saluted? Father's heritage was very much a part of him. He, like most Greeks, had a great sense of pride in his native country. He spoke the Greek language flawlessly and believed it vital that he did, to the point of having gone to school to perfect it. The language spoken by second- or third-generation Greeks, diluted and Americanized, was not for Label Cassivitis. He wanted perfection. But his heritage was much more than a desire to speak the language fluently. If anyone was ever the quintessential Greek man, it was him.

Years later, when I saw Anthony Quinn portray Zorba the Greek, I realized that in many ways I was watching my father. Both were proud and grand, boisterous yet brooding, complicated and opinionated, gentle and cold, determined even when afraid, confident even while insecure. And the funny thing about my father was that he was all that every day.

And so the man I idolized made it very difficult for me to quite comprehend him as a person. I primarily saw him as a celebrity. I perceived him as such until the day he died. Others did as well. No matter how old he was, when he walked into a gathering he was a formidable presence, literally sucking the air out of the room. All eyes were directed at him even when the occupants of that room were real stars! I remember cohosting the *Mike Douglas Show* once in the mid-seventies. One of the guests that day was, ironically, the great film star Omar Sharif. Leo Cassivitis walked into the green room where Omar and I sat talking and Omar looked up startled, partly at the similarity in looks but partly at the way Father dominated.

"Oh, my God!" Omar said. "Who is that?"

"It's my father," I said with a smile. "He does resemble you, doesn't he?"

"I'm moving over," Omar said with a laugh.

Later that day, when the show had taped and Omar and I again talked privately, he told me he had felt electricity fill the room when Father came through the door. He had been charmed just as I had been throughout my life, and just as the workers at Stone Furs and the cabbies and shopkeepers of Seventh Avenue had been.

My father's stature follows me still. I feel it to this day when I travel through the country. Father traveled with me for much of the seventies and off and on in the eighties and nineties, and people remember him. I'm just amazed at how many people ask about him decades later—skycaps in Philadelphia, doormen in New York, bell captains in Los Angeles. The funny thing is, I'll have to look at the man a moment, then realize how much time has passed. It will be a guy my father spent time with in airports or hotels, and the man will now have gray hair, and is maybe a little bent over. After all, twenty-five years have passed.

Just this past year, as I was checking in at the Tropicana in Atlantic City, a doorman walked up and reintroduced himself. I hadn't been at the Tropicana in a couple of years, but the doorman asked if my dad was out in the car. When I told him that Dad had passed away a year earlier, the man actually got tears in his eyes. That was the effect this man had on people.

Sometimes, after I've dressed for a show and checked myself out in a mirror, I still see myself trying to be as classy as Leo.

My parents had a brief, off-again, on-again marriage. That shouldn't be a surprise, because according to my mother, Ruth Estanislaw, she basically told him to take a hike the day he first approached her. Mamma had known Leo Cassivitis for years, since their families lived in the same building, and Leo was a great friend of her brother, Orlando. Then one day, when Mamma was about to turn seventeen, she stopped by the local candy store, her future husband came over to the jukebox and asked her what songs she'd picked.

"That's none of your business!" she shot back, a bit of Puerto Rican fire in her voice.

Even with a shaky beginning, Leo won her over. He was hard to ignore. He was the jokester, the prankster, the guy everyone wanted to be around. But, as Mamma says, she married him for the wrong reasons. In those days a young woman couldn't wait too long before marriage, or she'd be called an old maid. And Mamma *was* seventeen.

I was born on April 3, 1944, three years after they married, and were living on West Twenty-sixth Street. I was named Michael Anthony Orlando Cassivitis. Michael, in honor of my paternal grandfather, a Greek restauranteur, and Orlando, in honor of my mother's brother. Uncle Orlando was in the navy when Mamma was pregnant with me. He'd called and said, "Name the baby after me!" Mamma said, "No! That's a horrible name for a baby! I'm calling him Michael." But she relented and went for Orlando as a middle name.

My parents were married seven years, but only lived together for about two of those. Each time they separated Mamma and I would move in with the whole Estanislaw family at a brownstone at 221 West Twenty-first Street. Divorced or separated women didn't usually get apartments back in those days. If something happened to their marriages, they moved back home, especially if they came from strict Puerto Rican families like the Estanislaws!

I was two when we moved to West Twenty-first Street the first time, and four when they separated for the last time. Mamma decided it was time to take a trip west and visit Uncle Orlando in Long Beach, California. We took a train to Chicago, then changed to the Santa Fe El Capitan. I remember very little from the first leg of the journey. It was when I saw the El Capitan that I came alive. It was silver and red, with an Indian chief painted on the side. I can still remember the excitement of standing there with our little suitcases, hearing the conductor shout, "*Allllll* aboard."

The dining car was like something from one of our movies. The white linen tablecloths were starched and pressed. The plates elegant, and the waiters all very still and professional. Again, I had that Sunday suit on, and knew to mind my manners.

The most impressive thing was when we came to the desert and saw those colors, that sweeping landscape. Sundown made the trip through the desert seem even more magical. I'd stare out and think of the western movies I'd seen, which had all been in black-and-white. Now, on the El Capitan, I could see them in living color. And I could imagine myself in them, too. I could see the image of a white horse running across the land, of riding across the desert in some sort of western adventure. It was wonderful.

I love New York. It has given me many dreams, many aspirations. The West, however, gave me color and awakened my imagination.

Not long after Mamma and I returned to New York, my parents got a divorce. I remember very little of what led to it, just a quiet that fell over the household of Leo and Ruth Cassivitis. I never felt that Leo stopped loving me or that I was a problem in their marriage, as so many small children feel. Even when they divorced and my mother and I moved in with her family, I believed Leo loved me.

After the divorce, Mamma and I moved to West Twenty-first Street for good. We called it a "sharing apartment," because everyone shared the seven rooms, the food, the love. With the addition of Mamma and me, we numbered ten in that apartment. Mamita and Papito—Juanita and José Estanislaw, my maternal grandparents—my aunts, Eda, Elsie, Delores, and my uncles, Joey, Orlando, and Johnny. Those people were the ones who made me feel safe and secure even after a divorce in the late 1940s, not an event many ethnic families liked to see.

I can still see that apartment with the hand-crocheted doilies, little painted figurines, and religious icons placed on end tables. I can hear the hissing of the exposed pipes, smell the chilies and onions cooking. In fact, if there is one thing beside the closeness of family that I remember about that brownstone apartment, it was the smell. People think of tenements as dirty, stinking places, but back then those apartments were clean and neat and the smell you associated with each doorway was of food. You could tell someone's ethnic heritage by the smell of the dinners they cooked. We Puerto Ricans might have chicken, rice, and beans cooking with onions and chili peppers. Or potato meat pies or a *sanocho* cooking in the pot, a stew so named because it means "burnt by the sun." Sometimes Mamita made *pasteles,* a Puerto Rican treasure made with bananas, chopped meat, and olives, and somewhat similar to the *chili rellenos* you find in Mexican restaurants now.

I've always loved the Christmas season, and on West Twenty-first Street the holiday was defined by two things: religion and food. Some small gifts were exchanged, but presents weren't the main point of Christmas. It was a time to celebrate Christ's birth, and cook so much food that we could have fed the neighborhood. The whole family participated in the cooking as well as the eating, with Mamita in charge of it all. New Year's was another big event in the household, a great night for singing. I still like to close my shows with "Auld Lang Syne."

Our entire family was musical. I honestly believe if they'd have put together a group of some kind they could have been as popular as the Jackson Five later became. To hear my aunts harmonizing was to believe you heard the angels singing. To this day, when I am onstage interacting with the audience, I am reminded of my Puerto Rican family, of parties at my aunt Delores's when we all sang together. There were the aunts, uncles, cousins, children, grandchildren, great-grandchildren. Sometimes I think that I try to relive those days every time I step on the stage.

But Papito didn't think music was a safe profession. So even though my uncle Orlando was a great opera singer, my grandfather tried to discourage any of us from the world of career musicians. Papito knew it was a tough business for females and suspected it was almost as bad for men.

"Get a real job," he always advised. "Learn a trade."

Papito wasn't the only one against Orlando going into show business. When he had an opportunity to sing at the Roxy, Uncle Orlando's wife was dead set against it. That's why he and his wife ended up moving to Long Beach, California, and raising a family of five.

Papito was a very wise man, and one who taught me many things, including my first understanding—or attempt to understand—death. I remember one morning when I was around seven years old, I was awakened by Papito leaving the house. I slept on a foldout couch in the living room, and when I opened my eyes I saw Papito standing in the doorway. For some reason, his walking out the door scared me. Maybe it was because my father had left, I don't know. I started to cry and he came over and sat down on the sofa bed with me. When he asked me why I was crying I admitted that it made me afraid when he left the apartment. Papito sat there and looked at me for a long time. He patted me on the head and said, "Michael, I'm coming back. But you must know that I am an old man, and I won't always be here. I could die any time, and you must not stay afraid when I'm gone on a long-time basis."

I hugged him and he said, "Michael, if I can tell you one thing that I hope for you it is this: Don't be just one of the crowd. Don't follow along with people. You make your mark whether I'm here to see it or not."

I can hear him saying that as if it was yesterday. "Don't be just one of the crowd." Those words are part of what kept me from joining the street gangs in nearby Hell's Kitchen and they kept me from completely messing up my life even during the times when I was coming close to doing so.

My father was the star, but Papito was my hero. He could have been anybody's hero. He had been a high school teacher in Puerto Rico, he enlisted in the military to fight for America, and then, on returning, he became a professional boxer and ended up being the champ of Latin America. Gene Tunny finally beat him. After his defeat, he decided it was time to move to the United States, and brought his wife and nine children to New York City, where he first found work as an elevator operator. Finally, he was working three jobs. He delivered milk in the early mornings, then went to his elevator job, then ended the day playing music. Using the stage name Leon Stanley, he played trumpet in Desi Arnaz's band before starting his own group, a band that found jobs at clubs like the famous Coconut Grove. He was an innovator, too. Papito invented a double-lip mouthpiece that enabled trumpet players to play very high notes, and one of the first horn players to use it was none other than Harry James.

My mother had to work at a variety of jobs, from packing biscuits at the Sunshine Company to cashiering at the Horn & Hardarts automat. Remember the Hardy Girls? Mamma was one. Like her father, my Papito, she once worked as an elevator operator at a store. It was big news on Twenty-first Street the day she transported actress Piper Laurie. Same with Margaret Sullivan. In my mother's absence, Mamita became like a mother to me. Mamma was always thankful for Mamita being there at home for me.

Mamita's name was Joan, and she had a picture of Joan of Arc on her wall right along with her crucifix. She didn't talk much about it but everyone knew that St. Joan of Arc was a personal hero to Mamita. She was a strong woman, who, in another day might have been a very political woman. She certainly believed that females were in no way subordinate to males. And I have always liked and been attracted to strong women, probably due in part to Mamita, my own St. Joan.

The biggest social blunder you could make in our household was to appear too full of pride.

"That one has the big head," my mamma would say about someone in the neighborhood.

"Yes, just watch her walk down the street like she's better than us," my aunt Elsie would agree.

"No one should have the big head," Papito would pronounce.

I've had many years to think about what made me the person I am, flaws and all. And I have to say that this anti egotism upbringing I had is one of the most important influences. In our household, acting like a big shot was not just a no-no—it was considered ugly. My family was self-assured, but never braggarts. My uncles and aunts were all very talented people. Some were musical, many were very creative, and all had pretty sharp minds. I believe they could have succeeded at almost any field they attempted. They didn't go into high-profile professions, but they were successful as people, and as parents above all. To them the act of giving was all-important. They gave their time and concern to everyone—family, friends, neighbors.

Did the family's disdain for egotism have anything to do with my then-absent father, Leo the star of the garment district? Who knows? He certainly had pride and he made no attempt at hiding it.

Years later, when my first marriage was failing and I was doing drugs, I often thought back to that brownstone at 221 West Twenty-first Street. I beat myself over the head many times, thinking, "This is not what Mamita and Papito taught you! What would Uncle Orlando think? This life is not what you were taught!"

Everything was a morality lesson on West Twenty-first Street. If the fellow down the street had a cousin who got in a gang, it was a lesson to us all to watch ourselves, and to pay attention to our companions. If the police had to take some fellow home for being drunk on the street, it was a lesson on the values of sobriety. Mainly, we were all reminded of how much those actions embarrassed and adversely affected the individual's family. Embarrass your own family? Bring disgrace on your heritage? Nothing could be worse. That's why I tried my best to stay on the straight and narrow. And I did, too, while I was a child and a young man. It's funny how things work. I stayed out of trouble in Hell's Kitchen, but it took Hollywood to get me off track. What I got from those morality lessons was a braking system, a way to—when I absolutely hit bottom—pull back and talk to myself, not to Tony Orlando, a singer and television personality, but to Michael Anthony Orlando Cassivitis from West Twenty-first Street.

Chapter 2

Out of Conflict Comes a Miracle: Our Rhonda

Part of the reason I became so close to my grandparents is that Mamma remarried about a year after the divorce. Mamma and her new husband moved to West Twenty-fifth, between Eighth and Ninth Avenues. I stayed with Mamita and Papito at West Twenty-first, since Mamma still worked outside the home.

In 1954, all of us at West Twenty-first moved to Long Beach to be near Uncle Orlando, who surely was the pied piper of the family. We got a place at 344½ Via Wanda Lane. I enrolled in Clara Barton Grammar School, which I attended until 1956, when we moved back to New York.

My life in Long Beach was wonderful. It was wide open spaces, year-round warmth, and greenery. I had my own bicycle, a Schwinn I named Lucy. I'd ride her to school every day from Via Wanda Lane to Clara Barton. At the time it seemed like miles, with my little legs pumping up hills all the way. Coming back home was better because I could coast downhill. I recently went back to make that same trip from my old home to school and it was about a block and a half. That hill I coasted home on? Less than half a block.

I enjoyed the time with Uncle Orlando even more this time than when Mamma and I had visited. Uncle Orlando was wonderful. He was tall and strong, and had the same charisma that my father had, only more accessible. Orlando looked like Jeff Chandler, the movie star, with a flashing smile, a strong physique, and an obvious love for his family. I worshiped him, and that made it all the easier, some years later, to change my name from Michael Cassivitis to Tony Orlando.

I was there for two years when we went back to New York. Papito loved being close to his son Orlando. But he missed New York. When you are a youngster, two years is a lifetime, so when I think back on that period, it seems like a great chunk of time. In reality, it was but a moment.

Mamma and Louis came to Long Beach at one point, but Mamma was pregnant and suffered a miscarriage. They were the first to return to the East Coast. In the summer of 1956 the rest of us drove back in a Henry J, a car made by Kaiser, and probably one of the first compact cars. It had a little fin in the back, with a fastback look to it. We were packed in like sardines, and it was a far less friendly desert than the one experienced during the El Capitan trip. There was no air-conditioning, no table linens, and no formal waiters to serve you ice water! All the way through the desert, on Route 66, there were people with stands handing out burlap bags filled with water so the cars could make it through. There's always a big difference between watching something through the looking glass, and being in the middle of it.

There was also a big difference between being safely tucked in with Mamita and Papito, and living with a stepfather. Not long after we returned to New York, I moved in with Mamma and Louis on Twenty-fifth Street, and started the seventh grade at St. Columbus.

One result of Mamma's second marriage was the child-support question. It wasn't official, but every week I was sent to find my father and collect three dollars from him. I was humiliated. It was like being a street beggar, holding his hand out to a celebrity. I hated it more than I can say. Still, I was raised to be polite and obedient, so off I'd go for those three dollars.

When I was around twelve, I attempted to break the three-dollar guilt-trip cycle. I was telling people I wanted to get a job. I'd never had one, but I knew if I could work for the summer, I could quit going for that payoff. My Uncle Albert said he could get me a job at the Manhattan Hotel. Little did I know that it was in the men's room. I stood there and handed out towels and cologne to men when they left their stalls. I didn't last very long.

Little by little, Leo and I grew away from each other. There were the missed birthdays, the lack of any father-son conversations. When I was about thirteen, I asked my father to come to my confirmation. His response was: "What? Does your mother want me to buy you a suit?" That hurt at first. But then as we started talking about it, I realized it was more of a misunderstanding than any active maliciousness.

I ended up rationalizing the divorce to both my father and myself. I'd say, "Well, you and Mamma were very young when you got married, and you didn't live together all that long. A lot of people go steady longer than that."

Then I'd think, *I guess I was the result of a relationship that didn't work. That's simple enough.*

Still, as I said earlier, I never felt like the divorce had been my fault. I know a lot of kids go through those feelings, and it's a sad part of so many divorces. Maybe the reason I didn't experience the guilt trip is that I never heard either Mamma or my father talk bad about each other. They never put each other down.

I don't remember feeling angry. Hurt from time to time. Lonely. But not mad. Obviously, a psychiatrist would read those words and say, "Come to my office for an hour and I bet I can find that anger." And I know they could. But *at the time* I never felt an emotion I could identify as anger. Years later, I paid for distancing myself from my emotions. And when I paid, it was a whopper of a bill.

When I first started this memoir I was still saying I had no anger. There were a lot of honest moments throughout the writing process. The anger issue with my father was one of these.

Leo and I began to get a little closer during the time I was making records for Epic. I remember him coming to Brooklyn to Palasades Park, when I had "Halfway to Paradise" in the charts. And he was obviously proud. Then, years later, he became a big part of my recovery from drug addiction and depression. He ended up going to work for me.

He had two wives after Mamma. He was remarried in the year following the divorce, to a woman named Josie. They moved to Brooklyn, where my brothers, Bobby and Stevie were born. The third time would be the charm as far as Leo's wives would go. He and Abby had my brother David and a thirty-year marriage.

My brothers couldn't quite grasp the difference between the relationship they had with Leo and the one I had. Their experience involved living in the same household with him. Mine was seeing him from a distance. But we never thought much about being from three different wives, probably because Leo's personality was so strong. We were *his* sons. Now, my brother David plays keyboards for me, and our relationship is almost as close as if we'd been raised together.

Still, after I got some success and some money in the bank, I know my brothers thought I bailed out on Leo sometimes. They'd heard him talk me up, and couldn't understand why I wasn't more involved. Leo and I ended up very close, but it took time to develop. And I had to adjust my thinking to realize that the distance wasn't anybody's fault. It just happened.

For example, my father loved to fish, and my brothers went fishing with him all the time. I could count the times on one hand when I went fishing with him. Tales of their fishing trips were hard for me to hear. When I finally got successful in the music business, I asked Leo to go to Cabo San Lucas. We walked along the beach, and since I'd taken a video camera, I had the opportunity to catch him and his thoughts on tape. He talked a lot about fishing, about respect for both the beaches and the fish. He talked about how important it was to toss the small fish back. He'd reach up and say, "Feel this air—it's free. Think about that when you are paying a lot of money for a car."

We got on a boat and went out to the sea for "the big one." Leo finally hooked a marlin. It put up a big fight, and my father fought him for an hour and a half. Suddenly, the fish came up out of the water, and seemed to dance on top of the waves. It was huge, maybe even a record-breaker. And it glistened with the colors of the rainbow. My father stared at the marlin, and finally called to me, "Cut the line, Orlando."

"Why'd you have me do that?" I asked.

"That was the most beautiful fish I've seen in my life," he said. "And I was about to take its life."

Mamma's new husband, Louis Schroeder, was from the old neighborhood, and Mamma was a good friend of his sister Teresa. Like my father, Louis was a friend of Uncle Orlando's, but he was as different as night and day from Leo Cassivitis. Louis Schroeder was quiet and kept to himself, making him difficult to know.

I never got close to my stepfather. Even when he played games with me, I had the feeling he didn't much like me, or that there was a competition going on. Part of that was probably because I always felt I was being untrue to my real father when I interacted with my stepfather. We played a little fast-draw game, and I remember feeling like I shouldn't be participating. I always felt he was insensitive, cold. And he never wanted me to sing. He was a diesel engineer, and firmly believed in working with your hands. And he was a World War II navy veteran who had a stiff military manner, at times.

Just as I finally got close to my biological father, I made peace with Louis. Unfortunately, it was just two years ago, in 2000, when he was on his deathbed.

Louis and Mamma were living in Las Vegas when he was stricken with cancer. It seemed to me that this must have been a very fast moving cancer, because none of us had heard about his condition. On the other hand, I'd been concerned with his health several times since 1997. His skin had taken on a gray coloring, and he seemed even more withdrawn than ever. I asked Mamma a few times about it, but since she'd had a quadruple bypass in 1997, I kept most of my questions to myself.

When Mamma phoned to tell me he was dying, I flew there to be with them and found my stepfather at the hospice, unable to eat or drink. He was literally dying of hunger and thirst. Finally, the doctors had to pump so much water into him that he ended up drowning in fluids. As I sat with him, I felt a need to reach out in some way, to explain my feelings in a way that had seemed impossible all those years.

I knew that, even on his deathbed, I couldn't hand him a lie. I had to try to honestly say what I was feeling.

"Louis, I am very sorry you are going through this," I began. "I know that we have never been close, and I'll be honest, I felt you weren't there emotionally for me, and even at times for Mamma. But you've been a good provider for her, you've stuck by her for over fifty years. For that I thank you. If there is anything—anything at all I can do for you now, please tell me."

Louis could barely speak, but he finally made himself understood. "Tony, there's an attaché case under my bed. It has instructions."

After he died, I went to Mamma's home, and pulled the case from under the bed. As I mentioned earlier, Louis was a navy man, and the case he'd told me about was military issue. He was also a German-Italian immigrant, and at no time was his Germanic penchant for organization more evident than in the content of his attaché case. There was a stack of envelopes, each one titled: "Instructions for the Car," "Instructions for the Bank," "Instructions for My Old Clothes," "Instructions for the Funeral." He'd been meticulous about everything, including the name of the funeral home he'd preselected, and the specific staff members to contact.

There was also a notebook with a carefully documented account of his health since 1997. He'd detailed every doctor's visit, every prescription, each treatment. "Today I saw the doctor and he said . . ." "Today my weight was . . ." One page began with "Today I've been tested for prostate cancer." I think he kept this diary because he had no one to talk to about the illness. Mamma had had that bypass in 1997, and he hadn't told her about the cancer until it was no longer possible to hide the illness. He hadn't wanted to worry her. It was almost as if he was a captain going down with the ship. I found that alone made him a tremendous man.

At the very bottom of the notebook, in very small letters were three words: "Love always, Louis."

I was astonished. I could never have pictured him saying that. And I was saddened. There had been so much wasted time. It made me wonder if I'd really given him a chance to open up, or if he was even capable of it. And it reminded me that too often, shyness is mistaken for aloofness, quiet for cold. I now knew that he'd cared on some level, yet I will never understand the whole picture. So many questions remain. For example, I donated $10,000 in his name to a home for retarded citizens in Las Vegas, in honor of Mamma and Louis's daughter, my sister Rhonda. Louis didn't even go to see the facility. Why didn't he ever say thanks for anything anyone did for him or for Mamma?

I've wondered if it goes back to our family. Maybe Louis just couldn't acclimate himself to that big, extended, charismatic Hispanic family. Maybe it overwhelmed him. And I'll never know, now.

But I do know that he loved my mother enough to keep the

dark, painful secret of his cancer from her when she was recovering from heart surgery. And I know something else. Louis's marriage to Mamma gave me the biggest gift of my youth—my baby sister, Rhonda.

Rhonda was born in 1954, and diagnosed a year or so later with cerebral palsy. The doctors told Mamma that Rhonda would never walk or talk. They said she probably wouldn't live long anyway, and the best thing to do would be to institutionalize her. The doctors didn't know Mamma. No matter what it took, Mamma was determined to care for her daughter at home, and to give her the best life she possibly could. Rhonda was our angel. No, she never walked or talked, but Rhonda communicated. And she was happy and content until she died at age twenty-one. She gave us all much more than she ever took.

I baby-sat for Rhonda a lot, and I honestly don't remember ever resenting her for it. I will admit that I resented the fact that Louis, her own father, seldom helped with her. He'd wander off to bed while Mamma and I held Rhonda during her frequent seizures. He seemed incapable of facing the reality of the situation.

Sometimes I'd stay with her so that Mamma could get a little break and go across the street to church to play bingo. Rhonda had to be fed, cleaned, diapered, but it never bothered me. Like I said, she was our angel. We didn't know how long we would have with her, so we wanted to make every minute count. The whole neighborhood loved Rhonda, too. Even the street gangs respected her, and left us alone when I'd take her to the park in her carriage.

I learned so much from Rhonda. Keep in mind, she had to be helped with everything she did. I got so I could pick up the signs when she had an itch she couldn't scratch. If the back of her head itched, she didn't have the coordination to scratch it. Can you imagine how awful it would be to try to scratch an itch, and be unable to do it? I also learned to appreciate simple things like being able to clap your hands and stomp your feet.

When you see me onstage, clapping and stomping, it's for Rhonda.

I got so that I could tell when she was getting ready to have a seizure. There's what they call an "aura" that occurs before a seizure. It's sometimes a taste in your mouth or sometimes colors appear to change. People who have seizures can often tell when they're going to happen. And their caregivers can sometimes tell. And, of course, now they have companion dogs that can "read" the aura.

The minute I felt that Rhonda was on the verge of a seizure, I'd hold her and sing to her. The seizures were so awful, so terrifying that I'd do whatever I could—anything to help ease her fears, to keep her from hurting herself. Then, all of a sudden, Rhonda would stop shaking, and put her arms around me. She'd look up and get this unbelievable smile on her face. It was as if she really was an angel, thrust into the depths of hell, yet capable of coming back out shining. I often thought, when things were going bad in my life, that I needed to remember the courage Rhonda displayed, to have that faith in those close to me. The most important thing I learned from Rhonda was that there really is light after a storm.

Caring for Rhonda, helping Mamma and Mamita, and being around all my wonderful aunts, gave me a sensitivity that I don't believe I'd have ever developed otherwise. Those women influenced me greatly. Later in life, when I nursed my great friend Murray the K through his final illness, it all seemed natural. I'm not squeamish about the realities of living or dying.

Rhonda is the reason I learned to play guitar. From the time she was a baby, she loved to hear me sing, so I got a guitar to accompany myself with. You always knew when she loved a song, because she rocked faster, and smiled that beautiful smile at the world. To this day, just like when I clap and stomp my feet and think of Rhonda, when I sing, I so often feel I'm singing for my baby sister.

Chapter 3

Doo-wop Fever

When I was a kid I wanted to sing like Frankie Lymon. Hell, I wanted to *be* Frankie Lymon. He didn't rack up a long list of hits, but his impact and influence cannot be underestimated. Frankie was a star. He was Michael Jackson before there was a Michael Jackson. We minorities who lived in the cities with very little except our dreams could look at his success as a symbol of hope. Just like minority kids today look at Michael Jordan or Ricky Martin as "a possibility," we looked to Frankie Lymon.

Frankie was the first black who became a teen singing idol, although he had lots of competition. There were thousands of working doo-wop groups, including some of my friends and I, who sang in a group called the Five Gents. In fact, legend has it that over fifteen thousand doo-wop groups recorded at least one single! If you look to the cool black harmony groups who influenced doo-wop, you'd probably cite the Ink Spots as the most important. The Ink Spots led the way for the Ravens and the Orioles, all precursors to rock 'n' roll. I would also have to say that groups like the Five Satins, the Drifters and the Flamingos are cornerstones of rock 'n' roll.

The Penguins' "Earth Angel" is generally considered the first actual doo-wop recording. I guess if I were to pick what I see as the top three doo-wop songs I'd list Frankie Lymon and the Teenagers' "Why Do Fools Fall in Love," the Five Satins' "In the Still of the Night," and The Flamingos' "I Only Have Eyes for You." Some of the other records and groups that impacted me were "Sincerely," by the Moonglows and "You're a Thousand Miles Away," by the Heartbeats.

It was the lack of heavy instrumentation that made doo-wop so attractive to guys like me, who couldn't afford a band, but who had friends who could sing harmony. A cappella groups took to the streets, especially in New York. They weren't all black, either. There were white kids and Latinos standing on the corners crooning to anyone who would listen.

Then of course, when Frankie Lymon became an idol, we could see even more attractive possibilities, like recording contracts and star status. Frankie's voice made the singers in many of the other groups sound almost like amateurs. Frankie's vocals were full, rich, smooth, and sophisticated yet youthful. And when we listened to "Why Do Fools Fall in Love" we could almost picture the girls swooning over us just like they did over Frankie.

Interestingly, the original title of "Fools" was "Why Do Birds Sing So Gay." It was a song the Premiers were working up and when they needed a kid with a very high tenor, they asked Frankie to put his voice on their song. He reworked the lyrics and wisely suggested changing the title to "Why Do Fools Fall in Love." Gee Records released the song on February 18, 1956, and it immediately headed up the charts. The Premiers changed their name to Frankie Lymon and the Teenagers and continued to record for Gee. While they only charted twice more, and never with the success of "Why Do Fools Fall in Love," Frankie's legend continued to grow. And when Frankie went on the Biggest Stars for 1957 tour as a solo act, he seemed to own the world.

Like most of the doo-wop groups and their stars, Frankie and the Teenagers had a clean-cut public image. Unfortunately, Frankie's life was anything but clean-cut. He was arrested on drug charges, and married several times without benefit of any divorces. I hope people remember him for his talent, not his excesses.

I was sixteen years old when I first saw Frankie in person. My first single, "Halfway to Paradise," was climbing the charts, and I had just come from a meeting at the Brill Building. There stood Frankie, talking to an old guy named Larry, who was a fixture on that street. I couldn't believe my eyes. I walked up, introduced myself, and told Frankie I was his biggest fan. Frankie grinned and said he knew who I was, and liked "Halfway to Paradise." Unbelievable. We talked awhile, and struck up a friendship. Even more unbelievable.

We didn't exactly run around together, but I'd pick him up every so often and we'd get something to eat. Sometimes I loaned him money. Slowly but surely I started to suspect that Frankie had some heavy problems hanging over him. For one thing, I couldn't understand why he was so often in need of money. I didn't know about all his wives, but I figured out about the drugs. It was the first—but certainly not the last—time that I saw an entertainer (including myself) headed for a train wreck. Frankie ended up dying of an overdose in 1968. But he was one of the personal heroes of my youth, and he is still one of my musical heroes.

Doo-wop remains an important music genre. Look at it this way—all those big records first came out in the mid-fifties, yet the biggest moneymaker for PBS's 2000 fund drive was a doo-wop show. And PBS has had concerts featuring everyone from Steely Dan to Pavarotti. Paul Simon has a song in which he says "I love the Flamingos," and he goes into more doo-wop favorites. The influence of this music is immense. I think that Frankie Lymon and the Teenagers were the prototype for the Jackson Five. I think doo-wop influenced groups like the Backstreet Boys, Boyz II Men, New Kids on the Block, and 98 Degrees. What is their deepest influence if it's not doo-wop? There's also a group called Rockapella that does songs for Folgers coffee commercials, so the music remains attractive to advertisers as well.

Of course, I didn't meet Frankie Lymon until I already had a record contract. Before that, I performed on the street corner myself, with the Five Gents. When I was twelve and in the eighth grade, I started the group with Mamma's brother, my uncle Johnny. Uncle Johnny was in his early twenties and he had some friends who joined us: Frankie Robels, Jack Sanchez, and Bobby Paybon. We practiced harmonizing in Mamita's living room or up on Tar Beach—anywhere there was an echo. We performed up and down West Twenty-first Street, where we were stars. When sundown came around, we'd start singing, and people's heads would start poking out of the tenement windows and people would come out and sit on the stoops. Every block had its own group, and West Twenty-first was our musical turf. It belonged to us just as various territories belonged to certain street gangs. And music bridged the gap between the gangs and kids like me. The gang members may have been tough guys, but, like everybody else on the streets, they loved doo-wop.

When we moved our practicing to West Twenty-fifth, after I began living with Mamma and Louis, our practicing became one of Rhonda's great joys. Music was consuming me by the time I started high school. I went to school for a month, didn't like it, and quit. There were two reasons I didn't like going to school. First, I was starting to feel less confident there than on the corner singing. And second, I was getting very little sleep. For a while there, Rhonda's seizures were coming fast and furious. And I seemed to be the one who could get her through them. But I won't begin to say that is the main thing that caused me to quit school. It was only a part of it.

My best friend at the time was a guy named Tommy Regan. Since I baby-sat so much, I didn't have a lot of pals. But Tommy would come and hang out with me while I took care of my sister, so we became very close friends. He formed a group, too. We'd compare records, sounds. Tommy sounded a lot like Johnny Maestro of the Crests. The two of us did make one record together. It was after I already had "Halfway to Paradise" out. Tommy and I cut a single, a remake of the old standard, "I'll Never Stop Loving You" on Colpix Records (Columbia Pictures). It was the first record I ever actually produced, and it's become kind of a favorite among serious doo-wop collectors.

Tommy's musical knowledge and his friendship were an important part of my growing up. I can still remember his phone number: Algonquin 5-5926. Tommy ended up having a terrible accident, resulting in brain damage. He never realized his full potential, and I believe that potential was great. Years later, when I wrote a musical called *Jukebox Dreams,* I put Tommy in as a member of the group. That's the only way I could try to make up for his own lost jukebox dream.

Probably one of the biggest thrills I had during that time—in my life, for that matter—happened when I was fifteen years old and singing with some guys who went on to be the Belmonts. I was singing a doo-wop-style harmony, when Kelly Isley came out of the Turf Restaurant, which was in the basement of the Brill Building. Lots of record producers and publishers used to come from the restaurant straight into the Brill.

Kelly stopped, listened for a few minutes, and liked what he heard. He said later that it interested him that I was a white kid, a Puerto Rican, singing soul music. He asked me if I'd come over to the Harlequin Rehearsal Studios, and I accepted the offer, of course.

He had me come back for two days, singing with the Isley Brothers and the great Solomon Burke. They showed me some turns, and how to hold my hands and slide my feet—I went to school on those guys.

But as much as I wanted to be a soul singer, I landed in the pop world.

Chapter 4
1650 Broadway

Although the Brill Building has received most of the press over the years, there were actually two very important music centers located on the 1600 block of Broadway. The Brill was at 1619 Broadway but the building where my first music mentor, Don Kirshner, headquartered, was at 1650. You couldn't miss the Brill Building, with its big brass art deco front doors. To a kid like me, those doors looked like gold. The Brill had an elegant, thirties-style lobby, with a small, understated directory off to one side. The 1650 building, also built in the thirties or forties, had been remodeled several times, and had a more sixties-style lobby, with a big, brightly lit directory that made you feel like there was a strange mixing of times and styles. But at 1650, when you walked into the lobby, showbiz hit you right in the face. That fluorescent directory listing the publishers, record companies, and management firms fairly screamed excitement. Then, when you went up to the different floors, all the doors were painted with a black gloss paint, with the company name in gold letters. It was something for anyone to experience, let alone a kid from Tar Beach.

The 1650 building never was as famous as Brill, yet in some ways, the music coming from 1650 was even more significant to the face of modern rock and pop. Brill's fame was from teams like Jerry Lieber and Mike Stoller, who wrote so many hits, including "Hound Dog" (originally for Big Mama Thornton), and had such huge success working with groups like the Robins and the Coasters. Doc Pomus and Mort Shuman, who wrote a great deal for Elvis and the Drifters, were a big part of the legend. A listing of their hit songs would include classics like "Save the Last Dance for Me" and "Don't Be Cruel." Brill also housed companies like Hill & Range, which produced much of Elvis's song catalog.

The building at 1650 represented a newer breed: Carole King, Gerry Goffin, Barry Mann, Cynthia Weil, Neil Sedaka, Harry Greenfield, Jack Keller, Bobby Darin. These were young, energetic writers who understood the youth market better than most in the Tin Pan Alley area. These were the writers who fed the teen market. Elvis, Carl Perkins, Jerry Lee Lewis, Chuck Berry, Buddy Holly—those guys proved to the industry that there was a big teenage market out there. Three recording centers jumped on it: Philadelphia, New York, and Hollywood. But their approach was product that was less radical, less edgy, and more middle-of-the-road American teenager than those rock records had been. That led to the relatively short-lived "teen idol" era, sandwiched in between early rock and Beatlemania.

The Brill Building started out as a clothing outlet and came to be a music center because of the Great Depression, when the Brill brothers were forced to rent space to other businesses. A lot of people were broke back then, but music was still happening, and it was song publishers who rented the space, starting with Southern Music, Mills Music, and Famous Music. By the time I began frequenting the Brill there were over a hundred and fifty publishers in that building alone. But it was the glitz of 1650 that held my attention.

Pop music was happening on that part of Broadway, and it was accessible even to a kid like me. For example, you could try to pitch your songs, get arrangements and lead sheets, hire singers to record a demo for you. It seemed like everything was located in that one area: record companies, publishing companies, managers, and agents.

The first time I tried to be heard in those buildings was when I had the Five Gents. But I couldn't get through the door back then. There were just too many doo-woppers out there. Then, Bobby Paybon died of cancer at twenty-one years of age. We didn't have the heart to go on without him in the group, so I went on alone. The only place I knew to start was on Broadway.

I started taking a bus from home to the Port Authority Bus Terminal, and then hoofed it down to Broadway. I'd begin at the top floor of both buildings and work my way down. I'd stick my head in every door and ask "Auditions?" If the receptionist nodded in the affirmative, I'd sing "La Bamba" for anyone who would listen.

It was one of Don Kirshner's songwriters, a great R&B writer named Eddie Singleton, who led me to Don at Aldon Music. And Brooks Arthur, the producer, led me to Eddie. Brooks had heard me singing on the street corner, and liked what he heard. It was the beginning of a lifelong friendship between Brooks and me. When he introduced me to Eddie, Eddie asked if I was a songwriter, and I said I was. He asked me to come on in to Aldon Music, Don's company, and play him something. I played him a song I'd written titled "Let There Be Love," and when I finished he told me he wanted me to sing for his boss.

Don's story and the story of the people surrounding him are worth telling, because so many of them played such big roles in pop music.

It all started in the late fifties, in a New York candy store, when Don met a kid named Robert Casotto, listened to his songs and ended up going into business with him. Robert Casotto soon changed his name to the more commercial-sounding Bobby Darin. The two started writing songs without much success, then got into the jingle business, hiring, among others, a young singer named Concetta Franconero. She soon changed *her* name to the more commercial-sounding Connie Francis.

About a year after Don went into business with Bobby he met Al Nevins, who was a big-time songwriter and musician. Nevins was recording some kids calling themselves the Three Suns at the time. Don convinced Al to go into business with him and Bobby, and start a company geared to writing and publishing songs for the youth market.

One of the most interesting things to me about this historical process, is the way the participants came in and out of the story, influencing each other, participating in each other's success, and literally building modern pop music.

When Kirshner and Nevins moved into 1650 Broadway, right across the street from the Brill Building, two of the first writers they met were Neil Sedaka and Howard Greenfield. These guys had been writing together ever since they met at Lincoln High School in the fifties.

There's a connection here to my later career, too. Hank Medress, who would later become my record producer, was part of the Sedaka story. At Lincoln High, Neil had hooked up with Hank, Eddie Rabkin, and Cynthia Zolitin to form a band called the Linc-Tones in 1956, and recorded some tunes for Melba Records. In 1958, Eddie Rabkin left and Jay Siegel joined the band. Cynthia and Neil left the Linc-Tones a little later in 1958, and Hank reformed the group, naming it the Tokens with Phil and Mitch Margo in 1961. By the time the Tokens had their huge classic 1961 pop hit, "The Lion Sleeps Tonight," Hank was the only original Linc-Tone left.

When Don Kirshner moved to 1650 in 1958, Neil and Howard literally stopped him from unpacking boxes in his new office. They played him a couple of songs that caught his ear: "Stupid Cupid" and "Calendar Girl." Neil signed with RCA in 1958, the same year he left the Linc-Tones and signed with Aldon. Two years later "Calendar Girl" became his sixth release and first top-five hit.

"Stupid Cupid" would be an important song for Don and Bobby's friend Connie Francis, who had released a big number, "Who's Sorry Now," as her MGM chart debut in 1958. It went to number four and was a best-seller. Everybody knows that you've got to follow a monster hit with another big song, or you may very well get tagged a one-hit wonder. Unfortunately for Connie, the follow-up to "Who's Sorry Now," 1961's "I'm Sorry I Made You Cry," didn't do as well. It went to number thirty-six in 1958, and while it sold okay, it didn't have the identity that her debut had had. Then along comes Aldon Publishing with "Stupid Cupid," a number fourteen hit and a big impact record.

So by 1959, when I met Don Kirshner, his company was a legendary star-maker. I walked into his office and couldn't believe it. He had this red piano that was also a bar, and a big wooden "hit list" where he could track his successes from week to week.

I still can't believe he even listened to me, because I was overweight and my skin was broken out. Don agrees that I didn't look like a potential star. But, according to him, he felt I had warmth, sincerity, and a burning desire. He also detected an ethnic quality that would add an R&B element to my records. He offered me a contract, and, since I was only sixteen years old, asked that I bring my mother with me to finalize the deal.

Mamma thought it was all a big scam. She'd heard stories about phony show business types who'd offer to sign up a kid for modeling jobs, then charge lots of money for photos and training. Once the check cleared, the families never heard from these guys. At first she didn't even want to go, but the family convinced her to at least go and hear what this Kirshner fellow had to say.

Louis came with us, but it was obvious to everyone concerned that my mother was the person in charge. I knew that Louis didn't think much of the whole idea, but Don catered to

Mamma from the start, so Louis's opinion didn't carry much weight, anyway.

Don's nice office and expensive suit went a long way toward convincing Mamma, but it was his earnest manner and a team of lawyers that sold the deal. He told her he believed in me, in my potential as a recording artist. And then he dropped the big one: Donnie told her they didn't want any money from me. In fact, they intended to *pay* me fifty dollars a week. She put her signature on the dotted line.

After Mamma signed the contract, Donnie pulled me aside.

"I want you in here every single day," he said, ushering me into a tiny little office furnished with nothing but a piano, a couple of chairs, and a telephone. "The fifty dollars a week I'm paying you is to write and to help out singing demos for yourself and our other writers. That's all I want you to do."

All? Was he kidding? That's all I wanted to do. Fifty dollars a week to do exactly what I dreamed about, and to do it in the company of such amazing talent. Not only that, but I could take a cab instead of the bus. I had a job! I had spending money! I wouldn't have to ask my mom for money to go to the movies.

The first day that I showed up to write, Donny pulled me aside again.

"I want you to work with a young couple I'm really excited about, Carole King and Gerry Goffin."

Carole and Gerry were teenagers when they'd married, and I don't know if Gerry would have got into the business if Carole hadn't had such a drive to make music. That's not to say he was less of a talent; he understood how to write a song as well or better than anyone I've met. But Carole was the one who believed it could work, and Neil Sedaka was the high school friend who led them to Don Kirshner. It was perfect that this married couple were both teens, because they were writing for a young audience. They wrote about heartache and young love in a way that an older writer might not be able to pull off unless he had a very good memory. At any rate, their material was on target for the market and Don knew it. Jack Keller, Don's young writer/producer, knew it, too.

When Don introduced me to them he said that he thought I could be a white version of Ben E. King, who sang lead with the Drifters in 1959 and 1960 and then went on to a solo career with hits like "Spanish Harlem" and "Stand by Me."

"I want Tony to sing all your demos now," Don told Carole and Gerry. "You just tell him who you want to pitch the song to and he'll make it work."

After I sang for them and they sang for me, we were convinced it was going to work.

Since I now had money, I took a cab when I first went to their house in Brooklyn, but soon we had a pattern down. Carole would be in Manhattan writing and she'd drive me to Brooklyn with her when she left town around five in the afternoon. Sometimes on a Friday or Saturday night I even slept there so we could work late if they got on a roll.

Gerry was the lyricist and Carole wrote the melodies. They could construct what I consider near perfect songs. The way it worked was this: They had a little four-track recorder and we'd do the demos live. Carole and Gerry would sing me the song, and we'd put it down. Carole would say, "Tony, this is for Bobby Vee," and I'd sound like "Take Good Care of My Baby." Or Gerry would say, "This is for Ben E. King," and I'd do his sound. I got really good at hearing how a specific singer might do a song and gearing the demo to them.

It didn't always come easy, though. I remember once when I showed up at Carole and Gerry's, he was having so much trouble trying to make his lyrics fit Carole's melody that he literally tore the ivory off the piano keys. He started yelling at the piano and ripping out the keys one by one. I guess looking back on it you could say that sometimes writing is like pulling teeth, even for people like Carole King and Gerry Goffin. Gerry may not have actually extracted a molar, but he damn sure was pulling out the ivories.

To say I learned a lot from writers like Carole and Gerry or Cynthia Weil and Barry Mann would be a massive understatement. Aside from honing my vocal skills with a variety of styles, I learned to appreciate songs in a whole new way. I learned to try my best to interpret the song while staying true to the writer's intent. Cynthia Weil would literally get tears in her eyes when someone nailed one of her songs.

Carole King loved songs with that same intensity. And she understood how to present a song. For example, she'd explain how to phrase the word "paradise" as "pair-a-dice," to make it sing better. She is a true genius in this business, as well as one of the most compassionate ladies. I remember one time when Carole and Gerry came to Mamma's house to play some songs for me. Rhonda was on the bed, rocking back and forth, as she did so much. Carole realized how Rhonda loved to hear music. She climbed right on the bed with Rhonda, cradled her in her arms and sang to her. It brought tears to my eyes. And a smile to Rhonda's face.

I'm so happy that the music industry is still honoring Carole for both her talent and her heart. In December 2001, Carole received one of the New York Heroes Awards presented by the Recording Academy at the Roosevelt Hotel on Forty-fifth and Madison. The awards are bestowed upon "individuals who are integral to the New York music community, and whose creative talents and accomplishments cross all musical boundaries." Those words certainly describe Carole.

Carole King, Gerry Goffin, Cynthia Weil, Barry Mann—these were the stars at Aldon Music. And, as I mentioned in the beginning of this book, I had been exposed to the star treatment just walking down Seventh Avenue with my father. But I was soon to be in the presence of something even bigger, the "superstar essence." You can't miss the ones who have it, and I'll never for-

get my introduction. It started one afternoon when Donnie Kirshner wanted me to accompany him to the Franconero house,
where a big Italian family kept close watch over their singing
daughter, Connie Francis.

I loved Connie's records, and was in awe of her vocal ability.
But I was not prepared for meeting her. Donnie and I got there,
and were greeted by Mr. and Mrs. Franconero. In a few minutes,
Connie walked into the room. It like a flashbulb had gone off in
everyone's eyes. She wore very high heels and one of her trade-
mark shirtwaist dresses, with a full skirt enhanced, I guess, by
crinolines. Her hair and makeup were perfect. She walked,
stood, and sat like a queen. I don't mean she was arrogant, it
wasn't like that at all. She was naturally at ease with being
royalty.

Being comfortable with celebrity is a subject that goes hand-
in-hand with the whole idea of having a superstar essence. You
never know how people will react to becoming a celebrity.
Some run from it, some act like jerks because of it, others wear it
with ease. I guess the person I know who is most comfortable
with superstardom is Muhammad Ali, arguably the most famous
living American icon. Ali enjoys being a celebrity and knows he
has the essence, still, he thrives on his own accessibility. If, for
example, you saw Ali walking down the street, he'd be signing
autographs, laughing, talking with his adoring public. And I
must say that Muhammad Ali is one of the nicest, most genuine
celebrities I've ever met.

Then you go to a more complicated guy, like Elvis Presley.
Elvis was another person who fell into the "nice guy" category. I
don't believe anyone who ever met him, under casual circumstances, didn't like him. Yet he was at the opposite end of the
spectrum from Ali. Elvis was not comfortable with his celebrity
status, his essence, if you will. In fact, I suspect it almost embarrassed Elvis that he had the power to walk into a room and
immediately become the focal point.

I remember playing Las Vegas once, when Elvis was in the main showroom and I was at one of the lounges. He tried to walk across the back area of the stage, where he thought he'd be concealed. I turned my head when the audience started whispering, and there stood Elvis. He'd made it across the stage and was standing at a little bar to one side. The place was closed, so he had his privacy, but he had no place to go! The only way back was to walk across my stage. I played it a little while, asking the audience "Who *was* that?" But I dropped it quick, because I knew that Elvis Presley was horrified that he was in such an exposed situation, and I wanted to make his exit as easy I could. It's no surprise that he became so isolated later in his life.

Bobby Darin had it. It's a funny thing, a lot of people have described Bobby as arrogant. I never got that at all. He was self-confident, sure of himself, and he did not suffer fools gladly. Bobby was very intelligent. He couldn't stand to be around stupidity or bullshit. It's the same with Barbra Streisand, Jerry Lewis—a lot of them. They are the ones who never let down their end of things.

The first time I met Bobby was, of course, through Don Kirshner. When I met him in 1961, Bobby already had hits with "Splish Splash," "Queen of the Hop," "Dream Lover," "Mack the Knife," and "Beyond the Sea." He was one of the biggest stars in America, and married to another of the country's most famous celebrities, Sandra Dee. Bobby was in town, staying at the St. Moritz Hotel on Central Park South. I'd mentioned that I'd give anything to meet Bobby, so Don arranged for me to come to the St. Moritz. I walked into the suite, and there was Sandra Dee, making spaghetti. Bobby was on the floor inventing a new kind of Monopoly game. He was all revved up about the concept.

Don had told me to bring my guitar, and right away he said, "Play that song you wrote called 'Old Napoli.'" It was a kind of Dean Martin–style tune.

I played it, scared to death. Bobby listened, turned to Don and said, "Donnie, this kid has a lot of raw talent." I spent hours trying to figure out whether the comment was a compliment or not.

Later, when I was on a West Coast tour, Bobby invited me to his house in Beverly Hills. I arrived by cab, just at dusk. This place was everything you figure a movie star's house should be: swank. A pool lit for the evening, a fancy dining room with china and silver, linen napkins. I was all of seventeen years old and stunned into silence.

The funny part of it was that there didn't seem to be a cook or anything. Sandra Dee served the meal: steak, mashed potatoes, and peas. I took my knife and fork, started cutting the meat, slipped the knife, and shot the contents of my plate onto Sandra Dee's lap. I was so embarrassed, so humiliated, that I covered my face. I actually had tears in my eyes. All of a sudden Bobby grabbed my hand away, looked at me, and freaked out.

"What's the matter with you? If you're gonna cry over mashed potatoes, you're in a lotta trouble. Mashed potatoes ain't crap."

That put him in a more serious mode, and he started to philosophize. He talked on about learning to differentiate between important things and nonsense. Sandra went and changed her clothes. And while I've teared up many times since, it's never been about the mashed-potato problems of this world.

That star essence, is an elusive quality. I never had it. I was always too much the kid from down the street. But I was just getting ready to learn about stardom, because Kirshner had decided to take me to Epic Records.

Chapter 5

The Short, Sweet Career of a Teen Idol

When I first started haunting the halls of the Brill Building and 1650 Broadway, I was looking for record companies. I thought you had to audition for a label's A&R executives. I didn't yet understand that you could get your foot in the record company door through publishing, especially with a sharp entrepreneur like Don Kirshner.

Kirshner and Al Nevins had been getting a paltry two cents on mechanical royalties from record sales, and Don didn't think that was fair. So he formed what would be the first independent production company that brought in finished product to A&R departments at labels. They'd started with a powerhouse: Neil Sedaka and his RCA debut, "The Diary." Once the labels saw that Kirshner and Nevins were hit-makers, the royalty changed to 10 percent. It worked to benefit their artists, too, because Don split the production royalty with his singers.

Don put me with Jack Keller, who was one of his rising star writer/producers. I admired Jack's personal style so much from the day I met him. He was brilliant musically, and very well spoken. Since I didn't even have a high school education, I emulated many of the professionals I ran into through my career. Jack was one of the first in my long learning process.

Don signed Jack to a deal when he heard Jack's song, "One Way Ticket to The Blues." That song has been a hit in every part of the world except America, and it still could be here. Jack was only nineteen years old when he signed with Don, but even as an independent teenage writer, he had twenty-five cuts on various artists. His first smash was "Just Between You and Me" with the Chordettes. But after that hit, the rest of his cuts never made top-10, so he decided to affiliate with an established company. Jack's hit catalog is impressive: "Everybody's Somebody's Fool" (Connie Francis), "Run to Him" (Bobby Vee), "Venus in Blue Jeans" (Jimmy Clanton), "When Somebody Loves You" (Frank Sinatra), and many more, including television themes like *Bewitched*.

The first deal Jack made with Don called for him to produce some sides, but without credit. Under that arrangement, Jack worked a lot with Neil Sedaka, and by the time he worked with me, he had moved up to being a credited, royalty-sharing producer.

With Kirshner and Nevins at the production helm, I went into the studio along with Jack Keller. For my first sessions, we cut live at the old RCA Studios, no overdubs, one song an hour. Carole King sang harmonies. We had strings and harps. We used the timpani percussion that got popular after the Drifters' "There Goes My Baby." It was like rock 'n' roll gone symphonic.

After "Halfway to Paradise," we cut another song by Carole and Gerry, "Take Good Care of My Baby," which Bobby Vee later had a hit with. There was still another Carole-Gerry song on the session that hit the charts without my help. The Drifters version of "Some Kind of Wonderful" was the one that climbed the charts. "Halfway to Paradise" was my first release, but that first session also included my second release, Barry Mann and Cynthia Weil's "Bless You." It was the first song the two wrote after they married, and would be my second hit on Epic.

One song I'd recorded didn't make the cut. I was positive that

Don would chose a Carole-Gerry song titled "Will You Still Love Me Tomorrow," because I thought it was a natural smash. "That lyric is something a girl would say to a guy," Don insisted. "No guy would say it." And so it was a number one record, Carole and Gerry's first, but for the Shirelles, not Tony Orlando, the name Don had decided fit a recording artist better than Michael Anthony Orlando Cassivitis.

Jack Keller was a big part of the sound we got on both of my first hits. When you look at the Don/Al team, Al was the producer while Don had the ears. Jack had the ability to translate what Don heard in his head to what Al was doing with the mechanics of recording. And he was as innovative a producer as he was a songwriter. We were required to use the new CBS studio by the time we recorded "Bless You." The facility was new, and everyone thought the first takes were sterile. Finally, Jack put this big electric bass guitar "Hava Nagila"–style line down just before he brought in the strings. It was exactly what we needed.

Don had a good relationship with Epic Records A&R chief, Dave Cappolette, and it was on CBS's Epic label that I was set to make my debut with Carole and Gerry's "Halfway to Paradise." This was a big step for Epic. The label had never signed a teen pop singer before. It was primarily a big band label—dance and ballroom music. They did have some vocalists, like Roy Hamilton, who'd had "You'll Never Walk Alone," "Don't Let Go," and "You Can Have Her." But they weren't aiming at the growing teen market. Frankie Avalon was on Chancellor, Annette was on Disneyland and then Vista, Paul Anka and Brian Hyland were on ABC-Paramount, Gene Pitney was coming out on Musicor. Kirshner persuaded Dave to jump into that market, and convinced him to use my record to do it.

But first, I had to get by Epic's public relations staff. I knew they didn't think I quite fit the teen idol profile, and so I was nervous about the publicity shoot scheduled in Central Park. Maybe people at the office sensed that I needed all the extra confidence I could get for that photo shoot, because Bobby Darin not only loaned me his tie to wear for the pictures, he decided to go with me to the Central Park location. Bobby made some small talk along the way, then, when we were almost to the park, he leaned over and said, in all seriousness, "You really are a wonderful singer, Tony." That was the shot in the arm that pulled a scared, overweight kid from the streets through a so-called glamour shoot.

Down the road, Bobby did me an even more meaningful favor. He stopped me on the street after he had open-heart surgery, and bequeathed me his rhythm section and his musical director, Bobby Rosario. Bobby was brilliant, a man with an Oriental kind of wisdom. But even his deep philosophical nature couldn't stop him from being devastated when Bobby died. We were working the Blue Room at the Roosevelt Hotel in New Orleans just before Christmas of 1973, when word about Bobby came over the television. I went to Bobby Rosario's room and heard absolute wailing. I started to knock on the door, but I just couldn't intrude on his private grief.

Back to 1961. Epic wasn't taking any chances. Don Kirshner may have shrugged off my weight, but those PR professionals had no intention of letting me look fat in my first publicity shots. They didn't have time to put me on a diet, so they solved it very simply. After the publicity stills were processed, a staff member in the Epic art department simply whipped out a razor blade and trimmed down my sweater! They'd decided to go for the Frankie Avalon look. They must have been satisfied with the resulting image, because they gave me tremendous radio and sales support.

The label decided to debut "Halfway to Paradise" on Dick Clark's *American Bandstand,* on March 21, 1961. They started promoting the appearance in *Billboard,* using a silhouette of my press photo, the same one they'd doctored to make me look like

Frankie Avalon. The copy read: "On March twenty-first Epic will introduce a voice you'll always remember, a name you'll never forget." Then the next week, they followed up with another ad, and finally, on March twenty-first, they showed the photo.

To get on *Bandstand* was the single most important thing you could do back then. Let's face it, Dick Clark was responsible for Frankie Avalon, for Fabian, for all those guys. The exposure he could offer was as good as it got. I think Dick Clark was the catalyst for most of the great performers we have had since the late fifties. He was color-blind from the first, too. He had Frankie Lymon on his show, Chubby Checker, Chuck Berry. That was taking a chance, given the climate of the time. He will go down in history as the greatest entrepreneur and music-igniter in the history of show business. And that was the guy I was getting ready to meet.

My debut on *Bandstand* was fine from a musical standpoint, but it had one glaring glitch, one that gave new meaning to "getting exposure" on *Bandstand*. It was my first professional appearance, the first time I really faced a crowd. Certainly the first time I was on television! I was scared to death. What if those dancers just stared at me? Worse yet, what if they wouldn't dance to the song? I gave myself a pep talk, got up, did my song, and they seemed to love it. Then the station went to a commercial, and Dick called me over for an interview. I was feeling pretty good about everything by then. He leaned over and handed me a note.

"Tony, your drug store is open."

I read it twice and still had no idea what it meant. "I don't understand," I began.

Dick leaned over and whispered in my ear. "Your zipper was open for the whole song."

I looked down, and there it was. My pants were unzipped and you could see my underwear. It's one of those things that is so mortifying you want to crawl off and die. All I could think about was my family, people in the old neighborhood, all looking at my underwear sticking out from my pants, and being embarrassed that I was making such a fool of myself. Dick must have seen the stricken look on my face. He shook his head.

"I don't think it showed up when you sang. Just fix it for the interview."

We did the interview, and I'm sure people wondered why I was so subdued after my big television debut. But when I left the studio I was about as down as you could get. You figure you get one big shot, and if you blow it, you can kiss everything good-bye.

But Dick must have been right, because nobody said a word. And believe me, somebody would have. My stepfather, for starters. Epic was thrilled. Kirshner was thrilled. So I just kept my head down and vowed to check my pants every time I stepped on a stage.

Years later Dick Clark gave me a great tribute on the twenty-fifth anniversary of *Bandstand,* asking me to host the show and be the opening act. What an honor. But he still reminds me about my inauspicious debut on the show. These days when he brings it up, I say, "Aw, Dick, it wasn't no big thing."

I don't know which was more exciting: the first time "Halfway to Paradise" played on the radio and the whole neighborhood started phoning Mamma and Mamita, or the first time I saw Papito come to a package show at Palasades Park, sporting a Tony Orlando button on his suit coat. It was also at Palasades Park, at a Clay Cole Show, an *American Bandstand*-type setup, that I met Frankie Avalon for the first time. I told him the story about the Epic Art Department taking a razor to my photo in the hopes I'd pass for a Frankie Avalon kind of guy. Frankie loved that. In fact I think my honesty about the incident kind of endeared me to Frankie, and we've remained friends to this day.

I had always had my feet planted in two musical worlds. On the one hand, I idolized the soul and doo-wop singers, Ben E.

King, Frankie Lymon, the Isleys. But on the other hand, I was a teenage kid who bought fan magazines. I remember trying to cut my hair like James Darren, wishing I looked as cool as Frankie Avalon, or, better yet, that I could meet Annette Funicello. And there I was, getting ready to be in their world. It was a pretty heady concept.

I found performing onstage very easy, a natural thing to do. It was rehearsals that scared me to death, and they still do. I hate rehearsing, especially when there are others involved. There's a kind of panic zone I get into, a feeling that the audience and the people I'm working with aren't going to like me. It's a little like how I felt in school, worrying that I won't measure up. So rehearsals were always a problem, and one that vanished when the curtain went up for the actual show. I have to admit, though, in the early days, rehearsals weren't the most frightening part of it all. It was the screaming girls that scared me half to death. I may have thought I wanted a Frankie Lymon–type swooning audience, but the truth is, I was in no way prepared for it.

One additional incident happened soon after "Halfway to Paradise" came out, and this one was big. It was so astonishing that I still don't know how to really relate the feeling. And my initial reaction will go a long way to explaining just how much effect those legendary writers working with Don Kirshner had on guys like me.

One day I walked into Kirshner's office and was handed a fan letter. It was short, but oh so sweet. The writer said he loved "Halfway to Paradise," and congratulated me on making a great record. The guy who sent it was Elvis Presley. I've heard over the years that this was not an uncommon thing for the King to do. He'd pass along congratulations or praise to a singer, a writer, or a musician, and I think it says worlds about what a good guy he was, about the level of respect he had for music. You'd think my first reaction would have been to phone Mamita, or Mamma, or some other family member I could share this with. But my initial response was to run through the halls of the office looking for Carole King and Gerry Goffin. It was, after all, their song.

Chapter 6

Murray the K

In addition to the Epic promotion push and *American Band-stand,* a third component to the success of "Halfway to Paradise" showed up in the person of one Murray the K, disc jockey and star-maker.

Murray "the K" Kaufman may not be a household name like Dick Clark these days, but during the fifties and sixties, he was one of the most flamboyant, innovative, and powerful people in show business. His clout was such that when Brian Epstein asked American acts touring Europe advice for breaking the Beatles in the American market, almost to a person, the acts pointed him in Murray's direction. Once in the U.S., the Beatles bonded with Murray to the point where he hosted a Beatles' show at Carnegie Hall, broadcast his radio program from their hotel room, and promoted them on air so much that he became known as the "fifth Beatle." He stayed close to them, too. He was the one who did the peace interview with John and Yoko from their bed.

Murray sponsored shows from a lot of locations, including Manhattan's Cheetah, San Francisco's Fillmore, and even an airplane hangar at Long Island's Roosevelt Field. He also put on some holiday shows much like those of another legendary dee-jay, Alan Freed. Not only was Murray the K my childhood radio idol, he inspired the writing of "Splish Splash," so there was a double connection for me and the Kirshner group. The idea for the song was born before Bobby had a recording career. He hung out with Murray a lot, and one Saturday night the two of them were at Murray's house, and for some reason Bobby started talking about taking a bath. Murray said, "Splish splash I was taking a bath." Bobby ran home and wrote the song, gave half the writing credit to Murray, and got his first hit out of it.

When I got to know Murray he was broadcasting from WINS and producing some of the most exciting shows in the nation from Brooklyn's Fox and Paramount Theaters. He was the king of New York radio, Murray the K's *Swingin' Soiree* and the Sub-marine Race Watcher's Club, named after the song by the Angels, Jiggs Sirico, and Peggy Davison. Or, as Murray used to say, when referring to submarine watching, "What's a cheap date but to take your girl out to park by the ocean and tell her you're gonna watch the submarine races? Just tell her, 'You can't see 'em, honey—but they're down there racing!' "

Murray had so much power in New York that once, when he said he was going to Plum Beach for a meeting of the Submarine Race Watcher's Club, the Belt Parkway jammed up for over ten miles.

And that's the guy who liked "Halfway to Paradise." Dick Clark and Murray the K—I was in Fat City. What a thrill it was when Murray offered me a spot on one of his Easter shows at the Paramount. He took me under his wing right away, and did everything he could to help me become a good entertainer. The best advice he ever gave me was to look the audience in the eye and never interrupt them. "Sing to the girls in the front row. Make eye contact with them, and make sure they make eye contact with you," he'd say. "If they're clapping, let them clap. If they're laughing, let them laugh. Don't step on their reactions."

Murray was more than a great deejay and show host, he was an entertainer in his own right. He could take the stage and hold it like a star. He could be outrageous, loud, funny—but always graceful. Fred Astaire was his idol, and it showed in the way he moved. So he was an integral part of these shows, which had an abundance of star power and a wide diversity of musical styles.

Murray only wanted the best, so King Curtis fronted the house band. King Curtis, who had started out working with Lionel Hampton in 1950, and moved from Fort Worth, Texas, to New York City in 1953, was one of the all-time great rock 'n' roll musicians. He's the guy Sam Cooke is talking to on "Having a Party," when Sam calls out, "Play that one called 'Soul Twist.'" And it's King Curtis on saxophone for the Coasters' "Yakety Yak." The headliners at Murray's shows never had to worry about a band—they had the best.

The first Easter show I appeared on featured headliners Jackie Wilson, Smokey and the Miracles, Jerry Lee Lewis, and Chuck Jackson, who had "I Don't Want to Cry" on Wand Records. Murray made a big deal out of the teen idol concept. We'd each be rolled out on a cart with a sign that read "Teen Idol," do our song, then roll off and make way for the next. On my first show, we had Brian Hyland, Frank Gari, who had "Lullaby of Love" on Crusade, and me.

We did six shows a day. They'd run a movie, then do a show, then run the movie again, then do a show. It was like the old days, when Mamma would take me to Radio City to see a movie, then stick around for the vaudeville acts. It made perfect sense that Murray the K liked to put on shows in this manner, because he'd been raised in vaudeville. His mother had been a piano player and his aunt a performer.

Jackie Wilson was the most memorable of all the acts I worked with on any of Murray's shows. What an artist. He was such a soulful singer. He'd come out with "Lonely Teardrops," do his spins, and the house would absolutely come down around him. And what a character. Jackie was like a black Jimmy Cagney. Jackie loved Cagney, he even had Cagney's moves down. Every so often when he was talking to you, you'd get this "you dirty rat" growl from him. He was light on his feet, like a boxer, and he was always dancing, as if doing roadwork.

I learned a lot from Jackie. There was a little slide left-right foot thing he did when he'd sing "My heart Keeps Cryin', Cryin'." I picked it up from him and you'll still see me do it in my show. It's a classic Jackie Wilson slide, and I loved it then and now.

In many ways, you become a composite of all the performers you really admire. When I did television sketches in the seventies, I could feel Jackie Gleason's influence. I can still tell when I slip into a Bobby Darin or Sam Cooke mode in my show. Sometimes when I'm onstage I can almost feel like I'm back at the Harlequin Studio with the Isley Brothers, trying to keep up while they're singing "You make me want to shout."

I remember Jackie Wilson in his dressing room warming up, going from his lowest note to his highest. He was the first singer who showed me how to get my facial muscles loose. He used to sit there and say, "Okay, go as low as you can—*me, me, my my, mo, mo, moo*. Then take it up a notch—*me, me, my my, mo, mo, moo*." Years later, when I played Broadway, where it's vital that you warm up before a show, I'd sit in the dressing room and think of Jackie. "Okay, Tony, go as low as you can—*me, me, my my, mo, mo, moo*."

Jackie Wilson was also very bright. I don't think he had much formal education, but he was well spoken, leaving the impression of an educated man. There wasn't a trace of a street kid in Jackie's talk. So it wasn't just Jackie's moves and vocal techniques that influenced me, it was his class.

Chapter 7

On the Charts and on the Road

"Halfway to Paradise" ended up a Top 40 pop hit, not as strong a showing as my next outing would make, but enough to get me on the concert trail. It also set the stage for my second release, Cynthia and Barry's "Bless You." That single went even higher on the charts, although I think people from that era remember me more for "Paradise."

By the time I started on my first big tour, I was well on my way to losing enough weight so that I was actually recognizable from the publicity photos. That first tour was something for a kid from Tar Beach. I expect it was something for all of us out there. One thing it wasn't: drugs, sex, and rock 'n' roll. We were a bunch of squeaky-clean types.

We were all to meet in front of the General Arts Corporation (GAC) on Fifty-seventh Street between Sixth and Seventh Avenues. The lineup included the headliner, Gene Pitney, Brian Hyland, Ray Stevens, and me. Mamma insisted on driving me to the bus, and made me bring my uncle Johnny along as a kind of chaperone. Then, at the urging of Mamita, Mamma and Louis drove to our first show, following the bus all the way along! That embarrassed me to death. I could just picture Pitney and Hyland snickering about the kid who had to bring his keepers along.

Luckily I got there first, and when Gene showed up he didn't seem fazed by anything. He was a great guy, kind of quiet. And I suppose it was silly to consider what any of them would think. None of them could have cared less that I had my uncle on the bus, or that my mother was determined to drive along for the first leg of the tour. Gene and Ray were nineteen. Brian and I were sixteen. We were all just kids.

Gene had "I Wanna Love My Life Away" out, but "Town Without Pity," the song that became his signature, wasn't released until around Christmas of 1961. Still, he was the big draw, and I felt lucky to be on the tour with just one song on the charts. Gene, a native of Rockville, Connecticut, started out with more of an ambition to write, than to sing. In fact, since he is such a vocal genius, some forget that he was, and is, a *great* songwriter. He was still a college-going teenager, majoring in electrical engineering, when he had songs recorded by Steve Lawrence, Tommy Edwards, Billy Bland, and Roy Orbison, before he decided to cut his self-penned song, "I Wanna Love My Life Away." One thing some might not remember is that Gene also wrote Ricky Nelson's monster hit, "Hello Mary Lou." Gene's now been inducted into the Rock 'n' Roll Hall of Fame, a long overdue honor.

Brian Hyland had the biggest hit of any of us the previous summer, when "Itsy Bitsy Teenie Weenie Yellow Polka Dot Bikini" went number one. Brian started out even before his teen years, in a band called the Delphis, in his home borough of Queens, New York. He was only a sophomore in high school when he recorded "Polka Dot Bikini." Brian is vastly underrated as an artist, probably because "Polka Dot Bikini," a novelty tune, was his first hit. Not only was he an excellent entertainer at a young age, his other hits, like "Sealed with a Kiss" and "Gypsy Woman," were brilliantly done.

Ray was just getting ready to release "Jeremiah Peabody's Polyunsaturated Quick Dissolving Fast Acting Pleasant Tasting

Green and Purple Pills." Ray was a Georgia boy, from a cotton mill town named Clarkdale. He, too, fronted a band while still a high school student. And like Gene, Ray first saw himself as a writer.

Since I was the new guy on the charts, I got the lowest billing—almost. Bottom billing went to our bandleader, who didn't travel on the bus, but took his car everywhere. Bobby Vinton was everybody's bandleader back in those days. He was from Canonsburg, Pennsylvania, the son of Stan Vinton, a local bandleader. Bobby made enough money playing in bands to put himself through college, earning a degree in music composition. He was the only really trained guy out there with us, and his expertise showed onstage. Bobby played piano, clarinet, saxophone, trumpet, drums, and oboe.

Bobby had made a couple of big-band recordings for CBS, but neither of them went anywhere. In fact, the label had started to drop him, but he reminded them that they owed him another shot in the studio. On the very day he reminded CBS of their obligation, he pulled a demo from the trash and heard a song he thought was radio friendly. By the time we started on that tour, Bobby had just recorded the song for Epic, and was hoping to hit the charts.

This story about the trip is especially funny if you've been around Ray Stevens. Ray is a major power in the music business, and one of the artists who built a real estate fortune with some wise investments that he made through the years, many of them with Chet Atkins. Ray is a sophisticated and savvy guy. But when I first met him he was a scared kid from Georgia.

Brian, Gene, and I were standing around in front of the building waiting for Ray, and the time to leave came and went. We thought maybe he'd made a mistake and was standing on the wrong street corner, or he had gone inside the GAC building, so we set out to try and round him up. Finally, I caught a glimpse of someone standing underneath a stairway at GAC. I went over, and sure enough, there stood Ray, practically shaking in his boots.

"What's the matter?" I asked.

Ray pointed out to the street, where New York's morning rush hour was in full swing. Cars were darting everywhere, cabbies were shouting. People were crammed into the streets trying to get to work on time.

"I never saw so many people in my life," Ray said. "Everybody's going in every direction and it looks like they're going nowhere! I can't handle it."

I looked out at the street and tried to imagine what it might have felt like if you'd never been in New York before. I had to agree with Ray—I might not have handled it very well, either. As it was, being from the city, the noise and confusion seemed normal to me. I got a kick out of Ray. He was very quiet, very shy—nothing like such releases as "Jeremiah Peabody" or "Ahab the Arab" might suggest. It wasn't that he was really frightened, just unnerved. And he'd done what most young kids do when they're unnerved: He went into hiding.

We finally got on the bus, and, ironically, it was my uncle Johnny who formed an immediate bond with Ray. Uncle Johnny was a singer, too. You may remember he helped me put together the Five Gents. But we all hit it off as friends and traveling companions right off. The chemistry on that bus was immediate, and that was a very lucky thing because it might have been a nightmare. It was a forty-day tour, and we slept in a hotel only a few times during the trip.

Bobby Vinton didn't stay in the hotels with us because the tour managers wouldn't pick up the bill for him and his guys. They traveled in his old car, and caught up with us at various points down the road. One day we were rolling down the highway just outside of Duluth, Minnesota, when we spotted Bobby's car pulled to the side of the road. He was jumping up and down and waving his arms, holding something in one hand. We were afraid somebody was sick or his car had broken down.

When we pulled over, he said, "Follow me! We gotta find a record store. I just got the acetate for my record!"

In those days, you could walk into a record store, go into a little room, and listen to records before you bought them. So Bobby led us through town, found a record store, and we all piled into a little soundproof room. Bobby was going on and on about how scared he was over the record. He had a one-shot chance with Epic. Like I said, they'd only just started into this end of the business, and they weren't taking many chances. He knew that if this didn't at least make Top 40, he was out of a deal. We all knew how iffy record deals were, and we were pulling for him. But I'll say this, we were all brutally honest with each other about our records.

He slipped the acetate on the player, and we all held our breath.

"Roses are red, my love, violets are blue. Sugar is sweet, my love, but not as sweet as you."

I looked over at Gene, and he immediately looked away, with an almost sick expression on his face. I looked at Brian, and he was grimacing. Ray Stevens wouldn't even look at any of us. He didn't want any part of it, and had zoned out. Finally I said, "Uh, Bobby. We're your friends, and we love you. But this is the corniest piece of crap I ever heard, and I think everybody else agrees. *'Roses are red, violets are blue? Sugar is sweet and so are you?'* You're crazy to bet your record deal on this song! You gotta go in and cut something else!"

But it was too late. Bobby's "Roses Are Red" had already shipped.

We didn't feel sorry for Bobby for long, though.

By the end of that forty-day tour, "Roses Are Red" had hit number one on the charts. It stayed there four weeks, and showed all of us "song experts" just how little we knew about anything. It wasn't long before the billings went BOBBY VINTON, RAY STEVENS, AND TONY ORLANDO, DRIVING THE CAR BEHIND THE BUS!

Ray later said the DAC tour was an awful experience that wore him out, but at least he saved enough money to buy a car. He had good reason to cast a dirty look back on that trip. The bus we traveled on had no bathroom, no bunks, no privacy. If you had to use the bathroom, you went behind a makeshift curtain in the back and peed in a Coke bottle. There were few comfortable places to sleep and we had a good natured war going on over the choice spots. The very best place to sleep was the backseat, which offered the most space to stretch out. At first, every time we stopped at a White Castle to get some burgers, everybody ran to get back to the bus first, and grab that backseat. In time we decided to take turns.

Ray decided to sleep in the luggage rack on nights he didn't get the backseat. Ray was pretty proud of himself for finding an alternative. (My own alternative was to sleep in one of the seats, and hang my legs over the seat in front of me.) But what Ray didn't think through was the fact that the luggage rack was smooth metal, not unlike a playground slide. If the bus stopped too fast, you'd zoom down the rack like a bowling ball. One night the bus came to a sudden stop, and I jolted awake just in time to see Ray go past me like a meteor. His eyes were about the size of saucers, and he was going headfirst to the front of the bus. That incident taught us a lesson. In the future, we slept with our feet toward the front of the bus to save a potential headache.

These trips gave us an opportunity to meet a lot of performers, whether they were on our specific tour or not. Once, during the Christmas season, Cleveland had a big holiday extravaganza complete with a basketball game featuring performers and deejays, and a postgame show. Conway Twitty played in the game, and since he'd been a professional baseball player, it came as no surprise that he was a solid basketball player. The guy who surprised a lot of people was Johnny Mathis. What an athlete! He was an amazing basketball player—and so fast you couldn't keep up with him! I believe that if Johnny hadn't been an entertainer, he could have been a pro athlete, and, in fact, we learned that he'd turned down a chance to run track in the Olympics because his singing career was getting started.

In comparison to Conway and Johnny, I was an overgrown klutz! I remember feeling so embarrassed running down the court, with my sneakers squeaking loudly every time they hit the floor. Then I fell down, and proved I *was* a klutz!

But the show turned out worse than the game, and I took a big chance at pissing off an audience. We performed the show at the same stadium where we'd played basketball. There was no band, and so we all had to lip-synch our records. During "Halfway to Paradise," the record player got stuck: *"halfway-halfway-halfway . . ."* Right away, the audience started throwing pennies. There were thousands of people in that audience, and a lot of 'em must have had pockets full of change. I was bobbing and weaving, but the pennies were hitting me anyway. Finally I grabbed the mike and shouted, "All right everybody, shut up!"

It was like turning off the radio. Somebody finally shut down the song, and the pennies and the yelling stopped. I said, "I just wanted to wish you all a merry Christmas." Then I started to leave the stage. If the record had a glitch in it, I didn't see any use trying it again. Right then, Conway Twitty, bless his soul, walked out and began clapping. Then Johnny Mathis walked out clapping. Then the deejays all came out. All of a sudden, that same audience was applauding. One guy yelled, "Put the record back on!"

So I came back to center stage and they started the record again. *"I want-I want-I-want-I want . . ."* I just laughed, took the mike, and said "Happy New Year!" The whole audience stood and applauded.

It was a risk to chastise the audience the way I did, and almost unthinkable to tell them to *shut up*! I also know that when I said, "I just wanted to wish you all a merry Christmas," I was basically laying a guilt trip on them. But it had been a gut reaction. What would have happened if I'd asked, "Would you good folks kindly quit hissing and throwing pennies?" The Cleveland audience would have eaten me alive. As it turned out, they didn't mind getting as they gave.

And it didn't hurt that Conway walked out clapping, either.

One of the most interesting times I ever had on tour in those days was when we went to England to play the Granada Theatre chain, in 1961. Bobby Vee was the headliner. The rest of the group was, aside from myself, Dusty Springfield (before the hits), and Clarence "Frogman" Henry.

Bobby Vee will never forget this tour, because I almost sliced his ear off.

We were all backstage, and like most guys our age, Bobby and I were fooling around, pretending to open-hand spar, jabbing at each other. I'd been learning to finger pick my guitar, and had let the fingernails on one hand get very long. As I threw my right hand, my nail shot through his earlobe! Thank God ears don't seem to bleed as bad as some other parts of your body. We slapped tissue around it, and Scotch taped it together. He still tells people I "cut him."

Clarence was a loner. He was older, a New Orleans cat. Very into his music, and very disinterested in us. A nice guy though. Just not into the "teen idol" scene. What a surprise, huh?

The most important thing that happened involved Dusty Springfield. Dusty was still with the Springfields at the time, still singing folk songs à la Buffy Sainte-Marie. She had "Good Night Irene" out in England. Dusty was miles away from her signature sound, and I am proud to say I played a role in its development.

I was sitting around singing a Sam Cooke song, and she said, "What's that you're singing?"

"You don't know who Sam Cooke is?"

Well, she knew the name, but she was too immersed in the folk scene to have sought out Sam, or some of the people I loved. The closest she'd come was Chuck Berry and Little Richard. So I went out and bought her a bunch of records: Clyde McPhatter, the Drifters, Sam Cooke, Ben E. King, Bobby Bland, the Isley Brothers. She fell in love with Sam Cooke. Then I played her "At Last," by Etta James. Dusty almost fell on the floor. Along the way, you could hear the change. It was astonishing to witness an act take shape that would be so important.

So later, when I was back in the States, I turned on the radio and heard Dusty sing, "Wishin' and hopin, and . . ." I said, "Oh my God! She found it."

Chapter 8

And Then I Had Lunch with . . .

Okay, I promised myself I wouldn't ever say, "And then I had lunch with." But I've got to say this, "And then I got to meet America's sweetheart," the girl every red-blooded boy in the country secretly lusted after: Annette Funicello. Just like every-body else, I was in love with her. I was head over heels for her. And keep in mind, I thought Frankie Avalon and Paul Anka were the coolest guys around, too. So you can imagine how excited I was when I walked into a New York restaurant one night and there the three of them stood. I was speechless. Moreover, because I had records out, they accepted me as one of their own! I probably could have died happy right then. And even though I didn't have much to say, when the trio started to leave, Annette turned to me and said, "Are you going over to Sal Mineo's party?"

Sal Mineo's party? Sal Mineo the movie star? I didn't say that, though. I tried to be cool.

"Yeah," I answered. "But I forgot the address."

"It's over on Fifty-seventh," she said, and noted the building and apartment number.

"And what time is it?"

"Around eight," she said.

I was way past being *halfway* to paradise. I was talking to Annette and heading for Sal Mineo's. If that wasn't heaven, I didn't know what was.

I found Sal's building, and knocked on his door, knowing I was a gate-crasher, and having no idea what kind of a reception I'd get. Sal opened the door, his girlfriend on his arm. It was still another movie star, Jill Haworth, the British actress who'd appeared with Sal in *Exodus.* I quickly stuck out my hand and introduced myself.

"Oh, sure," Sal said easily. " 'Halfway to Paradise.' " Oh, the power of a hit record. I was in.

I talked with Sal and Jill for a little while, and was struck by how much he reminded me of the people he played in movies: shy, vulnerable, sensitive. The way he talked about people in the room, his friends, I had the feeling that he was a very loyal person, just like he'd been in *Rebel Without a Cause.* The times I ran into him after that, I kept that first impression. He was a nice guy, a genuine guy you could trust.

Then I turned and saw the real deal—the guy who outshone all others in the "cool" department. Fabian Forte. He already had a bunch of hits out there: "Turn Me Loose," "Tiger," "Hound Dog Man." And the movies were setting him up as a screen idol, too. But the main thing about him was that *look.* Other than Elvis Presley, I never saw such a beautiful man. Everything about him was perfect, from his sculptured hair to his gleaming, toothpaste-ad teeth. Like Elvis, he looked like a walking god. I'd feel embarrassed talking this way about another man if I hadn't heard others, guys like Carl Perkins, say the same thing about the first time they saw Elvis in person.

Fabian was sitting on the floor, kind of leaning back, looking over the room. He was way too cool to be glad-handing or "working" the room. He had that star essence I spoke of earlier—with a touch of cool, to boot. He motioned to me, and I went over, as if summoned. I sat down, introduced myself, and again, he knew my hit. I guess all of us kept on top of the chart situation back then. We sat there and talked music until he got bored with the party.

"Hey, I got a new car," he said. "Want to go for a ride?"

"Sure," I said.

Then he got his girlfriend, though I never did quite get her name. And through some other set of circumstances I wasn't in on, Jill Haworth came along, too. It seems she and Sal had had a fight, and she wanted to go. So here I am, a guy who's hardly been on a date before, riding along in Fabian's new Buick, with Sal Mineo's movie star girlfriend on my arm.

It didn't take long for me to realize that Fabian was crazy. Not insane, just wild. Trust me, he was the James Dean of all the teen idols. All of a sudden, he jumped the car on the sidewalk and we burned rubber through the financial district, bringing a whole new meaning to the sidewalks of New York. My heart was in my stomach, especially when I looked at Fabian's face and realized he had absolutely no fear. The film *Rebel Without a Cause* kept flashing back in my mind, not only because of Sal Mineo. I was reliving the scene where those guys are playing chicken in cars. Somehow I knew that Fabian would never be the one to swerve. I've got to admit, when he dropped me off, I was only too happy to get out of that Buick alive.

Fabian was the toughest, most macho guy I ever met—and that includes the gang members in Hell's Kitchen. He was the *real* Italian stallion, Stallone's got nothing on Fabian. He would have waded into the middle of a gang fight with no fear whatsoever. And I have no doubt that he'd be standing at the end.

Here's a little example of what Fabian was all about. It's a story that doesn't start with him, but with Jerry Lee Lewis and Jackie Wilson. As I mentioned earlier, Jackie was a boxer. He was fast, and he was strong. I wouldn't have messed with him. But Jerry

Lee Lewis didn't mind doing it. I've heard stories about Jerry Lee going nuts on people, but I never saw it firsthand. I did see people backing down from him, just because of the underlying threat of craziness. Jackie Wilson, of all people, was one of them.

It started the way most of Jerry Lee's altercations did—over who closed the show. Jackie was supposed to, and Jerry Lee thought he was entitled to. No fists flew, but Jerry Lee closed that night.

The thing about Jerry Lee was you got the feeling he didn't care if he lost a fight, but he was gonna hurt you. When he came at a person, they'd better be ready.

There was this one time that someone didn't back off, and that person was Fabian. It was at a radio appreciation day in Houston. Mickey Gilley played the show, as did I. It started just like the Jackie Wilson thing started—over the closing spot. Only this time, Fabian closed. Jerry Lee didn't go for him, either. Fabian was crazy, but not mean. And to tell you the truth, I don't think Fabian would have really allowed himself to get into a fight with Jerry Lee, especially right before a performance. First of all, he was too much of a professional. But like I said, Fabian had that look. The look that said, "Don't screw with me." And Jerry Lee didn't screw with him. At least to his face.

Remember the famous story about Jerry Lee setting fire to the piano to upstage Chuck Berry, when Chuck was the closing act? Then he walked by Chuck and said something like, "Follow that."

What Jerry Lee did at that show in Houston was to finish his set, then throw up in a malted milk cup, which he left onstage. Then he walked by Fabian and said, "Your turn."

I believe he was out of the building before Fabian finished his set, though.

If I was ever in a situation where I faced enemy fire, or on an airplane with a terrorist, Fabian Forte's the guy I'd want beside me.

• • •

I thought about that wild car ride with Fabian a year or so later, while I drove out of Manhattan to my mamma's home in Union City, New Jersey.

I was almost eighteen years old before I learned to drive a car. My driver's education classes started down at the America Hotel in a studio called Mirror Sound, where my friend Brooks Arthur was engineering a record on Guy Mitchell. I hung out there for a while, and when I left I ran into this drop-dead, beautiful woman in the lobby of the hotel. I struck up a conversation with her, and at some point in the talk, she invited me to her room. I had no idea she was a hooker.

On the second day I was with her, I picked up a mono-grammed cigarette lighter with the initials "FS" on it.

"It's Frank Sinatra's," she said.

I must have looked confused, so she started explaining.

"Sometimes I walk into a club with Frank, not as his date—just for the 'look.' "

"Get *outta* here," I said. "You don't know Frank Sinatra."

"No, really. That's his. Look at the initials."

" 'FS'? Could be Fred Silverstone."

She just shrugged, and I laughed it off.

On the third day, I heard that Bobby Darin was going to be at the Copacabana, where my uncle Carmine was the maitre d'.

"How about I take you to the Copa to see Bobby?" I suggested.

"Oh, yeah, I'd love to go."

I'd never driven a car in my life, but she suggested I drive her Cadillac to the Copa. I couldn't stand the idea of admitting I didn't know how. She handed me the key, and I desperately tried to figure a way to weasel out of the situation.

"The car's in a parking lot over on Eighth Avenue," she said. "It's a white Cadillac."

"That's crazy," I quickly said. "We're right here. Let's just jump in a cab and go."

"Okay."

What a relief.

We get to the Copa, and Uncle Carmine dropped his jaw.

"Come over here, kid!"

"Hey, Uncle Carmine," I said. "Pretty girl, huh?"

"I want you outta here right now," he ordered. "Frank was in here with her just the other night! If you think I'm gonna let my own nephew bring Frank's girl to this club, you're crazy. Get outta here!"

He ushered me out the door and put me in a cab. And I still had her keys in my pocket.

"Don't you even dare to come back here," he shouted as the cab pulled away.

As soon as I got back to the hotel, I called the Copa and asked to speak with her.

"I'll just leave the keys here," I said.

"No," she said casually. "I gotta go away for the weekend. Keep the car and have some fun."

I didn't know what to do. So I finally went down to Eighth Avenue and got inside the car. I pulled the car out okay. After all, I'd watched like a hawk while Fabian drove like a maniac through the streets of New York. Surely I could maneuver those same streets if I drove carefully. Lucky for me, a Cadillac is the easiest car in the world to drive.

I was afraid to try to change lanes, so if I needed to go in a different direction, I made right turns until I was on the correct track. I finally was going toward Ninth Avenue successfully! I had the hang of it! I was so pumped! I decided to drive back to Union City, New Jersey, where I was still living with my mother and Louis. I aimed the car through the tunnel, cruising down the road to Union City, where I knew some explanations were in order. Not only was I driving, but I was driving a brand new white Cadillac owned by a hooker, and Uncle Carmine had thrown me out of the Copacabana.

Luckily, I didn't get the third degree. I guess Mamma just figured it was all part of show business.

There's another story about the Copa that I want to share with you. It happened years later, when I played what was to be the last show played in that building. I hadn't known about the closing; it wasn't advertised as a "last night" situation. But I sat at the bar after the show, and saw an amazing display of loyalty. The waiters all walked in, took off their fancy Copa uniforms—right down to their shoes—threw them in a pile, and lit them on fire. This crew looked straight out of *Goodfellas.* They then said, to Jules Podell, "Boss, this is for you." It was the end of an era.

Chapter 9

Beatlemania Sinks the Teen Idol Ship

What none of us realized during those early 1960s was that a musical invasion was about to hit the U.S. with as much of a surprise factor as the attack on Pearl Harbor. I don't think American music's power brokers ever saw it coming, and while it wasn't an actual war, it would expand boundaries and change the country's musical landscape forever. I think to understand a big part of the Beatles' appeal you have to understand the musical climate that produced them.

European fans, and especially British audiences, were very different from those in the States. When I was on tour in Europe in 1961, I was surprised when fans would come up and ask if Carole King was going to be singing background vocals on my next record. They'd ask if Jerry Chester was playing drums on some Carole King demo. They cared as much about the musicians as they did the stars.

Most American teenagers were buying a specific song or artist, with little concern about who was playing on the records. They didn't pay attention to the fact that, say, Joe Osborne was playing bass with Ricky Nelson or that the guy who played saxophone on "Locomotion" was Artie Kaplan. While American teens were reading personality profiles in *Sixteen* magazine, the

Brits were devouring music magazines that discussed in depth the pickers and the history of the music. They were interested in *the band* as a whole.

American record-buyers did have a great appreciation for what I call "the originators"—Little Richard, Elvis, Gene Vincent, Chuck Berry, Bo Diddley. They loved what the musicians contributed, too. But with the exception of Elvis Presley, they didn't *read* much about those people in the mainstream teen magazines. So when the Beatles finally hit American shores, part of the appeal was their upfront admiration of the rock genre and the people who invented it. They understood the blues side of rock's roots and they understood and appreciated the country roots, as well. The Beatles seemed more knowledgeable than half the people who worked in the business! They revered the Crickets, Carl Perkins, Elvis, Buddy Holly, Chuck Berry. They were aware of all the pickers and tipped their hats to them. They talked up Motown, the Drifters, and sang "Chains" by Carole King and Gerry Goffin. John Lennon loved Elvis; Paul McCartney loved Little Richard. Chet Atkins, Buddy Holly, and Scotty Moore influenced George Harrison.

Let's face it, the Beatles fit into American music more than many American musicians.

The Beatles had a passion for this music called rock 'n' roll, and it showed. When they got to America, there was no missing the band's admiration for the originators. Make no mistake about it—the Beatles were a retro band whose first love was the blues. In 1970 John himself explained it to *Rolling Stone* in explicit terms. "The blues is a chair, not a design for a chair, or a better chair . . . it is the first chair. It is a chair for sitting on, not for looking at or being appreciated. You sit on that music."

John's attitude, I think, makes it clear why it's important that artists, songwriters, and musicians understand what they're sitting on—where their roots are and what influences they draw from. As John went on to say during that 1970 interview, the

Beatles were building their own sound, but they knew where it started.

Since that time I've heard executives says, "Oh, the minute I heard the Beatles, I knew that they'd own the market." Don't believe it. I was there and here's what I heard from executives: "Who are these guys?" "She loves me yeah yeah yeah—what's that about?" "It's a fad. It'll be over in a month." And the big one in music circles: "What's with those haircuts?" It seemed to me that the hair is what threw everyone. They just couldn't believe that kids would actually dig what they considered goofy hair. More disastrous still, they didn't get the music. But the kids dug it big time. They loved the music, hair, the clothes, the accents, and the "yeah yeah yeahs." They also picked up on the band's respect for the roots of rock. Plus, the Beatles were solid players and tremendously talented writers. The writing team of Lennon and McCartney still ranks among the industry's finest. George Harrison was a great intuitive guitarist who never stopped exploring and innovating, as he did with his sitar work. Ringo is an underrated drummer. He was solid and steady, providing the rhythm that was the band's backbone.

Add to all those components the fact that the Beatles had a very smart general named Brian Epstein running the invasion. Brian not only made sure they got the Ed Sullivan gig, he took out a full-page ad in the *New York Times* that read like an interview. I suspect that 80 percent of the people who read it thought it was a *Times* piece. Still, many in the U.S. record business thought it would pass. Maybe they should have listened to Brian Epstein, who said as early as 1962 that the Beatles would be bigger than Elvis.

By the time the majority of U.S. record executives realized they'd been "attacked," radio was no longer particularly interested in the so-called teen idol singers. Oh, the dates were still available but they were for less money and smaller venues. My reaction? The first thing I remember thinking when the Beatles were all over the charts and acts like the Dave Clark Five and Gerry and the Pacemakers came along was this: *It's payback time.* There had been the time that only the very biggest European acts, people like Cliff Richard or Cilla Black, could compete with American artists on the American record charts.

The positive side of this for American pop artists was that European fans are very loyal. It seems like on our side of the pond we're always looking for the next big thing, the newest trend. Europeans may love a good trend or a fad, but they aren't as likely to throw out the old to make way for the new. The fans are also into diverse forms of music. They might listen to a Chet Atkins recording followed by a Beatles tune followed by a Carl Perkins. And while American radio went cold on American artists, those acts remained hot overseas. Guys like Gene Pitney and Paul Anka had a steadfast European audience. They could get big bookings and sell out major venues. It's just that after around 1965 they couldn't get much support from American radio, which had moved on to the Beatles, Motown, and Bob Dylan.

The Beatles' attitude fit right in with the growing Bob Dylan-style antiestablishment feelings growing among American teens. People watching televised interviews saw John, Paul, George, and Ringo saying whatever came into their minds, sometimes smoking on camera, and wearing whatever suited their fancy. The Brits basically had two different types of antiestablishment crowds—the mods and the rockers. The mods loved the outfits that we first saw the Beatles wear, the velvet vests and the ruffled shirts. The rockers wore leather, like the Stones. But both were definitely questioning authority.

When I saw some of those interviews, I marveled at their openness. When I'd started singing I'd been put through what a lot of people call "star school" or "media training." Believe me, we were scripted. We wouldn't have talked about religion or politics or anything that smacked of controversy. If we smoked or drank we'd have never admitted it or done it in public. And we certainly never talked about having any specific girlfriend. Our answers might be more along the lines that we were "still searching for that perfect girl." The girl our mammas would like.

The British Invasion ended up bringing us an eclectic bunch of artists ranging from the R&B-oriented Rolling Stones and Rod Stewart to the pop of Tom Jones. It became difficult for radio to categorize the new waves of music because often an act would flow from one genre to another. It wasn't like the teen idol days when the sounds were more similar. I loved this because it's when music gets great—when it's not boxed-in or pigeon-holed. That's when the innovations come, when chances are taken and barriers broken down. I wish the name was just "music"—with far less attention paid to the categories like AOR (album-oriented rock), easy listening, and others that are used in marketing and airplay pitches.

As the Beatles progressed, their lyrics changed radically from the "yeah yeah yeah" tunes to sophisticated and powerful themes. Both the Beatles and Dylan ushered in a new respect for serious songwriting and tackling social problems in song, instead of just aiming for the "hit." Thank God for people like Paul McCartney, John Lennon, Bob Dylan, and Joan Baez. Their lyrics reflected the youth's discontent and it gave them both an outlet and a voice, just as Marvin Gaye's great song, "What's Going On," did in 1971. As the antiwar movement grew, music was marching in step right there at the front. What guys like Lennon and McCartney, and Bob Dylan were writing really *was* the sentiment "blowing in the wind."

It's hard to look back and remember that a great many adults were angered at Dylan's antiestablishment songs and what they perceived as his general disrespect for authority. It was probably the same naysayers who thought Elvis was singing the devil's music, which brings me to the subject of rap music.

I believe that the same attitude is found among those who

hate rap music across the board. I'm not saying I find it pleasant to hear rap songs about killing police, raping, and robbing. But that music reflects, as Marvin Gaye might have said, "what's going on." We should always at least be aware of what's happening on the street.

And there are some messages from the streets we should hear. First, there are rappers who aren't about violence. Additionally, there's a discontent in the cities, in the neighborhoods, and we'd do well to listen and try to affect change somehow. Let's not forget that at one time Bob Dylan was called anti-American and a communist for writing songs about injustice, about the social fabric of the country. What he was writing was folk music—music of the folk—and we might want to take a look at some rap music in that light. Listen to the streets. When music makes you think it's more than doing its job within the art form.

There's another thing that gets me going, and it's when people turn their noses up at artists just because they are the current rage or phenomenon, like today's boy bands. Anyone who says the Backstreet Boys can't sing is crazy. They're probably just reading some highbrow critic who hates anyone the general public embraces. I'm sorry, but those boys sing their butts off. They work hard on their choreography, and on their harmonies. Their tracks are tight and solid. Their songs are musical and memorable.

When the Backstreet Boys recorded "Ain't Nothing but a Heartache" I read some criticism of it. Yet if Celine Dion had recorded it everyone would have applauded. But because the Backstreet Boys are marketed at a specific age group, they take some cheap shots. The record companies want to sell to the teen market, but the critics trash artists who make that music, no matter how successful they are—or maybe because of it. Britney Spears suffers from this syndrome, so that now you can see her trying to say, "Look at me, I'm now doing grown-up songs."

I remember when some were calling the Bee Gees a cartoon act. When they trashed Elvis for playing Vegas. Every act that gets huge goes through it. Cher? She's still here and making hit records. I think it all goes back to this concept: Some critics believe if it's "popular," it can't be good.

And God forbid that a hugely popular artist take a chance. Do that and the arrows will be in place and the bows pulled before you leave the studio. I was one of the first people who bought a copy of Garth Brooks's *The Life of Chris Gaines* CD. Frankly, I was curious. I'd heard he was going for a movie soundtrack, a greatest hits project from a fictional pop star. To pull that off would be formidable. First, you'd have to capture a variety of sounds. No greatest hits package is going to reflect just one standpoint—musically or emotionally. Second, even though the songs were supposed to have been recorded at various times through this fictional star's career, there still had to be a flow throughout, because the glue that held it together was this one pop guy's vision. I couldn't wait to see how it would be pulled off, especially by a country singer.

When I worked in music publishing, I had an office in Nashville, and gained great respect for it as a songwriting center. It really has become Tin Pan South. When I had the television show, I had a lot of country stars on, and they never failed to pull good ratings—even during the early seventies, when pop was supposedly the reigning god of the music world. I had Johnny Cash, Tammy Wynette, Tanya Tucker, Minnie Pearl, Buck Owens—all of them living proof that country is in no way the redheaded stepchild of the music business.

But I was interested in seeing how the current country king could pull off this ambitious *Chris Gaines* thing. I popped the CD in the player and was thunderstruck. He'd done it. I was there through the years he was dealing with, both as an artist and as a producer. He damn well succeeded, and succeeded beyond all reason. Imagine my surprise when I read negative comments in the press. You know what? They didn't get it. It's that simple. Garth and Don Was didn't miss. Those music critics missed, and missed big.

I'll get off the soapbox now, except to say that the rich musical tapestry that evolved in this country owes much to the British Invasion. We had the country music, the blues, the rock—and the Beatles inspired other artists to meld those styles, to take the chances and to shrug off the nonbelievers. And that's why I say, when someone takes a chance, when they try something, cut 'em a break. They just might be the next Fab Four.

It's with some pride I later learned that the Beatles were aware of my early music. John Lennon came over to me at the Grammy Awards one year and told me he'd been at the show I did with Frogman Henry and Bobby Vee at the Granada Theatre. "Bless You" had been at the top of the British charts.

"Was that in sixty? Sixty-one?" He asked.

"Nineteen sixty-one," I said. Then I admired the diamond Elvis pin he wore on his lapel.

John didn't talk much. He didn't seem one for making a lot of small talk, though he did appear to be in an almost giggly mood, possibly from smoking something before he got there. A lot of glad-handing and casual conversation goes on at big industry events, but John Lennon didn't expand on his initial comment about coming to our show at the Granada. He didn't say "I was there with my family" or "I was with such and such a band at the time" or "I loved the show" or any of that usual stuff. He just said, "I thought 'Bless You' was a funky tune, you know."

Having said all this, I have to add that the Beatles put me out of business.

Chapter 10

From Mr. Mom to Management

I met my first wife, Elaine, at one of Murray the K's extravaganzas at the Brooklyn Paramount Theatre. Elaine was Jerry Lee Lewis's fan club president, and since Jerry Lee was headlining the show she'd come to the theater to meet him. She was very close to Jerry Lee and his family. In fact, after the return from that disastrous English trip, when fur was flying about Jerry Lee and his thirteen-year-old cousin/wife, Elaine was with the wife in their hotel in New York. I was attracted to Elaine right off and asked her out, never suspecting she was anything but a teenager like myself. It turned out she was twenty-one years old.

We went out that night with her sister Geri, but I didn't see her for several years, when we met again at Hill & Range Publishing, where I was supposed to be meeting with Burt Bacharach to listen to songs. We went on another date, this time minus sister Geri, and started seeing each other exclusively.

We got married in Mamma and Louis's living room and had a nice reception with about fifty people in the backyard. Mamma did her best to make the day a special one, even though she was dead set against it. I was only twenty years old and far too young to be a husband, in her terms. But Elaine and I were in love, and, like so many young people, we thought it was the thing to do.

I'm not gonna go out of my way to bash my ex-wife here. She is, after all, the mother of my son Jon, one of the lights of my life.

As in any marriage, neither of us was a sweetheart for the duration. She was and is a strong-minded woman who follows her own path. That path included throwing her wedding ring under a truck on our honeymoon, and dumping all my clothes in the street two weeks after we got married. For me, seeing the wedding ring so easily discarded was clearly symbolic. I don't think I ever felt quite the same about the marriage. Elaine was convinced I had a wandering eye from the beginning. Years later, I did cheat on her, and it's something I'm not proud of. But back then, I was interested in no one but my wife.

When we first got married, we moved into a tenement on Featherbed Lane, in the Bronx. Now, I've got one of those "I was so poor" stories for you. It's really a slumlord story, and I fear this kind of slumlord still exists in damn too many places. Our building had old, old plumbing that went out every so often. We had running water, but half the time the toilets didn't work. No matter what you did, how much you complained, the landlord wouldn't fix it. So Elaine and I—along with everyone who couldn't afford to move—sometimes had to do our toilet business on newspapers, roll up the paper, and take it outside to the Dumpster. Ain't that a landlord and a half? And they wonder why ghettos get bad.

I was still trying to hang on to my record career, despite Beatlemania, but work was scarce, and I was down to collecting pop bottles for train fare for Elaine to get to work, and me to get to 1650 Broadway. Finally, it seemed useless.

Bookings started to get fewer, money for shows seemed to dry up for those of us who'd been called the teen idols. I have always tried to avoid wearing blinders when the handwriting was on the wall. After stumbling through some months of a shrinking market, I decided to make a change. I quit when the quitting was good. Keep in mind, I wasn't a prolific songwriter who was getting royalties from BMI, ASCAP, or SESAC, organizations that monitor radio and record companies, collecting royalties for airplay and sales. I was the kid from Tar Beach who felt lucky to have had his fifteen minutes of fame.

Elaine had been married before, to the great songwriter, Ken Neil, who wrote "Candy Man" and "Somebody's Talking," among others, and they had a young son, Kenny. I stepped easily into the parental role. Since I was out of a career, and Elaine had a good job at Hill & Range Publishing, I stayed home to care for Kenny. In some ways, I think I saw Elaine as more of a mother figure, and the arrangement gave me a chance to play at being a kid again. Years later, when I was in therapy, my doctor told me that it seemed as if I identified with the single-mother-only-son concept, and in some way wanted to reverse the bad relationship I'd had with my own stepfather. Kenny was fatherless, as I had once been or had felt. And I said I was not going to be the distant stepfather Louie Schroeder had been to me.

I was bullshitting myself.

This is one of the hardest things for me to admit in this book—another come-to-Jesus moment. My whole life, I've talked about being Mr. Mom for a period of time, and I know a lot of people thought, "That's wonderful." Truth is, I don't think I was a very good father figure to Kenny. I don't think I realized that until I started work on this memoir and really took a hard look back. In some strange way, I acted out my own conflicting feelings about what a father, or a stepfather, was supposed to be.

Sure, Kenny and I went to the park, we played ball. I helped him with his schoolwork. I always worried that Kenny didn't get much outward affection from Elaine. She was never demonstrative, at least as far as hugs went. Not like my family. So I tried to be more demonstrative.

I didn't really know anything about being a parent. Oh, I'd baby-sat Rhonda, but that was far different. In many ways, it's easier to comfort a handicapped child even when they are having a seizure, than to figure out how to raise a good "normal" one. I was way too hard on Kenny, and he was a good kid. I'd never let him get a bit out of step, and I'd paddle him if he did. Not hard, not even close to a rough spanking. But a paddling is a paddling, and I think it humiliated him. I never did that with my son, Jon.

So you can see the hypocrisy of me saying Elaine wasn't enough of a hugging-type parent. I was home being a disciplinarian, which didn't really come naturally to me. I've seen many parents over the years who think that a stern attitude is the only way, but I don't believe it for a minute. And I made a mistake in doing it.

The other factor is the loss of my career. I've always said that I didn't mind moving into the Mr. Mom role. Maybe that was jive I was selling myself all this time. Maybe I resented it, after all.

I really liked Kenny. But I was too tough on him, and I regret it. He was better off when I quit being Mr. Mom.

Why did I quit? Well, while I saw it as being a parent, some people, including my mother, saw it as being a deadbeat. This was long before "Mr. Mom" was considered respectable. One day Mamma dropped by, and found me mopping the kitchen floor. It was almost more than she could take.

"Tony! What do you think you're doing? You gotta get a job."

After that mandate from my mother, I started job-hunting. One of the first people I talked to was Wally Schuster, a long-time song plugger and very respected in the New York song-publishing world. I said, "Wally, I gotta get a job. Can you help me?"

Wally knew me, was well aware of my time with Don Kirshner and Carole and Gerry, and knew that above all, I loved good songs. He gave me a job as his assistant at the publishing arm of MGM—Robbins, Feist & Miller—for a hundred dollars a week.

The first thing Elaine and I did was move out of that no-toilet slum. We found a little apartment in a two-story motel-type building in Union City, New Jersey. The rent was $113 a month, and even as we moved our stuff in, we worried that we wouldn't be able to come up with the money regularly. At least I wasn't out collecting pop bottles for train fare.

I cut my publishing teeth at Robbins, Feist & Miller, where I learned how the game was played, how to stay on top of which artists were looking for songs and what type songs they needed. Having had the experience with Kirshner turned out to be invaluable, too. I applied everything I'd learned with him to my new job. With Wally I ended up getting to work with Arnold Maxim, who went on to be president of MGM, and talents like Eddie Snyder, who wrote "Strangers in the Night." That was one of our songs. What a great catalog we had!

Going from star to publishing assistant didn't bother me. I really loved the music business—all aspects of it. And I'd learned at Aldon Music that songs are the heart and soul of the business. I didn't miss the star trip a bit, but I know it took people a little while to see that I was doing more than just marking time until I could get back onstage. I worked like hell and when people realized I was sincere about a career in publishing, I was taken seriously.

My initial problem was that I had never worked anywhere. You couldn't consider singing demos and writing songs for Kirshner work. In fact, the closest I ever got to a real job was back when I was twelve and took that short-run gig at the Manhattan Hotel's men's room—handing towels and cologne to men after they wiped their asses. Singing and the men's room—that was the extent of my résumé. When I came to work with Wally, I didn't even know how to open a file cabinet. The first day, I followed the secretary around and waited until she opened one. Then I acted like it came perfectly natural to me.

I lucked into a deal though, and it made me a player in the publishing world. Arnold Maxim took a liking to me, and I hung out in his office a lot, always interested in the synergy between the film and song industries. MGM had a film coming out called

Valley of the Dolls, with a theme song written by Andre and Dorie Previn. I listened to the song, and immediately thought of Dionne Warwick.

Andre shook his head. "You'll never get Dionne," he said. "She's exclusive with Burt Bacharach."

She had worked with Burt since 1962, when he took a demo tape of Dionne singing a song he'd written with Hal David to Scepter Records. Scepter turned down the song, but wanted Dionne. Down the road, the team of Warwick, Bacharach, and David had thirty hit singles and twenty or so big-selling albums. By 1967, when we were looking for a singer for "Valley of the Dolls," Dionne had top-ten hits with "Anyone Who Had a Heart," "Walk on By," and "Message to Michael."

I went to Arnold Maxim's office, and he repeated Andre's sentiments. "You'll never get Dionne Warwick."

But I kept thinking, "Why not?" I knew Burt well. He was a friend of my wife Elaine's through her work at Hill & Range. And he'd produced a record for me on Epic, a song called "To Wait for Love." Burt was one of the guys. I figured it wouldn't hurt to ask, especially since this was a song for a film, not the usual single-release type thing. So I went to Burt and gave him a hypothetical.

"If MGM had a movie theme they wanted Dionne to sing, what would it take to get you to record it with her? I mean if it was something you liked and thought she should do."

He smiled and said, "A *lot* of money."

Then I ran right back to Arnold Maxim and told him we could cut the deal with Burt.

"How?" he asked.

"Offer him a lot of money."

"What's a lot of money?" he asked.

"How should I know?" I answered. "I don't live in the world where a lot of money comes into play. You do though. What's it worth to you?"

Then I had another idea. "Tell him it can be the B-side of her next record. Then, when the record comes out, we'll hire some promotion guys and promote 'Valley' ourselves, as if *it* was the A-side."

So Arnold picked up the telephone and offered Burt $25,000 to record "Valley of the Dolls," and said it could just go on the B-side.

Burt took the deal. Then I picked up the phone and called Cal Rudman, who had a very powerful promo sheet called "The Cal Rudman Report." "Who are the top record promotion guys in the country, and what would they cost me a week?" Cal knew me from the old days when I was an artist on Epic, and he helped me round up one hell of a team.

The A-side record, "I Say a Little Prayer," was released on November 4, 1967, and went to number four. But with our promo team swinging into action, "Valley of the Dolls" started getting airplay. On February third, Sceptor Records went ahead and released "Valley" as a single. It went to number two and stayed there for a month. It was Dionne's biggest record to date, and we had publishing on it.

Arnold and Wally ran all over New York singing my praises. They hyped me so much around town that the big publishers starting sniffing me out. Ultimately I was approached by the people at April Blackwood Publishing, which had been created by Mitch Miller, and was owned by CBS. They offered me five hundred dollars a week to be the company's general manager. I was stunned at their offer and unsure what to do, because I loved working with Wally and Arnold. But since Wally was a fair guy, he told me I'd be foolish not to accept that kind of money. And since Wally was smart, I followed his advice.

Overnight I went from making four hundred dollars to two thousand a month. We moved again, this time to a nice apartment in North Bergen. It was a big step up from the Union City place, and worlds away from Featherbed Lane. For the first time, we stopped worrying about paying the rent. We stayed in

Bergen Park even after Dawn was put together, and I started touring.

Thanks to the success at Robbins, Feist & Miller, I was put in charge of the creative end of the company. Neal Anderson was the business head of the company, although, like his mentor, Clive Davis, he was great in creative, with some of the best ears in the business. I wasn't an attorney, like Clive or Neal, but I did want to learn everything I could from both of them. In publishing, if you can study at the feet of people who combine top legal minds, business acumen, *and* great ears—you've got some kind of a classroom situation.

I'd gained back up to well over two hundred pounds when I went to work for April Blackwood, and Clive Davis made no bones about how he felt about obesity. During one meeting, he passed me a note that said, "Tony, you're too fat."

I couldn't believe it! I wasn't an artist. Why was my weight an issue? So after the meeting I confronted him about it.

"Clive, that was pretty rough stuff you just sent me! I know I've got a problem with my weight. It's not like I don't *want* to lose it."

Clive had an even stronger answer: "I'll tell you why you are going to lose that weight. If you are not going to be loyal to your own body, how do you expect people to think you'd be loyal to this company?"

I sputtered around some, and he went on. "You're in your twenties. It's not like you're a middle-aged man. Here you are, a young executive in this company, and you've got a forty-two inch waist. Take more pride in yourself."

I lost the weight.

Other than that, I never once had a run-in with Clive Davis. I worked for him for four years, and had nothing but respect and admiration for the man.

Clive took some criticism early on because he was a lawyer, not what people considered a "music guy." Nothing could have been further from reality. Clive Davis is a music guy of the first order. He knew songs, he knew artists, and he knew what it took to make the business end of it work. And he was always willing to stick his neck out for his beliefs, even when it might mean immediate criticism.

The Blood, Sweat & Tears song "Spinning Wheel" is a good example. In its first incarnation, the song was seven or eight minutes long. Now, Clive was a great proponent of having some lengthy songs on an album, if it was right for the album. But he also knew that any song longer than three and a half or four minutes would suffer at radio. If he believed the song was a potential hit, and could be cut down, he'd ask the artist to try to do it. He understood why radio wanted shorter songs, from their concern for how many tunes they could program, to the question of how long the listener would pay attention to a song on the airwaves.

Sensing it was a classic, Clive insisted that the engineer try to cut "Spinning Wheel" down to airplay length. Back then, you didn't edit by computer, you edited by razorblade. You had to be very careful to make the cut without a glitch. Add to that the fact that "Spinning Wheel" was a tough song to cut down. But in the end, the song became a classic, one that would not have been heard on Top-40 radio as an eight-minute song.

Calls like that made Clive's reputation. He built Columbia as a commercial label.

One of the most amazing record executives I ever met was the president of Columbia, Goddard Lieberson. Goddard had an air of elegance and style that outdistanced almost anyone. He taught me one of the most important lessons any record or pub-lishing executive can ever learn.

"Never tell an artist or writer that you are turning them down because of a lack of talent," he said. "When you turn down a song, keep in mind that you are turning down a piece of the writer's heart. And that can do serious damage to the creative process."

Goddard wasn't simply being a sympathetic soul, although he did care about the fragile egos that so many artistic types possess. He had sound business reasons. The same writer you turn down one week may have a gem you'd kill for the next.

Here's another reason to treat songwriters and artists with respect: You never know where they'll wind up from a business standpoint. There's an old show biz adage: Be careful whose toes you step on while you're climbing up the ladder, because they may belong to the guy whose ass you'll have to kiss on the way down. Tommy Mottola, now head of Sony Music, comes to mind.

I was a publishing hot dog when I first met Tommy, then a would-be artist. He had this great Frankie Avalon look with dark curly hair, and he was a fantastic singer. If he'd come along a decade earlier, he might have been another Frankie Avalon or Bobby Vinton. But I knew that the days of the teen idol were gone. I'd been there, done that.

Oh, I could have signed him up, kept stringing him along. But there would have been no honesty in it. And anyway, I talked quite a bit with him, and knew he had great music instincts. I had a feeling that Tommy was so hip, so smart, that he could be another Clive Davis if he just gave it a shot.

One day I said, "Tommy, this ain't gonna work. You're good enough to be a star, but the English groups have run us out of business. You're too sharp to keep knocking your head against a wall. Why don't you go over to Chapel Music and do what I'm doing? Learn the business."

He went to Chapel, and believe me, Tommy Mottola learned the business.

The flip side to that is my own experience. I went the other way, and ended up back on stage. But the reason I was able to pull it off is that Bell Records came up with a niche for me, the right sound at the right time. It's all about making the decision, figuring out the right move. It's always a tough call, though. Like Yogi Berra said, "When you come to a fork in the road, take it."

When I got to April Blackwood, I knew that my first obligation was to the company's song catalog. It's too easy in publishing for a new guy to come in and start signing writers without understanding what songs and writers he already represents. When that happens, a lot of good songs get ignored, and some great writers overlooked. I spent an entire year familiarizing myself with every song and every writer that April Blackwood had ever signed.

In the process of doing this, I came across a project called the Flying Machine, a group formed in 1966 by two guys from Martha's Vineyard. Their names were Danny "Kootch" Kortchmar and James Taylor. The songwriting talents of James Taylor on songs like "Rainy Day Man" and "Night Owl" particularly struck me. It appeared that we hadn't done much with him as a writer, so I decided to try and find out what this guy was up to. By the time I tracked him down, he'd signed the Flying Machine project to the Beatles' new label, Apple Records. The downside to that was that I believed we'd missed the boat with James Taylor. The upside was that the Beatles were launching their new label with an album of April Blackwood songs. Or so I thought.

I tracked down the acetate of the upcoming Apple album, and to my surprise, all of James Taylor's songs were credited to Maclen Music, John and Paul's publishing company. I knew this was big stuff, so I went straight to Clive Davis and told him I needed to pay Apple Records a visit. With Clive's blessing, I jumped on a plane and headed for London, acetate in hand. I walked in the building, introduced myself and dropped the bomb.

"I believe there's been a mistake on this Flying Machine album. April Blackwood owns James Taylor's songs. We've got this entire project in demo form at our New York office."

Well, it was like a shock wave went through the entire building. All of a sudden George Harrison walked in, and I said hello to him. And that's when it really hit me that I was in the big leagues of publishing. Here's a guy who just over a year earlier didn't know how to open a file cabinet, and I was standing in Apple Records' offices with the goods on their first release. They didn't argue about it. And I'm sure the error was just that, a mistake. James Taylor certainly wasn't the kind of guy who paid attention to detail, and he probably didn't know or care where his songs were published. Apple thought they'd hit the jackpot.

When I got back, the entire April Blackwood staff stood and applauded. It felt every bit as good as when audiences were screaming for Gene Pitney, Brian Hyland, and me.

James's Flying Machine project didn't do as well as Apple had projected, and he was soon back in the market for a label. He sent a tape of some current material to April Blackwood, and Neal passed them along to me. I told Neal that I believed the new songs were out of this world.

" 'Fire and Rain' is probably one of the best songs I've ever heard."

Neal wasn't sure. " 'Sweet dreams of flying machines in pieces on the ground'? It's about the group breaking up."

"I don't care," I said. "We've got to do everything we can to sign this guy and his new songs."

So Neal said I should take it to Clive. He wasn't sure either.

"I don't know," he said. "The Beatles couldn't break this guy even though he was their flagship artist. What makes you think we can?"

"He's come leaps and bounds, Clive."

Clive smiled. "Then go ahead. Let's sign him." But just before I left his office Clive called me back.

"Tony, you know those cartoons where a guy is sitting out on a limb, sawing himself into a fall? That's you, buddy."

It was one of the very few times I ever knew Neal and Clive to miss something on the front end. I promise you very little ever got by either one of them. As you probably already guessed from my "Roses Are Red" experience, and you'll see during my Tony Orlando and Dawn career, I've missed countless hit songs. But I almost never miss a *great* song, and James Taylor had great songs. Of course, you never know whether "great" will translate into "hit," but I was willing to bet that in this case it would.

We missed it, anyway. By the time we made our move, Mo Austin at Warner Bros. had already signed James Taylor. *Sweet Baby James,* was a multiplatinum release, and "Fire and Rain" became a classic, one of pop music's all-time biggest songs.

Both Neal and Clive were quick to give me credit for having seen it coming. I have been very, very lucky in my professional life. So many times upper-level executives will take credit for what others do. Not so with the men I was fortunate enough to work with during my early years: Don Kirshner, Al Nevins, Jack Keller, Wally Schuster, Arnold Maxim, Neal Anderson, and Clive Davis. I would meet more people of that integrity, and each one, in their own way, reiterates the sentiment of that song I once sang in the upstairs room near the Wing & Fin: "You never walk alone."

I take no credit for James Taylor. He was already in the door before I heard and loved his music. That also goes for Laura Nyro, another great writer I worked with at April Blackwood. I signed some good people, guys like Donnie Fritz, who's played with Kris Kristofferson all these years, and Chip Taylor, who wrote "Angel in the Morning" and "Wild Thing." And I signed a guy off the street, a guy who couldn't get arrested when I met him. From the first time Barry Manilow sat down at the piano and played a song for me, I felt he could be a songwriting and performing force in the business.

Barry was playing the bathhouses with Bette Midler when he first started coming to April Blackwood, and I signed Barry to April Blackwood publishing, and got him a deal with Bell Records.

I also wanted to sign Bette Midler, because I believed her talent was unstoppable. Unfortunately, Larry Utall, the president of

Bell had seen Bette on the *Tonight Show* and she reminded him of Dodie Goodman. Barry and Bette met with me at Eskow's Coffee Shop on Fifty-seventh Street, just around the corner from Bell Records, and I had to admit that Larry had passed. Bette wasn't fazed. "The guy has no vision," she said, and strutted out of Eskow's. The next thing I knew, she was signed to Atlantic. Down the road, Barry came to me and said he was leaving Bell for Arista. I couldn't believe he would be that disloyal to the label that first believed in him, and said so. He said it was a move he had to make. Clive Davis entered the picture, and it turned out to be the best move Barry ever made.

Nobody at the label thought anyone with the name "Barry" would make it at radio, so I suggested he use a group-type name. Barry agreed and we went with "Featherbed," since I lived on Featherbed Lane in the Bronx. I may have hated the apartment, but I loved the name of the street.

The name wasn't the only concern Bell Records had regarding Barry. They felt some of his songs weren't commercial enough to fly on pop radio. One song in particular was so esoteric they turned it down: "Could It Be Magic." I listened to it several times more, and finally had a talk with Barry.

"Listen, we've got to get this into a Top-Forty vein or radio won't play it," I said. He suggested we work it over together, so I rewrote the lyrics, and the melody, turning it into an up-tempo tune. I knew it was a little bubblegummy, but thought we'd see if it would fly with the record company. It didn't, so we split the copyright and put it on the shelf. That wouldn't be the end of it, though. The song would end up costing me eighty grand a few years later.

April Blackwood was happy with the job I was doing, so much so that Neal called me in, and gave me the exciting news that I was being promoted to vice president. I'd been working in publishing for about four years.

Then I got a phone call that would change everything.

Chapter 11
A New Day Dawns

My old friend Hank Medress, from the Tokens ("The Lion Sleeps Tonight"), was one of Bell Records' producers. He phoned me one day and said he was unhappy with a vocal he had down on a song called "Candida," written by Toni Wine and Irwin Levine.

"It needs an ethnic feel on the lead vocal, Tony," he said. "I thought maybe you'd lay down a track."

"It's for a release?" I asked, unsure just what he was asking me to do.

"Yeah," Hank said. "It could be a smash with your voice on the track."

"I can't do that, Hank," I said. "I'd lose my job if I recorded for another company. I'm on the verge of getting a big promotion. I'm not gonna screw that up."

"You won't screw anything up," he said. "It's just a single, and since the harmonies are so strong, we'll put it out as a group. Nobody will ever know."

I didn't like the idea at all. I had no burning desire to be a star, not even a wistful longing to get back on the stage. Like I said, the applause I'd received from the staff at April Blackwood after my London trip was plenty for me. I loved being behind a desk, signing writers and artists. I loved being behind the board in the

studio, cutting demos and records for other people. I loved finding songs my writers wrote, and pitching them to appropriate
acts, like matching Laura Nyro songs with Blood, Sweat & Tears.
I didn't need this complication.

"Come on, Tony," Hank kept on. "I really need you to do
this."

Finally, figuring the song would bomb anyway, I agreed, and
together with Hank and coproducer Dave Appell, slipped into
the studio where I put my voice on the prerecorded tracks.
Dave, by the way, is one of the unsung heroes in the music
business. He was an unbelievable talent, a brilliant musician,
arranger, and producer. I'd like to see the industry honor him in
some way.

I didn't think any more about it until one day Elaine and I happened to be out driving when "Candida" came on the car radio.

Elaine frowned. "That sounds exactly like you," she said.

"It is me," I admitted sheepishly.

The song was a smash. According to *Hits* magazine editor Roy
Trakin, it combined the magic of street corner doo-wop, barrio
Latino, and classic Brill Building pop. What a strange sensation!
The street was buzzing with talk about this group Dawn and the
hit song "Candida." But I couldn't say a word to anyone or I
knew I'd be fired.

The idea of getting fired was horrific to me, because on September 8, 1970, my son Jon had been born. I took the responsibility of fatherhood very seriously. I will never forget that day. I
had this great concept of becoming a new father. I'd pictured
myself seated in the fathers' waiting area with other guys, smoking cigarettes, nervously waiting for a nurse to appear and tell us
if we had a son or a daughter. For months, it had played like a
movie in my mind.

I hadn't wanted to go to work that morning. I had the feeling
it was the day. But Elaine said she'd been through it all before
and was days away from delivering. Well, I *hadn't* been through

it, so I took her word on it. I shouldn't have, because when I got in to the city, Elaine called me and said the pains were coming fast. I didn't see how I could fight my way back out of the city and back to North Bergen fast enough. So I called Marvin Lasheber in the Bronx. Marvin was my brother-in-law, married to Elaine's sister, Janet. I told him I didn't know if I could get back through the Lincoln Tunnel in time, but he could use the Washington Bridge, which was faster.

"Let's go *now*! One of us will make it in time!"

The race was on. I drove like a maniac through the tunnel, along West Side Drive, through Hoboken, Union City—the New York skyline on my right. None of that had been part of my new father movie scenes. I pulled into our driveway, and there was Marvin, pulling in right behind me. I ran to the apartment, got Elaine, and off we went to Englewood Hospital. We got in that car around 12:50 P.M. and by running stoplights and speeding, I made it to the hospital around 1:04. They took Elaine, and Marvin and I headed for the fathers' room. I hadn't even lit the first cigarette when someone announced, "Mr. Cassivitis, you have a son."

We didn't exactly name Jon after the songwriter, John Christopher, but that's where the name came from, anyway. He's written hundreds of songs, including "Always on My Mind," which Willie Nelson had such a hit with. Elaine had seen the name "John Christopher" on a Brenda Lee album, and thought it had a beautiful ring to it.

And young Jon Cassivitis *was* always on my mind. He was especially on it during the time when I wasn't sure what to do about becoming an artist once again. Frankly, it was a roll of the dice that I didn't think I could take.

Hank Medress soon came back to me with another song. I thought it sucked. I listened to "Knock Three Times" and couldn't believe Hank was even bringing it around. "What's it mean, Hank?" I asked him. I mean the lyrics were talking about knocking three times on the ceiling or twice on the pipes. What pipes? Who had exposed pipes anymore?

Medress kept up the pressure. Once again I agreed to sneak into Bell's studio and make a record and once again, the fictitious Dawn had an out-of-the-box chart-topping, million-selling single. This time *Hits* described it as "Ben E. King meets the Ohio Express."

Bell Records found itself with a hit act that didn't exist. Dawn was me and a group of session singers: Toni Wine, who'd written "Candida," Linda September and Jay Siegel from the Tokens. By the time "Knock Three Times" hit number one in England, there were five or six groups billing themselves as Dawn and claiming to be the original.

I was torn up trying to think what to do. I had a good job that I loved and was secure. I was about to be promoted to vice president, which would have made me the youngest VP at the label. But there were those two hit songs out there and there were a bunch of guys taking credit for them. It's wild. I hadn't figured either one of 'em for a hit, yet there was something special about the vocals and Hank's production. Hank told me I was gonna have to go out on the road fast. Of course, what Hank didn't tell me was that he and his partner had *put* some of those bogus bands on the road to help promote the songs.

There was another problem I had to consider and that involved Bell Records' lack of album promotion. Bell was primarily a singles label. It wasn't like signing with Clive Davis at Columbia where you'd get a bunch of tour support. Even though Hank and Bell had put some groups out there doing shows, they'd never spring for the major tours we'd have to do once we were acknowledged as the real Dawn. I realized that when all was said and done, I might be responsible for fronting a lot of the money I earned just to keep Dawn on the road. That's how it worked, too. By the time we got the television show I'd put over $800,000 into our act and was about to go under financially. But in the beginning, I made the decision to jump in with both feet. I believed it was doable and if you're an artist with a number one song out there—you leap.

Like the champ he is, and has always been, Clive Davis gave me his wholehearted support for the career change. Clive didn't merely give me his blessing. True to form, he asked me if we had an album's worth of material. I said we didn't, and he said. "Well, just make sure four or five April Blackwood songs are on it!"

Bell Records left it up to me to decide who and what Dawn was. It could have been just me, or me and a bunch of guys, or whatever. But I figured we had something going with my lead vocals and the two female backup singers, so I decided not to mess with success. I had to find a couple of female harmony singers.

Just after making the decision to put a group together, I happened to be in the studio producing a single for Barry Manilow. He decided the song "Run Rosie Run," needed a more soulful sound, and asked a friend to recommend an R&B backup group. Tony Carillo, who'd just done the arrangements on Gladys Knight and the Pips' "Midnight Train to Georgia" recommended Isaac Hayes's backup group, Hot Buttered Soul, which had a young singer named Telma Hopkins. Deciding to include her in Dawn happened faster than I would have dreamed, although signing her was not easy.

I was sitting in the studio when Telma and two other girls came into the room. My God, I was just struck dumb! Telma Hopkins was the most stunning woman I'd ever seen. She had this velvety skin and wore a long wig like Tina Turner. She had on high boots and this little short dress. I didn't even have to hear her sing to know I wanted her for Dawn. Telma didn't waste any time making small talk, though.

"We want our money in cash," Telma said, not skipping a beat. "We don't work for no W-2's and all that. Cash. Understood?"

I understood all right, and I agreed right off, knowing that the

Hot Buttered Soul sound would be the best thing that could happen to Manilow's record. But the more I was around Telma, the more I started thinking of her as a member of Dawn.

"Listen, Telma," I began, when she was taking a break. "I've got two hits out there right now under the name of Dawn. 'Candida' and 'Knock Three Times.' I gotta put a group together to start touring and was wondering if you might be interested."

Telma was barely paying attention to me. She just stretched out there in the chair, eyes kind of narrowed, looking like an incredibly bored lioness. "Uh-huh," she finally answered.

"I'm real serious. There's a bunch of bogus groups out there saying they made these records, and if I don't do something right now, the time's gonna be gone."

She just looked at me in a disinterested way and said, "Hmm, I don't know. Maybe."

I decided to take that as a positive and press on. "Are there any more like you at home? I need another singer, too." Of course, what I was really saying was: *Are there any more at home who look like you?* I wasn't any dummy—if Dawn was made up of me and two goddesses, we'd certainly be a step ahead of those other groups out there on the road.

Telma acted as she so often did. She sat there as if she hadn't heard me until I was almost ready to start begging. Finally she said, "Yeah. My cousin Joyce is a singer. But I don't think I want to be in a group. I like what I'm doing. Gives me a lot more time." Then she pulled herself out of the chair and took a leisurely stroll back in the studio.

After the sessions were over I tried again, pursuing her like a love-struck teenager, which is kind of how I felt.

"If you're going to be in town tomorrow maybe we could have lunch and talk about Dawn," I suggested.

"Maybe."

"Could I pick you up at your hotel?"

"Have you got our cash?"

I scrambled around and got the cash to pay her and the other girls. That seemed to please her.

"Okay," she said, with a slow smile. "I guess since you played straight with me and paid up I can have lunch and hear about your deal. I'm staying at the America Hotel." Then she swept out of the studio like royalty. You very seldom see that kind of unconcerned confidence. Here was a backup singer who simply carried herself with the aura of a diva, a superstar. I really wanted her in Dawn.

I showed up the next day a little before noon. As I was dialing the house phone I looked around the place and noticed that it was a little shabby. Surely she wouldn't turn down being a part of a hit group!

The phone rang and rang and rang, and when she finally answered she sounded surprised when I told her I was down in the lobby.

"Oh. I'll be right down, honey."

Well, at least I'd gone from the guy paying for the Manilow sessions in cash to "honey," so I figured I was a step ahead of the game. Little did I know. I was never gonna catch up with Telma Hopkins.

I sat down and waited. And I waited and waited. Now I tend to be a pretty responsible kind of guy. If I set a time for a meeting, I try to make sure I'm there on time. But on the other hand, I had been around show business long enough to know other people don't quite have the time thing going for them. Telma was one of those, and I was willing to wait. I waited for an hour, and then it got to be almost two hours. I looked at the clock and it was nearly two in the afternoon! I finally called the room again.

"Telma, it's Tony. I'm still in the lobby. You all right?"

"Oh," she said, absently. "I'm taking a karate lesson. And I have to leave for the theater at six."

I couldn't believe it. But I was determined this woman was

going to be a part of Dawn. "Well, I really want to talk to you and I'll wait all day and night if that's what it takes."

"Okay," she said and hung up. Since Telma is such a professional, I have to believe the delays were all about her lack of interest in my group.

I kid you not, Telma didn't stroll out of the elevator until a quarter till six. But when she did, she was so breathtakingly beautiful I almost couldn't speak, let alone raise hell with her for making me wait all that time. She looked a little surprised to see me. "Are you still here?" she asked, her head tilted in an almost mocking gesture. She devastated me, and she knew it.

"I told you I wasn't leaving. Can we just talk for a few minutes?" I answered.

"I guess I can stretch it a little," she said. "Let's go across the street."

We went over to a restaurant and ordered coffee. I gave her my whole sales pitch again. I told her about Bell Records, about the hits, about the bogus Dawns running up and down the road. Finally I got down to the biggest problem of all.

"I'm not gonna lie to you Telma, I got a big problem," I admitted. "I've got a tour booked to Europe and I don't have my group in place."

It was as if I'd said the magic word, hit the jackpot. Her eyes lit up, she put down her coffee cup and leaned across the table. "Europe? You got a tour in Europe already booked?"

"Yeah, and if I don't have Dawn put together and rehearsed I'm in a lotta trouble."

"We'd have to rehearse a lot? How much time are you talking about?"

"Only enough to have the songs down," I promised. "Then we can get the kinks out of it while we're in Europe. By the time we get back to the States we'll be ready for the big rooms, some television appearances."

Big showrooms and television appearances didn't impress

Telma. But she did like the idea of a European vacation. "Okay. I'll go to Europe. But if I don't like it you have to pay my way home."

"Sure," I said, quickly. I'd have promised anything at that point. "Now tell me about your cousin Joyce. Does she look like you? Is she a good singer? What's she been doing?"

Telma looked at the clock on the diner wall and started getting ready to cut out for the theater. "She looks just like me. And we've been doing that Motown thing. I'll tell you what. You come to Detroit and I'll pick you up at the airport."

That was all I had to hear. I booked a flight for Detroit the following week, but I wasn't taking any chances. I informed Telma I'd take a cab from the airport. When Telma brought Joyce to meet me, I figured on Polynesian goddess number two.

Well, don't get me wrong—Joyce had a beautiful face. But she turned out to be a shy skinny girl who, if you met her today, you'd swear had anorexia. Her level of energy was about like someone who'd just got out of a hospital after several months in traction, and she didn't seem interested in much of anything. Of course, Telma was a little on the disinterested side of things herself!

Still, I couldn't imagine how Joyce, with her overwhelming shyness, would be able to get onstage and do a show!

I didn't know what to do. I was positive Telma was the person who would steal every show no matter who was on stage with her, and I didn't want to mess up my arrangement with her by insulting her cousin. Oh, yeah, I already had a big crush on Telma. As we later said, I was "Telmatized." So I agreed to hire Joyce along with Telma, figuring I could get her teeth capped and keep her a bit in the background.

I got to talking with Joyce and it turned out that she did have one little concern. Her maiden name was Vincent and that's how she first introduced herself. A little later in the conversation it came out that she was getting married and her married name would be Wilson. She felt conflicted, because while she wanted to be known as Joyce Wilson, she simply wasn't ready to give up her maiden name. That was an easy one as far as I was concerned.

"Let's just bill you as Joyce Vincent Wilson," I said.

And in a manner that I came to know and love about Joyce, she smiled a little sweet, almost childlike smile, and said, "Oh! That'll be nice."

The first thing I did was get her teeth capped.

Joyce turned out to be the least demanding and the biggest talent in the group. I quickly saw that Joyce sang circles around both Telma and me. We'd be onstage and I'd realize that she could be giving Dionne Warwick or Gladys Knight a run for the money. So even though it was Telma who'd first caught my attention, Dawn without Joyce would have been unthinkable. The three of us found our sound, which was eclectic and fresh, but with a nod to much of the music we loved.

Hits magazine later described the act this way: "Tony Orlando and Dawn stood at the center of seventies pop music—a bubble gum bridge between urban a cappella, R&B, and Spector Wall of Sound—with which they cut their teeth to the nostalgia of ragtime and the glitz of Vegas-style dazzle."

And, I should say, the act would never have done what it did without both Telma and Joyce, they were such talents, and both charismatic in their own way. They even passed the West Twenty-first Street test. The minute Mamma met them, she said, "Those are good girls. They aren't *stuck up.*"

Joyce became like a sister to me. And Telma became my lover.

Or maybe I should say, I became her lover. Nobody ever has control over Telma in any way, shape, or form. She's the one who always takes control. I don't mean she's controlling. She's just in charge of her life, and I respect the hell out of her for it. She has the same effect on both men and women, so it's not all sexual. She could just take over people and they'd do her bidding. I never saw anything like it. Telma was so different from any woman I'd ever been around. She was a perfumed goddess.

What does a kid from West Twenty-first Street know from perfumed goddesses?

Telma put a stop to our fling. She had a moral aversion to messing around with a married man, especially because she knew my wife. I was still devastated by her, and would have kept right on with the affair. My reluctance to give it up created some tension in the group from time to time, and I'll take full blame for it. All that was yet to come.

Chapter 12

Show Me the Money . . .

I spent the entire advance from Bell Records fighting legal battles with the phony Dawns out on the circuit, and—just as I'd suspected—I spent almost every penny I made on our tours paying expenses. Ah, the glamour of being a pop star. Somebody once asked a rich and famous entertainer if it was better to be rich or famous. He supposedly said, "Are you kidding? If you aren't rich, you can't *afford* to be famous!"

Still, there's something about hearing, or reading, that you're kicking butt with your career, your "sound." We had the sound down. We needed to get the *show* down.

We didn't play a single gig before leaving for the European tour. We rehearsed with Rene DeNite, who'd been the vocal coach of the Fifth Dimension. I got to know him through Mark Gordon, who'd managed that group. Mark was a friend of Larry Utal, the president of Bell Records, and Mark ended up managing us in the early days.

Mark asked to have Rene work with us for the two weeks before our first European show, a two-week gig at Barbarella's on Majorca. Rene worked with us in New York on choreography, staging—the whole concept of working as a group. I'd always been a solo act, of course, so we needed training. I also hired Richard Delvy as our musical director.

I really wanted this tour to go well, and for more reasons than just the immediate impact we'd have. I knew that the only reason Telma was in the group was for that European tour, and I wanted her to remain interested enough to stay in Dawn. Telma's attitude, by the way, didn't come from arrogance or lack of professionalism. It stemmed from the fact that she'd been around music business jive for long enough to know there are a lot of people who are full of shit. And the jury was still out on me. I also felt considerable responsibility toward Joyce. She'd just married Rock Wilson four days before going on this trip— and in the middle of the wedding preparations, had gone through having her teeth capped! Joyce's willingness to trust me was almost a bigger pressure than Telma's skepticism.

The first show was hilarious. What none of us had thought about was that the first show was in a Spanish-speaking country. Somehow, when I thought *European tour* I thought *England*. That was probably due to the old 1961 tour I'd done, when we played the Granada Theatres.

When we went on the stage at Barbarella's that night, nobody understood a word we were saying. It didn't matter so much with the songs but I had to announce them, and talk between them. When I saw the blank looks on their faces during my setup, I switched to Spanish. I could have kissed Mamita and Papito for making sure I knew the language of their homeland. But the trouble didn't end there. By speaking Spanish, the girls and the band were clueless. I don't know how we made it through. But we got about four standing ovations that night, due in no small part, I'm sure, to the fact that the audience loved an American act doing Spanish setups.

We all went backstage after the show and congratulated each other. We were high on encores! "Oh, yeah! Baby! They loved us! We were great!" Mark Gordon came backstage, and patted me on the back.

"That's the worst show I ever saw in my life. Forget the standing ovations. Technically speaking, it was sloppy. You shouldn't be taking bows. You should be taking notes."

It was a good lesson. There was no question that we were dealing with a major leaguer in Mark. When you think of the discipline of the Fifth Dimension, you can see Mark's influence. An audience may forgive you for being sloppy but that doesn't mean you get to keep it up. Mark's influence on us is a major part of the reason we were a tight, orchestrated, professional group by the time we got back to the United States.

From Majorca, we went straight to London, where we played mostly television shows, like *Top of the Pops*. We were already a huge charting act in England, and I felt we should try to do more television appearances than entire performances. That way we took far less of a chance to embarrass ourselves in a country where we were already stars. We played a few promotional dates, but no place where we'd be reviewed.

The actual shows we played were mainly at U.S. military bases, another very forgiving audience. It was when we went to Germany to play Lindsay Air Force base in Wiesbaden, that we got our first taste of racism. Telma, Joyce, and I were sightseeing in the city, and some guy on the street actually spit on us. It was so unforeseen that we could hardly react. Later, I always stepped up to the plate. And I'll tell you something else—little, shy, quiet Joyce Vincent Wilson stepped right up, too. When we got back to the States, we were standing in a coffee shop at one of the hotels around the Detroit airport. Some guy made an incredibly ugly racist remark and came toward us in a very threatening manner. I jumped in front of the girls, but Joyce didn't leave me out in front for long. She picked up a beer bottle, busted it on the table, and stood her ground. Needless to say, the guy backed off.

Joyce figured that Detroit was *her* hometown. She wasn't going to take any shit, especially on home turf.

I've always known that if I ever needed anything, if I was ever really in trouble, I could call on either one of the girls, and they'd be by my side. And I'd damn sure be by theirs. Even when we ended up having some ups and downs, we'd try to keep it between ourselves.

Dawn went back to Europe four or five times over the next few years. Before we got the television show, we played far more in Europe than we did in the United States. Prior to that, we were a record act—a singles driven pop act. Radio was what was important. When we became a television act, we worked more U.S. shows as a cross-promotion between the music and television audiences. It was only after we hooked up with David Geffen at Elektra that we became an album-oriented act, and did the kind of sales promotion/support touring we see as common now.

In 1973, Dawn was a hot pop act with a few chart-topping hits: Like so many of our contemporaries, we knew that popularity is fleeting, and it would be easy to slip off the radar screen. Especially since we'd had no "career" release.

Chapter 13

"Tie a Yellow Ribbon Round the Ole Oak Tree"

There are very few life-changing experiences that you can point to in any career, but a record became one for me. Almost like flipping a pancake, "Tie a Yellow Ribbon Round the Ole Oak Tree," flipped my life over. Every entertainer loves the idea of a signature song, a career song. Bobby Darin had "Mack the Knife." Bob Hope had "Thanks for the Memories." Glen Campbell had several: "By the Time I Get to Phoenix," "Rhinestone Cowboy," among them. We had ours in 1973.

I'm proud to have been a part of the phenomenon that became "Tie a Yellow Ribbon Round the Ole Oak Tree." It brought people together when the Vietnam POWs were returned in 1973. It became a rallying point for the country during the Iran hostage crisis, when Americans were held captive for 444 days in 1979 and 1980.

Irwin Levine and L. Russell Brown didn't write the song about American hostages or MIAs—the song is about a guy coming home from serving a prison term on a bad check charge, and his concerns about being welcomed by his wife. The hostages and MIAs had no worries about their welcome—this country desperately wanted them home.

But before the hostage crisis turned "Yellow Ribbon" into an anthem, it was simply a pop hit for Tony Orlando and Dawn, spending over a month in the number-one spot on the pop music charts in 1973. Ultimately, it became one of the most recorded songs of the rock era, with *Billboard* listing over a thousand cover versions. At the 1st American Music Awards in 1974, "Yellow Ribbon" won Song of the Year. It also won a Grammy at the 16th Annual Grammy Awards. You'd think I'd have been fighting to cut a song like that, but it was exactly the opposite.

Medress thought the song was a smash, and by 1973 we needed one. "Knock Three Times" had spent three weeks at number one December–January 1970, but our follow-up singles had died in the twenties and thirties: "I Play and Sing," "Summer Sand," and "What Are You Doing Sunday." I'd been fronting most of the expenses for our tours, and was about tapped out. We'd talked about giving up the group. Hank was determined he had found the song that would save us from the pop band scrap heap.

I didn't like it, at least for me. Like "Knock Three Times," I thought the lyrics were corny. Hank saw it in a completely different light. He saw "Yellow Ribbon" as an American story, like a novel, with tragedy, hope, suspense—and, naturally, a love-conquers-all happy ending. He thought a song like that couldn't miss.

I passed on it anyway. My problem in listening to songs for Dawn was that my tastes remained R&B. I was very capable of missing a radio record. But a strange thing happened with "Yellow Ribbon." I could not get that song out of my head. I'd find myself singing it in the car, in the shower.

So I started thinking that even though it was wrong for Tony Orlando and Dawn, *somebody* could have a hit with it. I played it for Jimmy Darren, who'd had such a big hit with "Goodbye Cruel World." He turned it down. Then I thought of my old pal Bobby Vinton, who'd gone on to have more chart success than anyone on that bus years earlier. It went through my mind that since he was attracted to "color" songs, like "Roses Are Red" and "Blue on Blue," maybe he'd do well with a little yellow on his song palette.

I called him up and told him I had a smash for him, completely forgetting about my first reaction to "Roses Are Red." When I played him the song, Bobby was silent for a minute, then repeated those words I'd said to him those years ago: "That is the corniest piece of crap I ever heard, and I think everybody else will agree."

I have thanked him many times over for turning down "Yellow Ribbon." And it just goes to prove that old music business adage: If anybody could really pick a hit song, they'd open an office.

We cut "Yellow Ribbon" at Century Sound in New York. It was a dark, rainy day and that suited my mood perfectly. It also suited Telma's. I was really upset. I thought, *Here I go with another novelty song like "Knock Three Times."*

I never, ever set out to be a novelty act, a singer associated with ditties or bubblegum tunes. Yet that was what was happening. "Yellow Ribbon" seemed like a novelty song to me. Even though I knew it had hit potential, it wasn't the kind of song I wanted to be defined by. I loved pop music, but I wanted to sing it with an R&B edge.

Telma hated the song immediately. She, too, wanted to find R&B-flavored songs. Joyce thought it was an okay song, but didn't place as much importance on it as Telma and I. But Joyce's sister, Pam Vincent, who sang on the record, saw things differently. Pam, in a way, was the fourth member of Dawn. She sang on everything we did, but was never part of the live group. She worked with a lot of people, including Aretha Franklin for many years. We played the rough for Pam. All we had down was my vocal and the rhythm track, with that little signature lick, *ba-bu-bu-bu,* that Frank Owens played on keyboards.

After she listened, Pam turned to me and said, "Honey, you just cut the biggest song of your career! You got a *smash*!"

"You're kiddin'," I said. "It may hit, but it's not going to do us any good."

"No!" She said. "That record's great! The *song* is great!"

I didn't hear it. Plus, I could just imagine the record press. They were tough on pop records right then—especially records they saw as lightweight. This country was volatile, political, at war, and on edge. Critics wanted heavy, they wanted a message. I figured I'd be out there justifying the record as soon as it hit. Oh yeah, I figured it would hit. It would hit us right in the face.

Back then—and it's still that way for so many entertainers—a ditty can get you put in a box you never escape from. You lose confidence. You start thinking that you can't sing, that you can't perform. You're left with the aura of being a no-talent. I saw it coming. And damn it, I felt Telma, Joyce, and I *were* blessed with some talent. We were eclectic. We could do a lot of kinds of music.

I braced myself for the bullshit.

Part of the overnight success of "Yellow Ribbon" was due to the failure of our prior release.

Rosalie Trombley was program director at WCKL in Detroit. Rosalie was considered to have some of the best ears in the business. When Rosalie picked a record, nine out of ten times, the nation went for it. She was amazing, one of the most powerful people in the business. The song we released just prior to "Yellow Ribbon" was a Peter Skellern song titled "You're a Lady." Peter had a big record with it in Europe, and it ended up being covered in the States by both Dawn and Paul Anka. That was far more common back then—people jumping on existing hits, hoping to duplicate the success. Hank Medress and David Appell seldom did that, but this time they were convinced we could have a hit with a cover tune. So I went to Rosalie with "You're a Lady."

She listened, sat back, and shook her head.

"I love your record," she said. "But I love Peter's record. And I love Paul's record. So you know what? I'm not going to play any of the records. But since you cut a great record, I'll listen very hard to your next one. If it's anywhere close to this good, I'd add it out of the box."

I couldn't ask for more than that. An out-of-the-box add from one of the most powerful stations in the country was the best you could do.

"Tie a Yellow Ribbon Round the Ole Oak Tree" was released on March 17, 1973. Right away I got a call from Kenny Beautice, the promo guy at Bell Records.

"Rosalie added the song."

Still another powerhouse, WKBN in Buffalo, New York, added it. We were on our way to a monster. And yes, we caught some flak. But one incident made me stop trying to justify anything to anybody.

The song was about halfway up the charts when I got a phone call.

"Tony, this is Bob 'Tie a Yellow Ribbon' Hope."

"Huh?"

"You heard me right. Bob 'Tie a Yellow Ribbon' Hope. I want you to sing 'Yellow Ribbon' at the Cotton Bowl in Dallas. There's gonna be seventy thousand people there, but they aren't the people you're singing for. You're singing for the POWs who've just come back from Cambodia and Laos."

"My God!" I said. "I'd be honored."

Bob had got my phone number from Tony Zoppi at the Riviera Hotel. Tony had booked the girls and I into the Riviera for our very first performance in Las Vegas. We opened for Don Rickles in the showroom. Tony had been impressed with "Yellow Ribbon," so when the Cotton Bowl POW welcome back event was in the planning stages, he'd suggested the song to Bob. He even had the record, and played it for him.

I swear that until we got there, I didn't get the full implication.

It was a typical Bob Hope show, with everybody in show business involved. The difference was that there were almost six hundred returning POWs seated on the fifty-yard line. When Bob asked us to open the show, I'd asked him why.

He said, "It's the opening line. 'I'm coming home, I've done my time.' That's every soldier's prayer. I don't think you understand the lasting impact of this song."

That was the first time I saw the song in larger proportions. For me, it had strictly been about a convict released from jail.

A major named Steven Long was among the POW group that day, a guy who'd been in the Hanoi Hilton, and who was one of four guys to make it out of Laos alive. That was a *war*. He'd told Bob that when he returned home, he was met by hundreds of yellow ribbons hanging in his neighborhood. And it turned out that others had as well. That was the first time I'd ever heard of the song being held up as a symbol of hope.

I sang the song, and when I got to the chorus, all of a sudden—like when Marines start singing "From the halls of Montezuma to the shores of Tripoli"—the POWs started singing with us. They got up and started walking toward the stage. I have never felt anything like it. The entire crowd erupted in applause for those men.

After the Cotton Bowl, I got together with a lot of those guys, and they inspired me like I'd never believed I could be inspired. Maj. Steven Long and I forged a lifelong friendship that day. He and many of the other men came to the Copacabana when I played the club's last show. I'd call the Copa "legendary" but it wouldn't sound right in the same breath as mentioning these heroes.

As I said, I never felt the need to justify the tune again. I can go back and tell you what I felt before that happened, but I would never again feel that way. "Yellow Ribbon" had taken on a whole new meaning. Little did I know how right Bob Hope had been about the song's lasting impact. I had no idea that it would resurface during the Iranian hostage crisis, and again during Desert Storm. It's become that same symbol of hope for the return of kidnapped children, runaways—any number of situations where someone may be lost.

It's become a significant part of American lore. During Desert Storm, Charles Kuralt did a study of where the concept of the yellow ribbon began. I'd been thinking it must have started during the Civil War because I'd seen that John Wayne movie, *She Wore a Yellow Ribbon*. It turned out that it hadn't happened in the Civil War, that it was a fictional thing. The first time that it became a national movement was during the hostage crisis, when Penny Langdon, whose husband Bruce was a hostage in Iran, tied a yellow ribbon on her mailbox. Her story broke, and the country followed suit. That was the marker.

The interesting thing is that the song's writers, Larry Brown and Irwin Levine, always believed the song had larger implications than the story of the returning convict. They *got* it from the day they wrote it.

Chapter 14

Keep on Dreamin', Kid . . .

Jilly Rizzo was a great friend of my father's brother Freddie. Jilly's was a famous club in New York, and I started going there with Uncle Freddie, then continued to patronize the club when I was in music publishing. I loved Jilly—everybody did. I brought Jilly all our new records, and since he was a toy collector, I'd sometimes find an unusual toy for him. And, after I had hit records with Tony Orlando and Dawn, I'd stop by Jilly's every time I had any time off from the concert tour.

The great thing about Jilly was that he made no distinction between a celebrity and the guy off the street. If Jilly liked you, he treated you like a king. I think that's why Sinatra thought so much of him. In many ways, Frank was the same way. If Frank liked the dogcatcher, then dogcatchers ruled. And if Frank thought a celebrity was an asshole, the celebrity was treated like an asshole. Frank's musical talent was exceeded only by his brutal honesty.

Jilly had heard me reminisce many times about the days when I'd try to dance down the streets of New York like Gene Kelly in *Singing in the Rain*. So when his friend Frank Sinatra, another regular Jilly's patron, was hosting a Friars Club roast for Gene, he asked Frank to include me. The stars participating included Cary

Grant, Liz Taylor, Don Rickles, Fred Astaire, Steve Lawrence, Eydie Gorme, Tony Bennett, Natalie Wood, Robert Wagner, Gregory Peck, Telly Savalas, Glenn Ford—you get the idea. It wasn't the kind of crowd that usually mingled with a pop singer who'd had a couple of hit songs. I couldn't believe he'd pulled it off—getting me on that lineup.

I stood off to the side with Jilly in the green room, just watching all the star power, marveling that even in that group of monumental celebrity, Frank Sinatra was the one who sucked the air out of the room. When it was time to go out and be seated, he grabbed a microphone and started giving people instructions to make it easier for them to find their place cards

"Cary, you want to get over here. Liz, behind Cary. Uh, Fred, you're next. Steve, Edyie, over here. Rickles, shut up." He went on down the lineup. I was the last name. "Orlando, follow me."

I couldn't figure that out. By going with Frank, I was at the head of the line instead of the end. When we got out there, the tables were in layers, up to the dais. All the stars were in order to be seated at their assigned seats, except me. Frank grabbed my arm, pointed to the place card that was a little behind the dais, but next to him, and said, "Kid, take Telly's card down and trade it with yours.

"*Telly Savalas's* card?"

"Sure."

Then he leaned over and added, "Welcome aboard, kid."

I know Frank did what he did because of his friendship with Jilly, but that doesn't diminish the act of charity he performed for a guy starting out. Sometimes Frank's legendary edge overshadows the kind side of his character. I would meet many people down the road who fell into that same category. Jerry Lewis is one of them.

Like I said earlier in the book, you never walk alone. To make it through this life, you depend on a few special professionals helping you along the way. Some make a big commitment to you. Some are the entertainers you learn technique from, and others give you a hand or a push when you need it. And you'll find that the right ones seem to arrive at the right time.

You might liken it to a fellow trying to cross a river. Sometimes a person will show up with a boat that can take him across. But the boat alone isn't always enough. Sometimes there's a person who understands the steering mechanism. Maybe somebody else understands weather conditions. Other times a person comes along who gets the boat back on course if it's veering too far in one direction. The fellow will ultimately have to pilot that boat himself, but it will be possible only through knowledge gleaned or directions received from others.

One more thing. Those people will keep you from getting too cocky, as well. Back in the days when I was dream-weaving on Tar Beach, I'd sometimes imagine my name on the same marquee with Frank Sinatra's. Of course, I'd see my name in HUGE letters, with Frank's name in little tiny letters below. One night I told that story on the *Tonight Show,* and the next day I got a picture of a Las Vegas marquee. It had been doctored to read:

TONY ORLANDO
WITH FRANK SINATRA

At the bottom of the photo was written:

Keep on dreamin', kid . . .
Frank

Chapter 15

Thanks to the Baby-sitter

The same person who was responsible for Sonny and Cher getting a television show was responsible for the *Tony Orlando and Dawn Show*—Fred Silverman's baby-sitter. Fred was then head of CBS television's programming. The baby-sitter had caught a special featuring Sonny and Cher, told her employer he should check them out, and once he did he offered them a network deal. Some time later she called him up again. "You better check out the Grammy Awards tonight. There's an act called Tony Orlando and Dawn that I think would be great on TV."

Fred did tune in to the Grammys, and he later said he liked what he saw. But he didn't offer a deal until he saw us live, and that was purely by accident. Ironically, we were filling in for Sonny and Cher at a Fifth Dimension show in Westbury, New York. The Bonos were scheduled to open the show, and had to cancel at the last minute. The same company that handled the Fifth Dimension managed us, so we were a quick substitute. Fred Silverman thought he was coming out from Manhattan to see Sonny and Cher, and I had no idea he was in the audience that night. But our act was ready for a television producer anyway.

I'd been thinking along the lines of a network show for quite a while, and had been reworking the act with that in mind. Not long before that fateful Westbury performance I'd approached Telma and Joyce with the idea of working up some skits and using more comedic characters in the live show. They loved it, and in fact, we modeled two of our most popular characters on their aunts: Effie Lou and Maureen. In our show they became Lou Effie and Moreen. Telma, especially, was a natural at acting. I kept thinking, *If we could get a television executive to come to one of these shows, we might have a chance*. Little did I know it would be a man with the power of a Fred Silverman.

I'd also given a lot of thought to the fact that television was ready for some ethnic shows. We were past the *All in the Family* day, when so many barriers were broken down by addressing them in public. Why not go for some real color on network television? A good way to start might be a couple of black women and a Puerto Rican. The funny thing is, until I started really playing it up most people thought I was Italian with a name like Orlando. But once I'd met Freddie Prinze, our identities as the Greek-O-Rican and the Hung-O-Rican became part of our schtick.

So that's where we were on that night of the Westbury show. Ready, willing, and able. Still, imagine my surprise when after the show a guy walked up to me backstage and introduced himself as Fred Silverman from CBS. He didn't have to tell me who he was, I knew. Fred asked me if I wanted to go get some coffee and maybe something to eat, and of course I jumped at the chance to talk to him. What was I gonna say? No?

So we went to a little seafood joint close by the venue, and ordered coffee and a big bowl of boiled shrimp. Fred made some small talk about liking what we did and the audience reaction, and I was just peeling my first shrimp when he asked me if I was interested in doing network television.

"Of course," I said, quickly. I was somewhere between feeling confident that my plans for television were about to come true, and being scared that I was dreaming.

"Let me ask you something," Fred went on. "You know that place in the show where you go out in the audience and stop singing and just talk to people? Then you start the song again, and go talk to somebody else?"

"Sure," I said. That was one of my favorite parts of the show, the audience participation.

"Is that all ad-libbed or do you rehearse some of it?"

"All ad-libbed."

Fred peeled a shrimp and thought about that for a moment. "We'd have to figure out a way to block that part. I like it and I think it would be great. But we'd have to block it."

I shrugged. "How do they shoot football games? You can't block that. You just follow the ball."

Fred smiled and kept on peeling shrimp. Finally he nodded. "Yeah, I can see your point. Just follow the ball."

I felt confident enough by then to really try to sell him on some of my show theories. "Think telethons. That's where I got the idea of so much audience participation in the first place. You know the last twenty minutes of the *Jerry Lewis MDA Telethon*. He goes into the audience and talks to them and collects money. It's all very personal. When I was a little kid that's the part I loved the most, more than anything I wanted to see Jerry interact with people sitting out there in that audience. I mean he just did a number on those people. They loved him after that. That's the part of it I didn't understand as a kid and the part I now understand as an entertainer."

I could see that Fred liked the explanation and felt we might be able to make it work in spite of a timing problem. "Variety shows aren't doing very well now," he admitted. "But I still believe in them and I want to try some out this summer. I want to get three acts, put one on in June, one in July, and one in August. Whichever one gets the ratings gets the spot for the next season. I'd like Tony Orlando and Dawn to be one of those acts."

Looking back on it, I think it was a courageous move on Fred Silverman's part. Despite my own belief that America was ready for ethnic shows, we were not the melting pot we are now. Martin Luther King Jr. had been killed in 1968. The country was shell-shocked from Vietnam. Watergate was all over television. And, as you'll remember, not only was I Hispanic, I was frequently having to step in when Telma and Joyce were met with overt racism. Even though I had a gut feeling that America would accept an ethnic-flavored television show, there was always a chance it wouldn't.

Since the show wasn't a sure thing for the long haul, I moved Elaine and Jon into the Beverly Comstock Hotel, where, ironically, Freddie Prinze would shoot himself several years later.

Fred Silverman decided to call the television show, *The Tony Orlando and Dawn Show,* instead of simply "Dawn." After all, we were up against two other shows with actual names involved: *The Bobbie Gentry Show* (to air in June) and *The Hudson Brothers Show* (to air in August).

The first time I met Sol Ilson and Ernie Chambers, who produced the show, we talked about the basis on which we'd do comedy. I believe that Sol Ilson was a theatrical genius. It was he and Ernie, another great talent, who shaped what the show was going to be like.

Their concept was to play to the kind of dynamic that Sonny and Cher had. Without the *Sonny and Cher Show,* there would have been no *Tony Orlando and Dawn Show*. They drew the map to follow. The difference with our show, was that we had two women's personalities to work with. We had the devil on one of my shoulders, Telma, and the angel on the other, Joyce. Telma would needle me, and Joyce would help get me out of tight spots.

The trouble was, I didn't want to be Sonny Bono! Even though his fumbling endeared him to the audience, they were left with the idea that he was, in real life, a buffoon. He wasn't.

Even though playing the Sonny role was the *right* thing to do, I fought it at first. I wanted to be more along the lines of a Johnny Carson—somebody cool. Plus, as all comedy is based on truth, I could see some of my less-than-cool traits being used as a joke. It's not an easy thing to deal with on a daily basis, either. I went with it, though, because I knew it was the best thing to do from a theatrical standpoint.

We started out ahead of the game, because from the early days on tour, Telma, Joyce, and I had used comedy. We took the electricity we had in our musical numbers, and translated it to sketches. The first time we tried a musical sketch was at a show at the Copacabana. *Super Fly* was a big movie at the time, so I played this Super Fly guy named Jack, and Telma and Joyce developed the Lou Effie and Moreen characters. The girls found out that Jack was dating them both, and that led to the song "Hit the Road, Jack."

I told that story to Ilson and Chambers, and we used it. That's how the planning process began.

For two girls who'd never done any television comedy or acting, Telma and Joyce were amazing. They got it right away. I thought Telma had the ability to become the black Lucille Ball. It turned out to be true. Just the other day I was talking to her on the telephone and I reminded her that she hadn't been off the air for four decades. First, there was our show, then *Bosom Buddies, Gimme a Break, The Odd Couple, Family Matters*—and she's still on in constant reruns. Her retention of lines was legendary on the set. Everyone else would still be working from the script, and Telma had hers down pat.

Joyce also had an immediate grasp of her character, and she played it to the hilt. She actually walked more of a tightrope than Telma or I, because by never taking sides she ran the risk of looking weak. Yet she took that shy, kinder, gentler role and made it powerful. She played it to perfection.

Fred Silverman wanted to use a lot of big names, current television stars to launch the summer replacement show. To that end, on the very first July episode, he asked Loretta Swit, who was huge on *M*A*S*H* at the time, and Rosie Greer, who was a beloved public figure, known not only as a top pro football player, but as the man who jumped in and held Sirhan Sirhan after he shot Bobby Kennedy.

In finding our niche, we had to combine our musical success with comedy. We did a parody skit with Loretta on the song "Sweet Gypsy Rose." Loretta played the character of Gypsy Rose Lee. We also wanted to show the diversity of our live musical show, so we did a doo-wop sketch with Lou Effie and Moreen, the old Silhouettes song, "Get a Job." We followed that with a sketch with me *getting a job.*

From that beginning, we developed a Walter Mitty character for me, where I got to live out some fantasy life. For example, since Telma had sung on the original *Shaft* soundtrack, we did a fantasy sketch where I wanted to be Isaac Hayes. That's Telma on the record, by the way, saying, "Shut your mouth."

"Don't you know who I am?" I asked Telma.

"No," she said.

"I'm Isaac Hayes!" I said.

Telma rolled her eyes and said, "Honey, you look more like *Helen Hays.*"

Here's where Telma parted company with the Cher-type character. She certainly had the same willowy look and sharp wit that Cher had. But she also had this Pearl Bailey persona, with a sassy delivery. The show dynamic remained Sonny and Cher, but Telma was Pearl Bailey.

That was part of the brilliance of Ilson and Chambers. They were able to pull in a "comfortability" of character for each of us. Except for me, of course. I wasn't so sure I wanted to be the foil, but they figured me out early on. Why would I want to be Isaac Hayes? To impress Telma, of course.

Secondly, the girls loved Dionne Warwick, so on that very

first show, I chose a Dionne medley for them: "Anyone Who Had a Heart," "Make It Easy on Yourself," "Walk on By," and "Breaking Up Is Hard to Do."

My solo song on the first show was "If," by Bread. So we were starting to pull in all our musical loves, in addition to our own music—our safety zones, if you will. It was all areas where we felt comfortable. And it was all contemporary: *Shaft,* Bread, Dionne.

Of course, we were lucky on the first show, because Loretta Swit already understood what it was to put scenes together. She was a solid actor, and we weren't. She became a very gracious teacher for all of us. And Rosie Greer was perfect as well, because of his warmth and ability to put people at ease. Everybody loves Rosie Greer to this day. In fact, I recently walked through an airport with Rosie, and couldn't believe how instantly recognizable he still is. Not only did people spot him, but people of all ages— kids to grandparents. He's a unique person.

The procedure forged in that summer series became a map set in stone, with the reliance on comfort zones so three people who'd never done a show before could pull it off. And guest stars who were not merely popular, but accessible both to the television audience and to Telma, Joyce, and I.

Chapter 16

Amateur Night in Dixie

The summer replacement shows were successful, and our show was picked up. The next thing we faced was the real season. And the season's opening program was crucial.

The first guest was all-important, and Fred Silverman was so confident that Jackie Gleason was the man, he paid him $25,000 for the one-hour episode. Those were princely wages in 1974, but Gleason was a television pioneer, a comic legend. Nobody was more excited than I about Jackie helping us kick off the show. Well, Mamma, who'd taken me to see Gleason do his vaudeville show all those years ago, was at least *as* excited.

There were slight problems that no one anticipated. Our other guest was Nancy Walker, a lady I truly loved for her dead-on honesty. She had a great sense of humor, a great comedic ability, and never lied.

The problem? Nancy and Jackie had been in a running feud since some incident at a Broadway show years back. We didn't know that when we booked the show. But Nancy's opinion of Jackie wasn't the biggest problem. And nobody saw the sucker punch coming.

Jackie Gleason was not the kind of guy who liked to rehearse, so he sat with the producers while we blocked out the scenes. I understood not liking rehearsals. As I said earlier, I didn't like them either, though I doubt Jackie Gleason felt insecure, as I did. Jackie probably felt his spontaneity might get lost in rehearsal. At one point I was sitting to the side, watching Telma and Joyce sing, and suddenly, the unmistakable voice of Jackie Gleason roars:

"Who are these *schwarzes* at the amateur night in Dixie?"

Telma and Joyce stopped short. You could have heard a pin drop.

All of a sudden I was mad enough to throw a punch at Gleason. I walked over to where he sat and said, "You owe these girls an apology. You can't come on our show and call them names. You owe me an apology, too. And I'm speaking as your host of amateur night in Dixie."

I don't know where I got the nerve to say that to Jackie Gleason, or what I expected him to do. What he did was stand up, and say, "I'm outta here, pal," on his way out the door.

It didn't take long for Fred Silverman to call me. "What the hell did you think you were doing? This is Jackie *Gleason*!"

By this time I'd dug my heels in.

"Look, Fred. I don't care if he wants to call me an amateur, if that's his opinion of me. But he is not coming here and calling Telma and Joyce *schwarzes*! We fought racist bullshit on the tour, and we aren't going to have to do it on our own show."

"Come on, Tony. *Schwarzes*?"

"Don't think they don't know that's derogatory, Fred. They do."

I never did find out what Fred said to get Jackie to come back to the show, but we got word that he was back onboard, and when time came for the final rehearsal, he was there. It wasn't over, though.

Jackie showed up with this sidekick, his personal assistant, who had this elegant white mustache and dressed in a double-breasted blazer, white silk shirt, and ascot. This guy's main duty seemed to be that of cigarette boy. It reminded me of my short-lived job passing out men's cologne at the Manhattan Hotel men's room. The fellow would walk around with Jackie, holding a pack of Parliaments, with several of the cigarettes pulled up so that it resembled a magazine ad. Jackie would snap his fingers, and the mustached assistant would hand him the pack, Jackie would remove one of the protruding smokes, and the guy would whip out a lighter for him.

Nancy Walker and I watched him strutting around, and she leaned over and said to me, "I want to get that son-of-a-bitch. I've been mad at him since 1949."

We ran through the scenes again, but never with Jackie participating. Then we all went to our dressing rooms to wait for showtime. Someone knocked on my door, and when I opened it, the Parliament guy was standing there.

"Mr. Gleason wants to see you now."

"Okay," I said, thinking he was going to apologize.

Not a chance. When I got there, Jackie wanted to go over the cue cards.

"Okay, Mr. Gleason," I said. I didn't want to blow this show, and if he was just going to sail on through, so would I.

"Oh, and kid, no ad-libbing. You got that? If there's any ad-libbing, it'll be coming from me."

Arrogant? Yes. Did he offer one word of apology about his racist comment? No. I kept reminding myself of what we had at stake, thinking: *Don't blow this, Tony*.

"I understand, Mr. Gleason."

What I *really* understood was that I was in the presence of a man who was absolutely sure that he was the Great One. But I'd decided to just try to get through the show.

Ironically, the first sketch we did together was a song called "I'll Teach You Everything I Know." It was all Jackie Gleason-isms, supposedly like this:

Jackie: "I'll teach you everything I know."

Me: "Even how sweet it is?"

Jackie: "I'll teach you everything I know."

Me: "One of these days, Alice—to the moon!"

But what happened was this: Every time we started the skit, Jackie would say, "Stop tape, stop tape. Let's go through it again."

It went on and on. Keep in mind, we had a studio audience. It was starting to look like I was blowing it, and the Great One was trying to fix things. Finally, by the third time, I'd had it. I said, "Stop tape."

Jackie stared at me.

"You're the Great One, Jackie. Can't you just ad-lib something?"

He kept staring.

The tape started to roll and I sang, "Now teach me everything you know."

So he came around and we sang the song and finished the sketch. Then he stormed back to his dressing room to wait for the next routine, which was based on the then-current hit series, *Kung Fu,* starring David Carradine.

The backstage people were all saying, "what the fuck were you doing?"

I said, "Look, the guy was trying to bust me. Leave it alone."

Jackie and Nancy Walker were both involved in the *Kung Fu* sketch. We were supposed to do a funny takeoff on the "Grasshopper" portions of that show, with Jackie clasping his hand down on my head, and blessing me. When we were getting ready for the scene, Jackie snapped his fingers for the Parliament man. The guy ran right out, and Jackie starts to light up a smoke. Those were the days when *a lot* of people smoked, including me. But during the actual tapings the studio was a no-smoking area. I knew how it felt, watching him get ready to have a cigarette when I couldn't. And I knew quite a few people in the audience were feeling the same way.

The audiences of my shows always rapped with me, from the very beginning. So I counted on them jumping in with me when I said, "Now, Mr. Gleason, you can't smoke if we can't smoke." And I looked at the audience and added, "Right?"

"Yeah," a lot of people called out. "If we can't, you can't." Jackie handed the cigarette back to his assistant, and glared at me.

The next scene we were to tape was the "blessing." Jackie brought that hand down like a sledgehammer, and nearly knocked me to my knees. I was dazed, and Nancy Walker knew it.

"Oh, great Grasshopper, try this," she said, and whacks Jackie.

The audience was rolling in the aisles, thinking this was all part of the script. So when we wrapped up the show they thought we were all comic geniuses.

I wasn't back in my dressing room five minutes before there was a knock on the door. Once again, it was the Parliament man.

"Mr. Gleason wants to see you."

And once again, I said, "Okay."

I went to Jackie's dressing room, but this time I had no idea what would happen.

There stood the Great One stirring a drink. He handed me the hardcover copy of the script that we left for each guest.

"Look at the first page," he said.

I opened the script, and Jackie had inscribed it: "Dear Tony, you're the greatest. I apologize."

I teared up, just as I've teared up every time I've told the story through the years.

"I'm sorry I disrespected you, Mr. Gleason," I said. "But I just couldn't handle those words. I just couldn't handle it."

Jackie took a drink, and said, "I was wrong. You did the right thing. You let those young ladies know how wrong I was." Then he got his things and started to go. "I'll be calling you," he said.

And from that day on, I received a telephone call from Jackie Gleason on tape day. "Hey, pal. How's it going? Any advice? You need any advice?"

The next time I saw Jackie in person was right after he'd finished shooting *Smokey and the Bandit*. We were staying on the same floor at the Riveria Hotel in Las Vegas, where I was playing a show. Jackie knew I'd be finishing up the show soon, so he left the door to his room open. As I started to walk by, I heard, "Hey, kid. Come on in, pal, and have a drink."

I wasn't a drinker, but I wasn't gonna say no. So Jackie poured me a glass of whatever he was drinking. I don't know what it was, but it was strong. When I took a sip of it, I almost choked. Jackie sat down in a chair by the window, which overlooked the Las Vegas strip.

"How'd the shows go tonight?" he asked.

"They went very well," I said.

"Yeah? You get any standing ovations?"

"I got a couple."

"Come look here a minute," he said, pointing down at the street.

I walked over and looked out the window. Jackie pointed at a guy standing outside. "You see that guy standing on the corner? He wasn't there."

I knew what he meant. No matter how many people applaud you on any given night, no matter what kind of a job you do, tomorrow's another day.

Chapter 17

Ain't Worth Your Salt Without a Little Jerry Lewis

Sammy Davis Jr. used to say, "You ain't worth your salt as a performer unless you bring an ounce or two of Jerry Lewis on stage with you."

Jerry was another hero from the old days when Mamma and I went to the theaters on Broadway. I always wanted Jerry to appear on the show, even though I kept hearing horror stories about him. Every time I brought up the idea of booking him, it was always the same.

"He's egotistical."

"He kicks water coolers over."

"He breaks tables."

And I usually had the same comeback: "Come on, guys. There's two people I want on this show: Jerry Lewis and Sammy Davis Jr. Let's do something about it."

Finally one day I was informed that Jerry Lewis would be guest-starring the following week.

I practically jumped up and down. "Oh, man! That's great!"

Nobody else was jumping. "You wait and see. Jerry will be tough as hell on you. This is gonna be a problem like you won't believe."

So on the big day, in came Jerry Lewis, looking like Jerry

Lewis ought to look—like a star. He was handsome, tanned, wearing a sweatshirt, crisp white tennis shorts, and spotless white tennis shoes. Jerry gave me a casual nod. He was so perfectly cast that he stunned me into complete honesty.

"Please tell me it isn't true," I blurted out.

"What's that?"

"Tell me you're not gonna be tough on me and that you're not gonna kick over water coolers and throw tables. 'Cause I love Jerry Lewis! I've dreamed about meeting you for years—*please* don't mess up that dream."

Okay, I admit it. I was begging.

Jerry kind of smiled. "Let me tell you something. Whoever told you that is right. I've done all that shit. But the only time I ever turn over any tables is when people ain't doing their jobs. I won't tolerate it. As long as you do your job, we're gonna be good buddies."

I did my job, and he was amazing. No throwing tables or tantrums. Just a class-A performance. I went to school on Jerry just like I'd gone to school on so many other performers from Jackie Wilson to Jackie Gleason. We did some sketches similar to the ones he used to do with Dean Martin, and it was a real thrill for me. I was in awe of Jerry.

But the strangest thing happened after the show. I went to his dressing room to tell him once again what a thrill it had been working with him. I paused outside the door when I heard what sounded like a sob from inside the room. I knocked.

"Jerry? It's Tony."

"Yeah, come on in."

I went in, and was stunned to see Jerry Lewis sitting there at the dressing table with tears in his eyes.

"What's wrong?"

"I've lost my timing. That was the first time in a long time that I did those sketches like I did with Dean. It made me feel like I was working with him again. And my timing's gone."

It was the first I ever heard one of my heroes express self-doubt, a problem I'd faced since my first record deal. On the one hand, it upset me, but in a strange way I felt like I wanted to hug him for reassuring me that self-doubt could hit anyone, even a legend.

I didn't know until later, when I read his autobiography, that when he was on my show, he was going through withdrawals from Percodan. No wonder he was filled with insecurities. And no wonder he was so easily reduced to tears.

In 1976 I did the *Jerry Lewis MDA Telethon* from Las Vegas. Word kept circulating backstage that something big was getting ready to happen. We kept hearing that Frank Sinatra was going to show up with Dean Martin. At that point, Jerry and Dean were still estranged. It was about time for me to go on, when all of a sudden I saw Frank Sinatra and Dean Martin walking down the hall. So just as Jerry thought he was going to introduce me, out walked Frank and Dean. That was when Frank made the famous "introduction"—"Dean, Jerry. Jerry, Dean. Dean, Jerry. Jerry, Dean."

It was one of those rare moments in show business that no one who was a witness will ever forget. I was still standing there, almost shaking from emotion, when they left the stage. I'd met both Frank and Dean before, so when Frank passed me, I said to Frank "Thank you so much for bringing those two together." But Frank just shook his head, said "Shhhhh," and walked on. I thought he meant "Don't ruin the moment." Dean was right behind him. "Dean, that was amazing—" I started to say. Dean shrugged, and said, "Fuck him."

I've thought about this many times over the years, about the intense joy I felt when the guys were onstage together, and that moment of complete letdown afterward. In retrospect, I can see that when Jerry and Dean were out there, it was Dean who held back. I know Jerry loved, respected, and missed Dean Martin. I can still picture Jerry in his house, sadly looking up at an old promotional clock with his and Dean's faces on it. But I don't think Dean felt the same. And, contrary to the popular perception, Jerry always seemed to be the one with the warmth, not Dean. At least in the dynamic between the two of them.

Jerry and I stayed friends. He even brought his mother to see my Las Vegas shows. One time he came backstage after the show and asked me if I'd like to host his Labor Day telethon from New York. Would I? It was like winning an Academy Award—from Jerry Lewis's mouth to my ears. I hosted the show, and continued to work with Jerry on MDA for years. They were wonderful years, all the more poignant because of my sister, Rhonda, even though her special needs weren't a result of muscular dystrophy.

One thing about Jerry Lewis—he has the same intensity about trying to save his friends as when he tried to save children on the telethons all these years. And once Jerry finally kicked everything and got healthy—watch out! He takes no prisoners.

Jerry came to my hotel room in 1984. I'd been able to leave the cocaine and caffeine behind, but I was back to smoking three packs a day. I'd been smoking in the room; there were ashtrays and crumpled cigarette packs everywhere. I knew I needed to quit, but didn't see how I could do it.

Jerry sniffed the air, and said, "It smells like a bear's asshole in here!"

He pulled open his shirt and showed me a huge scar that ran down his chest.

"You see that, Tony? They took a Black & Decker to my chest. Took my ribcage and pulled it open, reached in, grabbed my heart and pulled that son-of-a-bitch out and stuck it in a pail of ice! Are you listening to me, you prick?"

He pulled up his pant leg to expose another huge scar.

"See that scar? They pulled out veins to put in my chest! Then they put the heart back, sewed me up, and I was in more pain than you can even think of. All because of smoking, Tony! The next day, when they asked me to cough, I thought I was gonna die. You're forty years old! The doctors told me that if I'd quit at forty I'd have had a fightin' chance."

I said, "You know, Jerry, my son Jon the other day just told me he couldn't stand my smoking anymore. He said he was having dreams about my smoking, and when he stayed at my house his shirts started stinking like cigarettes." Jon had pleaded with me about the habit, saying, "Dad, I don't want to have you die young on me!"

And I told Jerry, "Ever since Jon talked to me like that I'd been on the verge of making the decision, of trying to throw these smokes down. Now you come in and put the final nail in my palms. You two have crucified me to the tree. I'm puttin' 'em down. I promise you that."

And I did. I never picked up a cigarette from that day on.

Fast forward to 2002.

I came back to Las Vegas to play a three-month gig at the Golden Nugget. Every night onstage I cracked jokes about the weight I'd gained. I don't know if there was any connection, but one night a few old show business friends came to the club— guys like Rich Little and Robert Goulet and a lot of Vegas press and bookers. When I called my son, Jon, onstage to introduce him, I did a fake sob, and said, "Look at that! I used to be that skinny, too!" The next morning I got a message from Jerry.

"Tony Orlando—you little Puerto Rican prick! I gotta find out from other people that you're in town? Call me—I love ya. Jerry."

I called him back. He started reminiscing about that old Martin and Lewis sketch he and I did on my show. Remember, at the time, he was on medication and was depressed. He'd hated his performance. Now, he says he's been watching the old tapes and wants to use them. He's decided they were great sketches!

"You should watch those, Tony," he said. "Because you should do what I did—*practice!*"

He got to his next point pretty quick.

"You gotta lose that weight. Remember when I went to the Desert Inn and saw you? You were saying you wanted to lose weight back then! Lose it! You're too old to be fat! You go over and kiss your little daughter, Jenny, good night, and you might as well be kissing her good-bye! How can you shave and comb your hair and not see what a hypocrite you are? You gotta take care of yourself! You're fifty-seven years old! That ain't nothing! I'm headin' for eighty, buddy, and I'm still kickin'. I'm layin' here with pneumonia, and I'm in good enough shape to beat it."

"I know, I know," I said, sheepishly. "I'm tryin'. I've been walking from the Golden Nugget to the Stratosphere every day, and that's about a two-mile walk."

"Can you afford fifty bucks? Then I'm sendin' my trainer over to work with you tomorrow!"

So we talked a couple more minutes and got off the telephone. A little while later it rang again. It was Jerry's trainer.

"Jerry Lewis just called me. I'm supposed to meet you tomorrow afternoon at four."

I said, "I'll be there." Tough love.

Thanks, Jerry—I've already lost ten pounds.

When I think about Jerry, I often think about Sammy Davis Jr. When Sammy died, it almost took Jerry as well. Sammy's funeral was one of the biggest events in show business history. Helicopters were hovering in the air. Every entertainer you could imagine showed up. Politicians. Sammy's widow, Altovise, looked so elegant. I sat in the pew with Jerry Lewis, Frank Sinatra, Dean Martin, and Wayne Newton. Jerry was so broken up they almost had to carry him out.

As we left the funeral, it occurred to me that show business, or at least an era of it, had died. Sammy bridged the gap between the old and new. He was able to work with Michael Jackson or Chicago or Blood, Sweat & Tears, and still be the Rat Pack guy.

Gregory Hines gave a eulogy that day. He talked about meeting Sammy at the Apollo Theater when he was nine years old, how he became his protégé. Gregory was one of the few people Sammy would be with at the end of his life. He couldn't stand the idea of people seeing him in such a deteriorated condition, the cancer rendering him literally speechless. But he would see Gregory. The day of the funeral, Gregory recalled that on the last visit, as he was leaving, Sammy tapped his cane on the floor. *Smack, smack, smack*. Gregory turned around, and Sammy took an imaginary ball and threw it to him.

When Gregory stood there at the podium, and held up his hands to illustrate the scene, I said, "Nice catch, Greg."

Gregory deserved to have the ball passed to him.

One of my most memorable show business moments came when I was in Sammy Davis Jr.'s dressing room at Bali's in Vegas, where Sammy and Jerry were playing. I rode down in the elevator with Jerry Lewis, and the ride seemed like it was in slow motion. I couldn't believe these guys treated me like one of their own. After Sammy had died, Jerry asked me to fill in on some long-booked dates.

When I first walked onstage with Jerry, he introduced me this way: "I've only had three partners onstage. Dean Martin. Sammy Davis Jr. And Tony Orlando."

Talk about show business dreams come true. When you think how lives unfold it's amazing. All those years ago, Jerry had endeared himself to my mother by holding a door open for her. Now, he held the door of a different kind open for her son.

Chapter 18

Someone's in the Kitchen with Dinah . . .

Dinah Shore first went on the air with *The Dinah Shore Show* on November 27, 1951. Her final series, *Conversations with Dinah,* was broadcast from 1989 to 1991. Through four decades of American television she became an icon of the medium. And she was a master at creating show business "moments," especially when she had walk-on guests. That's how, in 1975, I met my great friend Freddie Prinze—on Dinah's afternoon variety show.

I first saw Freddie Prinze when he appeared on *The Midnight Special,* and I soon became a huge fan of his television show, *Chico and the Man*. Freddie and I had a lot in common. We were both from New York, had started out young, and were lucky enough to have someone of importance take an interest in us early on. Freddie had grown up in Washington Heights, not that far from my old stomping grounds. We both spoke Spanish. I got a record deal with Epic at age sixteen. Freddie was working at the Improv at age sixteen. He debuted on the *Tonight Show* in 1973, and a year later had a hit comedy series on NBC.

The irony about *Chico and the Man* was that Freddie played a Mexican on the show, and many Mexican Americans complained about him being a Puerto Rican. That bothered Freddie terribly.

Freddie had a knock-you-in-the-face impact on a person. In some ways it took me back to the old neighborhood in New York. You remember the story I told about the Wing & Fin, the exotic pet shop I always stopped by on my way home from the movies. Part of the reason I stopped there was the air-conditioning, which was nice when you'd been walking around in the afternoon heat. On the other hand, there was nothing like the feeling of walking back out into the street and getting blasted by the heat rising up off the pavement, the smells of the butcher shops and bakeries, even the carbon monoxide fumes from the city buses. It was a wild kind of exhilaration, where the city smacked you in the face with its reality and you loved it. Knowing Freddie Prinze was a little like that.

He was one of the true geniuses of our time. He was only twenty-two years old when Johnny Carson asked him to host the *Tonight Show*. Can you imagine? *Twenty-two!* I was on the show that night, and so was Bob Hope. When Bob came backstage he shook his head and said to me, "I've just met a comic genius." I don't think Bob Hope often gave that kind of praise. And Freddie was funny in person, too, not just when he was on stage. Half the time when you talked to him you didn't know if he was serious or if he was playing some colossal joke on you.

A lot of people said they got the three of us "ethnic" types confused from time to time: me (the Greek/Puerto Rican "Greek-O-Rican"), Freddie (the Hungarian/Puerto Rican "Hung-O-Rican"), and Geraldo Rivera (the Mexican/Puerto Rican "Mex-O-Rican"). Freddie and I were often mistaken for each other.

So Freddie showed up at my house one day and said, "Man, I about freaked out in West Hollywood yesterday. I had to use the bathroom, and the only one I could find didn't have anything but urinals. I'm standing there with my pants unzipped, and see all these guys staring at me kind of funny, like maybe they're gay."

"They make any moves?" I asked him.

"Nah, but they looked at me," he said.

"They recognize you?"

"I think so."

"Man, what'd you do?"

"What else could I do?" Freddie asked, with wide-eyed inno-
cence. "I started singing 'Tie a Yellow Ribbon Round the Ole
Oak Tree.' "

That was one side of Freddie, the light side. I'd soon get to
know the dark side.

Another of those show business moments happened for me
when I did a walk-on with Muhammad Ali on Dinah's show. The
minute Dinah told me she was having Ali on, I went nuts.

I don't know what it is about me and boxers, but I love them
as people, as friends. Maybe it's because Papito had been a
boxer, and I grew up respecting the great ones of the sport.
Mamita loved boxing, too. I remember she talked about Joe
Lewis a lot. Papito had always said Lewis was the greatest boxer
ever. So it was a real thrill that he usually came to my shows in
Las Vegas. One night in the late seventies, when I was working
at the Hilton Hotel, someone came back and told me Joe was in
the audience. Joe had been through a stroke, and was in a wheel-
chair. Mamita was also in the audience that night. Papito had
died a couple of years earlier. We all still missed him mightily.

I could see in Mamita's eyes that meeting Joe Lewis would
almost be symbolic, that Papito would somehow be alive to her
for a moment. Joe was dressed in an expensive suit, a Dick
Tracy–type hat, and was wearing a gold Las Vegas coin medal-
lion. Someone rolled him up to me, and I said, "I want you to
meet Mamita!" I asked him if he remembered me mentioning
Papito's career, and how much Papito admired him. Joe said he
did remember, and would be honored to meet Mamita. When I
introduced them, Joe did the most astonishing thing. He took his
hand, which was crippled from the stroke, raised it, and took his
hat off in a gentlemanly forties-style show of respect for a lady.

Mamita's eyes glistened with tears, and that's just one reason I love boxers. And I've never seen a dark side to any of them, even Mike Tyson.

So you can see that a man like Ali would be a great hero to me. I wanted to meet him more than anything, and was willing to beg to do it! *"Please,* Dinah, can I walk-on during the show?" She agreed, and we came up with an idea. *The Tony Orlando and Dawn Show* had a lot of recurring characters, like Telma and Joyce's Lou Effie and Moreen and my Kid Ghetto. The Kid was a boxing character, so it was no stretch of the imagination to decide to stage a fight between Kid Ghetto and Muhammad Ali.

I walked out during the show, dressed in my Kid Ghetto garb—a cloak and boxing trunks.

"All right, sucka," I said to Ali. "Come on, come *on.*" Then I started dancing around doing an Ali imitation.

Ali got a big kick out of it, and he jumped up to spar with me. The trouble was, I didn't know how to fake spar any better than back when I almost sliced Bobby Vee's ear in half. Ali was joking around, not paying attention. All of a sudden, my hand connected with his face. *Slap!* You could hear the audience's breath intake. And you could see Ali's eyes get as big as saucers. I think it kind of embarrassed him. I *know* it didn't hurt him. But what it did do, with all certainty, was turn him from variety show guest into fighter. He immediately went into fight mode, and I felt like a train was coming straight at me. Ali was the El Capitan, the Santa Fe, and he was coming at me at nine hundred miles an hour. *Boom, boom!* He took a jab at my arm and threw me into the camera.

Ali's friend and spiritual adviser, Drew "Bundini" Brown, was there and he started playing it for all it was worth: "Champ! It's Tony! It's just Tony! Ease up on him!"

Well, I have to say that getting punched by Muhammad Ali was one of the greatest moments of my entire life—it was a kid's dream come true! Ali and I became friends as a result of that show, and he started inviting me to the track meets he sponsored for charity.

Once, when I was running down the track with Ali at one of these events, I got this rush. I thought, *Man! Here I am on the track, Marvin Gaye's up there ahead of me, Chick Ellis there behind me. Lavar Burton is right up there—and I'm running equal with the champ, Muhammad Ali! He's got to be in the best shape in the world! And I'm keepin' up!*

Ali must have read my mind, because, he suddenly looked down at me, grinned and said, "Tony, good-bye, sucker!" And he was *gone*.

Ali even called me at home sometimes. If there is any rush in the world better than having someone say, "It's Muhammad Ali for you," I don't know what it is.

I spoke of Ali's ease with celebrity in an earlier chapter. He is completely comfortable in his own shoes, and that comfort makes him an accessible star. If there are two insights I would want to pass along about Ali, they are his disarming accessibility, and the fact that as your friend, he will minister to you. I don't mean in a religious way, but in a personal, uplifting way. He's a great motivator, a great leader of people. And if he sees a friend in trouble, he'll try to save them.

Which brings up the lighter subject of great showbiz "saves."

One of the best saves I ever got, came from George Burns. Telma, Joyce, and I had been asked to perform at a Director's Guild show naming George man of the year, hosted by Rich Little and Bob Hope. Telma, Joyce, and I were the last act. Seated at the very first table were George Burns and his young date, Jackie Gleason and his wife, Gregory Peck and his wife, Gene Kelly and his wife, Kirk Douglas and his wife, and Fred Astaire.

Our manager, Dick Broder, had warned me that this was an *important* event. I was nervous as hell. But we seemed to get the audience right in our hands from the first song. So I decided to end the show a little different than I'd planned, with Joe Cocker's "You Are So Beautiful."

While I was singing, I thought, I'll end this song as a tribute to Gracie Allen! I'll say, "Goodnight, Gracie." Man! George Burns would love that!

So when I came to the end, "You are so beautiful—to me," I looked out in the audience, and added, "And in your words, Mr. Burns—"

At that point, I made a fatal mistake. My eyes switched momentarily from George Burns to Jackie Gleason. And I said, "Good night, *Alice*."

The audience sat there staring at me. When what I'd just done sunk in, I could have crawled off the stage, and practically did. The stricken look on my face said it all. I was slinking out, I heard Rich Little introduce George, then George took the stage, and said, "I want to thank Rich Little for the wonderful introduction. I want to thank Bob Hope for the usual Bob Hope job that he always does. And I especially want to thank that youngster, Tony Orlando, who had the class to recognize my date, Alice."

There was a rumble throughout the crowd, then applause. I stopped in my tracks. I couldn't take it in, except to know that George Burns had turned me from an idiot into a hero. Later, I went over to his girlfriend, and asked, "Is your name Alice?"

"No," she laughed.

When I found George, I started thanking him. He stopped me, patted me on the back, and said: "That's what we do in this town, young man. We save each others asses."

Chapter 19

"He Don't Love You (Like I Love You)"

We exited Bell Records in 1975, after Bell's promotion guy, Steve Wax, left to go to Elektra. Our last number-one record had been *Yellow Ribbon* in 1973. We charted four times between 1973 and the move to Elektra, and the erratic chart positioning proved that a hit television show doesn't always translate to chart-topping singles. "Say, Has Anybody Seen My Sweet Gypsy Rose" went to number three, "Who's in the Strawberry Patch with Sally" topped out at twenty-seven, "Steppin' Out (Gonna Boogie Tonight)" brought us back to the top ten, and "Look in My Eyes Pretty Woman" peaked at eleven. Both Steve Wax and Hank Medress were determined we could cut a number-one single as our Elektra debut.

While we were recording that first session for Elektra, Steve Wax called me at the studio with some news that really excited me. Barry Manilow, now on Arista Records, had cut our song, "Could It Be Magic."

"It's going to be the single," Steve said.

I just about freaked out at the thought of being a writer on what I believed would be a big hit.

"Oh, my God!" I told Steve. "That's the best news I've heard!"

"I got better news," he said. "I've got a copy of it. Come over to the office and listen."

I ran right over to Steve's office and he pulled out the acetate. The record didn't have any album art or title information attached. He played the song and it was done as a ballad, but he kept most of our lyrics, including the chorus I'd written.

Then, when the record came out, my name was nowhere to be found. I called my attorney, who by this time was also representing Barry.

"Wait just a minute," I said. "I have a forty-five of 'Could It Be Magic,' with me and Barry listed as writers, and Orlando/Manilow Music as publishers. You wrote up the contract! This record has another publisher listed."

I filed suit over it. I hated to do it, but I'd cowritten the song, no matter what new arrangement they added.

The lawsuit went on and on, and finally my *new* lawyer called me and laid it on the line.

"You know that you're into this lawsuit for eighty grand, don't you? Why not just drop it? This ain't 'Stardust.' Who cares?"

"Well," I said. "It's the principle of the thing."

"Forget principle," he said. "Your legal fees are ridiculous."

I dropped the suit, but I didn't forget about it. It was a very unhappy experience with an old friend.

Finally, one night I was in Las Vegas to do a Dean Martin roast at the MGM Grand. I walked through the lobby and saw a big sign advertising a Barry Manilow show. It was right about the time Barry had a big hit with "I Write the Songs." I thought it was ironic.

Later, when I was asked to appear at a Stevie Wonder tribute, and ran into Barry, I went straight over to him.

"Barry, I just wanted to tell you that I'm proud of all you've done. I knew you were a star the first time I heard you. Let's shake hands and forget that whole song mess."

I stuck my hand out, and Barry shook it.

"Thanks, Tony. I appreciate that."

When Barry's autobiography came out, I was happy to see

that he was complimentary of me, and mentioned that I'd given him his first real break. I admit, that helped ease the old anger. Then, just a few years ago Barry put out a box set. Not only was 'Could It Be Magic' in the box set, it was the original one with my production! And right there in the booklet, with the historical liner notes and photos, there's a picture of the original forty-five with both our names listed as writers, as well as a photo of *Billboard*'s review, predicting it would be a hit. I was still in a state of shock when I read through the booklet, where he did a one-eighty on me and my contributions to his career. Unlike in his autobiography, Barry said I tried to make him a bubblegum singer and almost ruined his career! What can I say?

Anyway, my name is on the record in Barry's box set. And I was glad to see it right there in print.

Despite my being sidetracked by seeing my name taken off "Could It Be Magic," we did cut a number-one hit during those first Elektra sessions. Our first release was a cover tune, much to the distress of the label head, David Geffen. He was convinced that doing cover tunes would keep Tony Orlando and Dawn stuck in the singles side of the business, instead of making us solid album artists. But Bell was a singles-driven label, and even though Hank Medress didn't usually like to cover songs, he was convinced that we could top the charts with "He Don't Love You (Like I Love You)," written by Jerry Butler, Curtis Mayfield, and Clarence Carter. It had been a top-ten hit for Jerry Butler in 1960, right after he left the Impressions to go solo.

As it turned out, both Hank and David were right. "He Don't Love You (Like I Love You)" went number one for us. But the single David wanted, "Morning Beautiful," was a more original sound, and would have helped market the album better. But "He Don't Love You" was a song all of us loved. It was Telma's favorite of any song we recorded. And it was R&B, which I loved.

David Geffen is one of those people with that superstar essence.

149

It's not just entertainers who have it. He's funny, philosophical, and disarmingly honest. I remember going with Steve Wax out to David's office not long after we'd signed with Elektra. He walked in the room and announced that he'd just broken up with Cher.

"That's it!" he said, throwing his hand in the air. "No more heterosexual life for me. Too much pressure."

Neither Steve nor I had any idea he was bisexual. I just thought it was a hilarious line. We just laughed, acting macho, like we "got" the joke. Of course, the joke was on Steve and me, because David was as serious as a heart attack.

David once told me a story that I've always loved. He said this incident happened when he'd just bought his big beach house in Malibu, and was bringing friends out to see the property. He kept seeing this guy out on the beach. The same guy would bring a blanket, a little sack lunch, and a beer. He'd just sit out there looking at the ocean. It seemed to David that the guy was there at any given time, morning, noon, or night. One day David approached him.

"Man, what do you do for a living?" David asked. "You're here every day on this beach."

The guy shrugged. "I don't do anything. I'm a surfer."

David said he looked up at his beach house, and thought about the twenty-hour days he'd put in to pay for the thing. Then he thought, here's a guy sitting on the same beach for free. They both ended up in the same place.

There's a power that emanates from David Geffen. He's one of the most important men in the industry now, and I think he understands playing the role. He knows that this is a business with a ruthless side, that it is an often-insensitive industry that will chew you up and spit you out once you are no longer the flavor of the month. David's learned to use his "power character" as a leverage device, so you sometimes think you're walking a fine line between being okay with him, and *not* being okay with him. He can keep other power brokers walking on eggs around him.

Two things he appreciates are hard work and loyalty. One time we were talking about Norman Brokaw, who, several years later, took charge of my career. David said, "You know what I respect most about Norman Brokaw? He eats, sleeps, thinks, sweats, and lives for the William Morris Agency. A company can't buy that kind of devotion. It just has to be there in the executive."

I liked working with him, and never once felt he treated me anything but fairly. In fact, when Barbra Streisand and Kris Kristofferson made *A Star Is Born,* and they wanted an artist for a cameo to present Barbra with a Grammy, David suggested me. He could have suggested a hundred others. The funny thing about that film is that David didn't pay me with money, but with a mustache cup! One of those cups with a little opening so you don't get milk on your mustache. I sure never questioned it. I didn't need the money right then, and I was grateful to be in the film. So I took the cup.

There's a showbiz moment I'll never forget that happened during the making of *A Star Is Born.* No other singer was intended to be in the scene where I was supposed to present the Grammy to Barbra and we get interrupted by Kris. But when I was waiting for them to shoot that part, Kris's then-wife, Rita Coolidge, walked up to me with an open copy of *Playboy* in her hand. She was upset, crying. There, in the pages of *Playboy,* were nude pictures of Kris and Sarah Miles, taken during the filming of *The Sailer Who Fell From Grace with the Sea.* It was obvious to anyone who saw them that things may have gotten out of control.

"I had no idea," Rita said.

I thought about it for a minute, then said, "How would you like to make this day one Kris is never gonna forget?"

She wanted to do just that. So I went to the director, Frank Pierson, and to Barbra, and asked if Rita could be in the scene. "One person doesn't usually give out the Grammy," I said. "It's presented by two people."

They agreed, and said to just ad-lib through it.

So we went out and did the bit. I'm sure Kris never forgot the day Rita saw that *Playboy,* either. But there was a side result I hadn't counted on. People only remember Rita on that stage! All these years later, if you ask someone about the Grammy scene in *A Star Is Born,* most will say, "Oh, yeah, when Rita Coolidge presented the Grammy to Barbra."

Just as I'd made sure Kris would never forget the moment, I'd aced myself right out of people's memories.

Even though I was on Rita's side in the *Playboy*/Kris/Sarah confrontation, I was far from innocent when it came to infidelity. I'd fallen so head over heels for Telma Hopkins that even without *Playboy* evidence, my marriage was headed for the same train wreck as was Kris's. The problem with seeing women you work with is that you still "see" them after it's over. You also see all the new men in their lives—I wasn't the only man who followed Telma around like a puppy. She had movie stars and professional athletes hanging out at the set just to be around her. I remember running into a pro football player one afternoon.

"What's up?" I asked.

"Just here to see Telma," he said gruffly, trying to act like it was no big deal.

I knew he wasn't gonna be a tough guy very long. He'd be Telmatized like every other man.

"I'm gonna bet you fifty bucks that within a month you'll be here picking Red up for Little League," I told him. Red was Telma's little boy. He was a great little kid, and, as a matter of fact, Telma was a great mother. She watched out for him, and was careful what kind of men she let around him.

The guy looked at me like I was nuts.

About three weeks later the guy showed up backstage. He was pacing around, nervous.

"What's up?" I asked.

"I gotta find Red and get him to Little League," he said.

Chapter 20

Don't Change that Dial!

So many people stand out in my mind from the television days. First of all, the network executives, who had but one mantra: Don't change that dial! With every guest, there was a question—what will this do to the ratings? Time and again, the executives were proven wrong.

One of their biggest errors involved George Carlin, who frankly scared the crap out of them.

In 1976 we changed the name of the show to the *Rainbow Hour,* and set it up a little like *Saturday Night Live,* with a cast of house players. They made the change to boost ratings, but I was never quite sure of it. It seemed like a bit of a rip-off to me. And while I believe they were going for a more "hip" show, I believed our audiences liked us a little less for it. We weren't about being hip. But, if we were going for *Saturday Night Live,* who better than George Carlin?

I had wanted George Carlin on the show since the beginning. He is a master, and I couldn't see where he'd do anything but make the rest of us shine. I got a call from Sol Ilson, who told me that George hadn't really been doing much television and that he'd sort of dropped from the radar screen. It had started when he did that list of "words you can't say on TV."

It almost felt like there was an unofficial banning of him because of those seven deadly words, which were just cuss words. You couldn't even use the word "pregnant" on our show, let alone anything stronger. The executives were scared that the public might turn the channel the minute I said, "It's time for George!"

I didn't care about all that. I was a *huge* fan.

I got the green light, and we approached him. He agreed to do the show as long as when he finished his bit, we went straight to commercial. That made it a five-minute George Carlin show—and that was fine with me. When we had our first meeting, I had to lay out the network's rules.

"Okay, George. They want you to cut your hair—"

George shrugged. "That's all right. I'll do that."

"And the suits are very nervous about what you're gonna do. I've told them that it's all gonna be cool, that we're lucky to get you. If you'll just prove me right, use those great facial expressions, like in the wonderful wino bit. Don't go to the seven deadly words. Whatever you do, you can't cuss."

"No problem, man."

So George went on the show. I looked out in the audience and every network executive in the company is there, all looking like they were on the verge of nervous breakdowns.

I said, "Ladies and gentlemen, *it's time for George!*"

George came out. He looked dead in the eye of the camera.

"You're gonna die. You're gonna *die*. I'm gonna die. We're *all* gonna die."

I never saw so many executives freak out. It wasn't dirty—but he went straight to death! Those suits all figured the whole country was gonna be switching the dial in unison.

Didn't happen. The audiences loved George, and the ratings showed it. He's still out there raising hell and eyebrows, and the audiences still love him for it.

I'm really proud of the work we did with George, because it

opposite of Archie Bunker, Carroll was like the character in other ways. He'd get angry, bark at you—there was a bit of Archie in him.

The night after he did that first show, Elaine and I went to dinner with Carroll and his wife. We listened for hours to stories of his schoolteaching days, as well as his politics, which were *staunchly* democratic.

The very next day we were sitting in the office, when I got a call from Betty Ford. Gerry was still president of the United States. By that time, I'd made two close friends in the Fords—but that story comes a little later. So I said, "Mrs. Ford, I'm sitting here with Carroll O'Connor, would you like to say hello?" Betty said sure, so I started to hand the phone to Carroll. He waved me off at first. That embarrassed me, because how could I tell the first lady that Carroll O'Connor didn't want to talk to her? He finally took the phone, and he was gracious. But when he hung up, he said, "I gave you the wave-off."

Then he got into a whole political tirade about civil rights, poverty, and his take on Republicans.

"You of *all* people, Tony! You brought an ethnic mix to this network! Who'd have thought of a Puerto Rican man and two black women headlining on a network show?"

"But, Carroll," I said. "Don't you see? Archie Bunker polarized the network and made it *possible* for them to put us on the air! That show was so far to the right, that we balanced it out."

Minnie and Carroll were far different from their characters, but Danny Thomas was just like we all thought he'd be—everybody's daddy. He was an incredible storyteller, a tremendously giving performer. Danny became a regular on the show. Everything he did onstage was to help the entire show, the entire cast. He was that way in his everyday life, too. Years after his appearances on the show, I sent him an invitation to my second marriage. He came and when he arrived, he said he had a gift for us. He got up and did a half-hour of standup, maybe one of the last standup shows he ever did. The subject was marriage, and it was one of the funniest routines I ever heard while at the same time it was full of wisdom.

I don't know if the younger generation today remembers Kate Smith, the great singer and American icon. She was like an ongoing first lady in this country from World War II forward. And even in the mid-seventies, she consistently got the single biggest ratings of any guest we had on our show. Every single time Kate appeared, the ratings went through the roof. Consequently, she appeared many times.

For those who remember Kate Smith, this scene will be as surreal as it was to me at the time: Kate and I singing "Bad, Bad Leroy Brown." I thought that moment had the potential to go down in show business history as one of the poorest song choices ever recorded. But we had a ball doing it, and nobody gave us a traffic ticket, so I guess we slid by.

Here's how the world goes around: As a boy, my Uncle Orlando auditioned with Kate and sang in the Kate Smith Choir for a time. Kate remembered him, and described his work with the choir to me as if it had been yesterday. Maybe because of that connection Kate took a motherly interest in me. One time when she guested on the show, I came down with the flu and was running a 103° fever. She sat next to me with rubbing alcohol to cool on my head until that fever broke.

I was en route to see Kate when she died. It nearly killed me that I didn't get there in time to say good-bye.

It's very interesting what happens with network television, and the perceptions held by those who run the show. Like I said with George Carlin, they are always scared that somebody's gonna change that dial. But they can't always read the public. Take what happened when I wanted to book Frankie Avalon.

Every career has arcs, and at that particular time, Frankie was somewhere in between hits or movies, so the executives didn't think he'd be a draw. I wanted him, because I didn't care about what his last hit was, he was still *Frankie Avalon*. I always thought Frankie's beach movies overshadowed his music, and made him a little underrated. I think he had a Sinatra-like stage presence, and I loved his voice.

I'd always wanted to work with Frankie, for two reasons. When I was growing up watching *American Bandstand,* there were two guys I tried to emulate: Frankie Avalon and Jimmy Darren. I tried to be as cool as them, to comb my hair like them. And then, when I finally met Frankie there at the Palasades Park, he treated me great, even though he was a *huge* star at the time. He had number-one records, he was a star on *Bandstand,* as well as a movie star. I had one song on the charts.

When we finally got Frankie on the show, it turned out to be one of the best, most fluid episodes we ever did. We sang the old Bobby Mercer/Bobby Darin song, "Two of a Kind," and we did a sketch about what the *Tonight Show* would be like in the year 2000. The audience loved it. As I said, he *is* Frankie Avalon.

Of all the guests we had, Ann Meara and Ruth Buzzi were the most comfortable sketch players. They were naturals. Ann had a hand in writing a sketch we did that was *far* out there, but brilliant. It was called the "Egg Sketch"—Ann played the egg yolk and I played the white. It was about us separating. What a concept to base a comedy sketch on! Ann is truly a comedic genius. I learned more from her about the spirit of comedy and how to play comedy, than with any single person. I also loved Ann because, with her thick New York accent, she could have been one of my aunts from West Twenty-first Street.

Ruth Buzzi went through a period of time in her career when she thought she might quit show business because it had just taken too much out of her. She wrote me a long letter about it, and I talked her out of it. It would have been a big loss to the entertainment world, as far as I was concerned. The world can't afford to lose another laugh. The day would come when I'd go through those exact same feelings and want nothing more than to hang it up.

When Freddie Prinze made his debut on the show, it was the first prime time network variety show he'd appeared on. He'd made plenty of other television appearances, but not in this precise format. I didn't realize that until he told me. Even though we'd met on Dinah's show and had become great friends, this was to be the first time we actually worked together, doing sketches.

Right away, he told me that he wanted to sing. He wanted to come out as Tony Orlando and Dawn and sing "I Got the Music in Me." He said he wanted to see how long it took the audience to snap to that he wasn't me. Well, first of all, Freddie was six foot four in flat shoes. I was six foot tall only if I wore those infamous seventies platforms! Fat chance they'd mistake us, with him towering over Telma and Joyce.

But here was the stunner—he sang his butt off. Then he ad-libbed and introduced *himself*, "Now, here is one of America's greatest comedians, Freddie Prinze!"

I stood in the wings shaking my head and thinking, *This guy is brilliant. He is too freakin' much!*

He stole the moment in the most unbelievable way. He sang great, moved great, looked great—and created the whole thing about introducing himself on his feet. Then he did a comedy bit with Telma like I only *wished* I could do! Then he walked off and said, "Man, I was so nervous."

I said, "Freddie, if that's what you do when you're nervous, you got no worries."

One scene Freddie did that never aired was a ballet. I don't know how, when, or why it got cut, because it was staggering. To my surprise, Freddie told me that his dream had always been to be a ballet dancer. He'd studied ballet as a child. I convinced the producers to let him dance, not as a comic segment, but played straight. I would give anything to find a copy of that piece of tape. He looked like Baryshnikov on the stage.

He did my show twice, and then I did *Chico and the Man* with him. When I walked out on that set, we circled each other like a couple of wary dogs, and finally said in unison, "Looking good!" That got the biggest studio audience laugh I've heard before or since.

One of the best sketches the two of us did on my show was one Freddie conceived of, and we both wrote, based on the old Bob Hope-Bing Crosby road movies. We called our version "On the Road to Puerto Rico." Freddie, of course, played the comic, the Bob Hope character, and I played the singer, the Crosby character. Adrienne Barbeau played the Dorothy Lamour role.

Sol Ilson and Ernie Chambers were both very close to Bob Hope, and asked him if he and Bing would do cameos. They agreed, and the two did a very funny bit from the corner of the TV screen, making fun of these two characters trying to do a road sketch. That bit meant a lot to me, because it showed the camaraderie, as the originals had done, between Bob and Bing. It played so well that Bob Hope called me and asked if Freddie and I would consider doing some road movies with him and Bing.

We might have done it, too, if we hadn't started down a very dark road in our personal lives.

Chapter 21

Starting the Journey Down

The years 1975 and 1976 were classic best of times/worst of times for me.

First, I was making all kinds of money with the television show and the touring, so I decided to try to put my family back together. My father was at loose ends, and Elaine suggested we ask him to move to Los Angeles and work with me. I believe her intentions were good, that she really believed this sort of arrangement could help heal old wounds that I wouldn't admit but she suspected were there. She also wanted me to move my brother Bobby to California. Maybe she felt I needed some family close by, I don't know. But I made the offer and they accepted.

Bobby started out working on the tour, learning as much as he could about the music business. He worked as a kind of valet/road manager, as a tech—anything to get a good all-around working knowledge of the business. Leo was another story. He was used to being Label the Furrier, the boss of everyone up and down the line. Slowly but surely, he started trying to get in charge. He'd pick up the phone and call Fred Silverman or another network executive and tell them about something wrong with the show. He called my accountants, my booking agents. Nobody told me about Leo's calls for a long time. But finally one by one, people started complaining. I was stunned. I thought, *Damn, I built this career without you, Leo. Don't muck it up!*

And when I talked to him about the calls, he said very little. In his mind, he was simply protecting me. Who knows why he'd started trying to get in charge of my life? Maybe it was because I was paying him a lot of money for someone who didn't know anything about television *or* the music business. Or maybe he was starting to try to be a father.

Reflecting back, now, I think Leo was 100 percent right on every count. The things he saw as problems *were* problems. If it were to happen all over again, I'd tell him so, too.

I felt awful every time I gave Leo a paycheck. It brought back memories of when I had to trudge over to find him and collect the three dollars of "child support." I kept questioning myself. Was I doing this because of my feelings about that three dollars I had to collect years ago? Was this some weird kind of payback?

On the upside of it, in 1975 Mamma and Louis decided to move from New York to Las Vegas. The idea had come from Uncle Orlando, who was still living in California. "Go to Vegas, Ruth!" he insisted. "You're gonna love it!"

And Mamma did fall in love the minute she saw the desert for the second time. In a way, she had the same reaction I'd had as a little kid riding the El Capitan—her imagination started to run wild. "How did the pioneers do it?" she wondered. Having lived in New York most of her life, she became entranced with the Indian culture of the Southwest, of the concept of pioneer families in covered wagons, crossing this vast, beautiful—yet potentially dangerous—desert. Then, when she actually saw a woman wearing an old-fashioned bonnet—well, she was hopelessly hooked.

I couldn't have been happier, because the move put her much closer to me in Los Angeles. Also, I spent so much time in

Las Vegas that I considered it a second home. It's always been a magic town for me. The city of Sinatra, of Elvis.

A shadow crossed over the move, though. Rhonda had been sick with pneumonia, but seemed to have recovered. Mamma asked Rhonda's New York doctors if there was any reason she couldn't make the move, and was told there was none whatsoever. But soon after the move, Rhonda got sick again. She only lived for about a month after they came west. I flew to Vegas for the funeral, almost comatose from the shock.

On the one hand, it didn't seem fair. But, I had to admit that she'd had the best life possible under the circumstances of her physical condition. She was twenty-one years old when she died, and that was twenty-one years longer than any doctor had predicted she'd live when she was born. She'd had chronic illness, pain, seizures—all things that you'd think would cause a person to hate life. Yet Rhonda loved so much. She loved her family. She loved music. She was dealt a hand of cards I wasn't in this world, a pretty sorry hand. Yet she played it well, far better than most do with far better cards. Certainly better than I was playing my own cards at the time.

Papito, too, was ill. He was still trying to come back from a stroke, when he suffered a heart attack. I took the first plane to New Jersey, but missed seeing him alive by minutes. Rhonda's and Papito's deaths were still more things in my life that I stuffed back into my subconscious and didn't really deal with like I should have. Like so many things, that grief simmered and stewed somewhere inside my head. With my sister and Papito gone, I started worrying about losing Mamita as well. I think that if I had to pick a time when I really started to zone out, it was then.

I'd been moving around a lot through the past few years, too. After the show got picked up, we moved to a place at Sunset and Beverly Hills, then to a Spanish-style home in Encino. The next house we rented was in Brentwood, and while we agreed to lease it, we hoped to buy if the price was right. Our real estate woman was Gig Young's wife, Elaine. She said the owner wouldn't budge off the $600,000 asking price. I couldn't see paying it, because the Tudor-style home was about half the size of another property offered for sale across the street. That house was ten thousand square feet and listed at $400,000. So we kept leasing.

Our realtor once joked, "Too bad you aren't a football player. The owner might negotiate. She loves professional football!"

From the first day Elaine and I moved into that Tudor house in Brentwood, I felt something amiss. I am going to call it an omen, but whether it was anything in the supernatural realm, or just coincidence, I don't know. But I felt it from the first time I walked inside, even though Elaine loved the house. Then on the first morning there, I opened the double doors of the master bedroom, looked down and saw two dead hummingbirds. I got an involuntary chill.

"I don't know, Elaine," I said. "This is a gorgeous house but there's a weird vibe here."

"Don't be melodramatic, Tony," she said.

So I shut up about it. But I never forgot that two couples who'd lived there before had had marriages that seemed sound, yet ended in divorce: Carole King and Gerry Goffin, and Carly Simon and James Taylor.

Finally I decided it was stupid to be paying rent in a luxury neighborhood, and bought the house across the street, the ten-thousand-square-foot monstrosity. I felt like I should be riding my old bicycle, Lucy, when I trucked down the halls of that place. Somehow, living in a place that big was isolating, divisive. It sure wasn't anything like our "sharing apartment" on West Twenty-first, and somehow, West Twenty-first had the better atmosphere.

One day I ran into the guy who'd founded the music industry publication, *Radio & Records,* Robert Kardashian. He told me that his friend O.J. Simpson was looking for a house in Brentwood. A memory of my conversation with Elaine Young, our realtor, flashed into my mind.

"Boy, you should tell him about the house I used to lease in Brentwood, on Rockingham. I moved across to Bristol because of the asking price. But the owner loves football players, so if anyone could negotiate the price down, the Juice could."

O.J. and Nicole moved in, and one day he and I were walking down the street.

"We're really screwing up the neighborhood," I said. "A Puerto Rican and a brother living across the street from each other in Brentwood."

O.J. just shook his head. "The only color that matters in an area like this is the color green."

Years later, as I watched that white Bronco race through Los Angeles, I kept flashing back to those two dead hummingbirds I'd seen that morning on Rockingham.

Tragedies like that make my problems during the seventies pale by comparison. But mine were hellish, nevertheless.

I was skinny as a rail during the Tony Orlando and Dawn days. It wasn't easy, because I've fought a weight battle all my life. I didn't wage a particularly healthy war, either, especially during the years we were on television. First of all, the workload was tough. We worked on the show twelve to eighteen hours a day. We recorded. We continued to tour. In the summer of 1976, during our break from the television show, we played thirty-two concerts in thirty-six days. My diet was as rigid as the workload. I ate nothing but steaks, not even salads. Plus, I was smoking three-and-a-half to four packs of cigarettes a day, and drinking one cup of coffee after another. I worked out. I spent hours in the steam room. Eventually, it took its toll on me. I was so exhausted from juggling my concert tour, television tapings, writing scripts and comedy sketches, rehearsing, and recording that I had to force myself to walk onstage or into a recording booth. Unfortunately, about the time I was winding down, someone showed up with a way to wind me back up.

I had just put on a chicken costume for the next sketch when Redd Foxx stopped by the dressing room for a visit. Redd took a look at me and shook his head. "You look like hell."

"I feel like hell," I admitted.

Redd pulled a bag of cocaine from his pocket.

"I don't do any of that shit, man," I said quickly. And I didn't. I'd grown up a streetwise inner city. Puerto Rican kid, but I'd never been a punk. As I have said, I had a tight family background and middle-class mores that had kept me aloof from the drug side of the entertainment industry. Then again, I'd never been that close to complete exhaustion.

Redd just laughed and said. "This stuff ain't gonna make you drunk or crazy or get you stoned. It's like drinking about fifteen cups of coffee."

I stuck the dollar bill up my nose and after a false start or two, snorted a line. I told Redd I didn't feel any better and he said, "Try another line and wait a minute."

I took another hit, and felt the old energy pump. It was bullshit energy, of course, but few people think of that when they start doing coke.

The very idea of me standing in my dressing room, wearing a chicken costume and snorting cocaine with Redd Foxx, could be the comic ending to a left-of-center seventies movie, if it wasn't the tragic beginning to my real life, sorry-ass seventies nosedive.

I continued to function, but underneath it all, I was a mess. Ironically, like a lot of entertainers, many people think of me and say, "Oh, yeah didn't he have a drug problem?" I did, for about a year. And I will say that it was the worst year of my life.

Freddie, too, was spinning out of control. One day he came over to my house and we started joking around.

"Come on, tough guy," I joked. "Let's box. I bet I can take you."

Freddie got this wild gleam in his eye, and before I knew it he'd kicked me in the gut and I was on the ground doubled over in pain. I thought he'd ruptured my kidney.

"What the hell are you doing?" I gasped. "I can't breathe!"

Freddie just laughed.

"You know something, Tony? You gotta learn how to take a punch," he said. "I've been taking karate. The first thing I did was tell my instructor to knock me unconscious."

"That's crazy! Why'd you do that?" I asked, still doubled over on the ground.

"I wanted to know what it felt like to get knocked out." He laughed.

"Well, I don't, man," I said. "I don't want to know how it feels and I don't want my damn kidney busted."

Freddie grinned and reached down to help me up. "Forget it," he said. "Let's go swimming."

I never kidded with Freddie about fighting again, because as much as he valued strength, he didn't know his own. Freddie was so complicated, such a combination of a child and a man. The child could make you laugh. The man could either give you backbone, confidence, or, at his worst, scare the hell out of you. You loved both of them. You couldn't help yourself.

Freddie loved JFK, worshipped the idea of him. And he loved the idea of Kennedy's Camelot, the myth of lords and ladies and heroic drama. Freddie considered the Kennedys to be American royalty, and he wanted to be royalty, too. That's why he picked a royal name—Prinze, spelled with a "ze" instead of a "ce," as a nod to his Hungarian surname, Pruetzel. He wanted to be the prince of comedy. Not the king, that was Bob Hope. Freddie had a streak of Camelot inside him. He was a trained ballet dancer, had stunned me with his grace when he performed on my television show. Beauty and elegance lived in Freddie, right next door to a bizarre craving for Washington Heights, slums, guns, and street violence.

Looking back on Freddie's too-short life, I wonder if the moment he crossed the line of reality was when he got hold of a copy of the Kennedy assassination film and started fixating on it. I remember one day when I went over to his house and found him watching the footage where the bullet hits the president's head. He'd get right up close to the screen when Kennedy slumped over in the convertible. Then he'd rewind the film and watch it over again. Or maybe it was when he saw DeNiro in *Taxi Driver*. He started buying guns and ammo, strapping them on in some bizarre commando fashion. He'd look at himself in the mirror, just like DeNiro did in the film, and get a glazed look in his eyes.

Or maybe it was just the drugs.

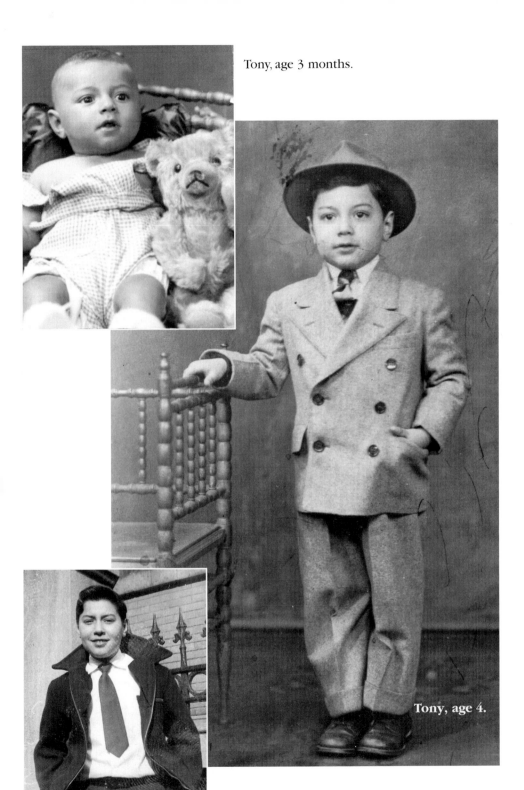

Tony, age 3 months.

Tony, age 4.

Tony, age 11.

Tony, mom Ruth, sister
Rhonda, and step-dad
Louis Schroeder (1955).

Tony Orlando publicity
photo (1961).

Tony's first
publicity photo
used on sleeve
cover for
"Halfway to
Paradise"
(Epic Records).

Tony signing autographs for fans (1961).

Tony signing autographs for "Halfway to Paradise" in a record store (1961).

Publicity photo, age 16 (1961).

Tony signing autographs at
Palisades Amusement Park (1961).

Tony leaving for
first tour (1961).

Tony performing onstage at
Palisades Amusement Park (1962).

Tony and "Mamita."

Tony and
son Jon.

Tony Orlando and Dawn (1973).

A classic Tony publicity photo (1975).

Tony and First Lady
Betty Ford dancing
at the White House.

Tony and
Freddie Prinze on
*Tony Orlando and
Dawn*, the "Road
to Puerto Rico"
sketch (1976).

Tony and Freddie Prinze.
Tony guest-starring on
Chico and the Man.

Freddie Prinze guest-starring on
Tony Orlando and Dawn (1976).

Tony and Freddie Prinze on
Tony Orlando and Dawn,
the "Road to Puerto Rico"
sketch (1976).

Muhammad Ali
and Tony at the
Muhammad Ali
Track Meet.

Tony and mom
Ruth at the
Riviera Hotel
in Las Vegas
(1977).

Tony performing on stage.

Tony in 1978.

Tony and Paul Anka onstage at
the Riviera Hotel in Las Vegas.
Paul surprised on his return
after Cohasset (1978).

Tony rehearsing for *Barnum* (1981).

Tony starring on
Broadway in
Barnum. Opening
night curtain call
at the St. James
Theater (1981).

Tony in *300 Miles for
Stephanie*, an NBC
movie of the week.

Tony Orlando
and Dawn's
"Reunion Tour"
(1988). Tony with
Telma Hopkins
and Joyce Vincent
Wilson.

Tony and Jerry Lewis backstage at the Hilton Hotel
in Las Vegas (1990).

Tony and Frannie's
wedding day:
April 29, 1990.

Tony and Frannie backstage at the
Hilton Hotel in Las Vegas (1990).

Tony and Jenny backstage at the
Golden Nugget in Las Vegas (1992).

Son Jon and Tony performing a musical tribute to *Barnum* at the Yellow Ribbon Music Theatre in Branson, Missouri (1994).

Tony, Frannie, Jon, and Jenny at Jenny's kindergarten graduation (1996).

Tony and daughter Jenny on stage at the Yellow Ribbon Music Theatre in Branson, Missouri, on Veteran's Day (1997).

Chapter 22

Mamita Makes Her Network Debut and I Do a Political
One-eighty

Even though I had started doing coke for the first time in my life,
I continued to function—at least on the surface—and Mamita
didn't suspect anything. It would have killed me for her to know
how I was messing up. Especially since I was getting ready to
make her a TV star.

One night Mamita came to see me at my apartment in the
casino. She sat in my old green rocking chair and started telling
me a story about a trip we'd once taken together. How I loved
listening to her talk, with traces of her Spanish accent.

"I'm gonna tell you about what happened the first night I visited you in one of those fancy hotels you always stay at, Mikey,"
she said. "You remember you always had those big rooms that
were like apartments?"

"Sure, Mamita, the suites."

"Yeah, the suites. They had a bedroom for you and one for
somebody else. And one night I went off to bed in my room and
I noticed that there was two beds in the room. I kept thinking,
now why would there be two beds unless Tony has more people coming? I went out into the living room of that suite and
looked around but you'd already gone into your room and
closed the door. So I went back in the other room and sat on the

bed waiting for the other people to come. I didn't want to be asleep when they came in. Nobody ever came and I never did go to sleep that night."

"Mamita!" I said. "Why didn't you knock on my door and ask me! Nobody was coming!"

"Well," she said with a slow smile. "There was a little sign on the door that said 'Do Not Disturb' so I didn't want to disturb anybody."

I didn't know whether to laugh or cry. That was so like Mamita. And I got to thinking how funny it would be if she told the story on the television show, about sitting up all night waiting for her roommates to show up. Because as I thought about it, that night might have been pretty awful since she didn't get to sleep, but now she somehow found humor in the telling.

Then she looked over at me with a kind of wicked grin on her face and a twinkle in her eyes. "You know what, Tony? I have a little crush on John Davidson."

That broke me up. You never knew what on earth Mamita might come up with. At age seventy-three she was so beautiful and I was so thankful for her that I started thinking about a way to show her just how much I appreciated her having been such a strong figure in my life.

The next afternoon I called the show's producers and told them about an idea that had been running around in my head for the past sixteen hours or so. It didn't seem like a particularly radical idea, and in fact, I didn't think anyone would blink twice at it. I was wrong.

"I want to have my grandmother on the show's Christmas episode," I said.

"Are you nuts?" was the immediate response. "Your *grandmother*? Sorry to break this to you Tony, but your grandmother isn't going to do shit for your ratings."

That really pissed me off.

"Okay," I countered. "I'll pay for the damn airtime. Figure up

what it costs for her to be on camera for a couple of minutes and bill me for it."

"That's a lot of money, Tony," they said. "We're talking prime-time television."

"Well, you can just hold my checks until it's paid off then," I said, even more determined that Mamita was going to be on that show.

I brought the green rocking chair from home, and put it down among the audience seating. Then I got the wardrobe lady to buy Mamita a beautiful green dress, and the stylists did her hair and makeup. She was so excited she just bubbled. That night when she came in and was seated, I had a spotlight follow her all the way to the chair and then announced, "Ladies and gentlemen, my grandmother!" The applause was thunderous and when she told the "Do Not Disturb" story it brought the house down.

Our ratings were never better and we got more mail about Mamita than we ever got about any star who appeared on the show. Nobody disagreed; Mamita was the biggest hit the show had ever had. Needless to say I didn't have to pay the network for the airtime. But I would have done so happily just to see the pride when Mamita later told people about being on television with Mikey.

Mamita had made a very distinguished fan that night, which leads me to the story of how I met the president and Mrs. Ford.

Not long after that show I got an invitation to dine with the president and his wife at the White House. Well, that just about knocked me over. First of all, I was a Democrat, a serious Kennedy-style Democrat. Secondly, I hadn't liked the idea of President Ford pardoning Richard Nixon and I sometimes brought up my politics when I shouldn't. So I wasn't sure if I was the right entertainer to go to a White House dinner! But I don't care what your politics are, when you go to the White

House and those trumpets play and they announce the president and first lady of the United States of America, you shiver right down to your toes. And later, after you have your steak dinner, when you're standing in line to be presented to the two, you really start to get cold chills.

I had absolutely no idea what to say and was worrying that I might come off like some idiot when President Ford looked over and said, "Betty! Look who's here! It's Tony!"

I almost fainted at that point, and stammered out some sort of greeting. Betty Ford sailed right in.

"Tony, how is your Mamita?" She asked with a great smile on her face. "Gerry and I were watching the night you had her on and we just loved her!"

I couldn't *wait* to see the look on Mamita's face when I told her.

After the introductions there was a dance, and I was standing there amazed and impressed by everything when President Ford came over.

"So, Tony," he began. "Who are you voting for in the election?"

Oh, great, I thought. *Here we go.*

"I won't lie to you, sir," I answered. "I'm a Democrat." Of course, you'll notice that I didn't come right out and say I planned on voting for Jimmy Carter.

President Ford grinned and patted me on the shoulder. "That's all right. Wait right here and I'll be back."

In a couple of minutes he showed up with a button that read "DEMOCRATS FOR FORD."

"Now, don't get me wrong. I'm not trying to sway your vote," he said with a grin. "But you can take this just in case you change your mind."

"It would be a one-eighty degree switch for me to vote Republican," I laughed.

He got a chuckle out of that as well, and it led to more conversation and a few stories and finally I couldn't stop myself.

"Uh, President Ford, what about the Nixon pardon?" I asked, bringing up the one thing I'd vowed not to talk about to anyone at the dinner, let alone the president of the United States.

I really don't know what I expected him to say, but his reaction caught me completely off guard.

"I didn't do it for President Nixon," he said. "I did it to clear my desk. Tony, what if I hadn't pardoned him? What if he'd ended up in court over Watergate? This country would have been in turmoil. Nothing would have been accomplished. I didn't know how long I had to serve the country as president, and I just didn't want to spend the whole time in the middle of prosecuting President Nixon."

I know that President Ford later explained his actions, using that very "clear the desk" line, but at that time, I had no idea what his motivation had been. I guess I just figured it was payback time. I look at that decision now, in light of the last two years of the Clinton administration, when so much more could have been accomplished, and I see the wisdom even more clearly. A presidency constantly embroiled in controversy cannot function like it should.

I spent a lot of time talking with President Ford that night and I came away with the strong belief that this was a man who'd been given a bum rap. First, he'd been severely chastised for the Nixon pardon, and I'd been among those who did the bitching. Second, he was not taken as seriously as he should have been. There was all the press coverage of incidents where he fell skiing or tripped. And yet this man was probably the finest athlete who ever served as president of the United States. I fear that when former president Lyndon Johnson made the comment that Gerald Ford had played one two many football games without a helmet it was one of those jokes that become part of the public consensus.

When I went back to L.A. I made it a point to read more about Gerald Ford and I will say that I came away impressed. True, he was more conservative than my usual politics, but his congressional record had been honorable and he hadn't seemed to play any games or compromise his ideals. I also realized that this man had not only inherited a presidency that had the taint of Watergate on it, he'd inherited a very unstable economy, and to try and turn it around in less than two years was almost impossible. One of the great things he did was offer amnesty to the guys who'd fled to Canada rather than fight in Vietnam. The most important thing I decided, though, was that he was a good and decent man. First, I decided to vote for him. Then, I decided to campaign for him.

You'd have thought I was announcing my new status as a serial killer when I told Freddie Prinze I was voting Republican.

"You're gonna do *what*?" Freddie threw up his hands as if in despair. "How in the hell can a Puerto Rican from New York vote Republican? How will you *live* with yourself? This man pardoned Nixon and you're gonna *campaign* for him?"

The truth is, I was just lucky Freddie was semistraight when I dropped my bomb on him because if he'd been messed up and packing his guns he might have shot me. From then on, throughout the campaign, Freddie would call up and say, "Is this my friend the Puerto Rican *Republican*?" Then he'd have to go through his whole list of reasons that any sane person had to vote Democrat. He made it into somewhat of a joke, but I know that deep down he was really mad about it. Freddie took his politics very seriously.

As I started helping out with the Ford campaign, I started taking politics very seriously, too. I really believed that given some more time, President Ford could have set the country straight again. I spoke with the president often throughout the campaign, and flew to various places to help whenever I could. The highlight of the 1976 campaign turned out to be the convention in Kansas City, when Gerald Ford defeated Ronald Reagan in a close race for the nomination. It was a good thing we celebrated after the convention, because we sure didn't paint the town when the final election votes were counted.

I flew to Kansas City's brand new international airport the night the convention opened and went straight to the Ford's hotel suite. Even though the troops were out of Vietnam and Watergate was behind us, it was a volatile time in 1976. Both Ford and Reagan had been greeted by groups of protesters from various special interest groups when they arrived, and according to the *Kansas City Star,* the police even thought they might face something like what happened in Chicago during the 1968 Democratic convention. With that in mind they'd purchased an additional 2,000 handcuffs, 1,000 gas masks, 250 tear gas grenades, fifteen quarts of liquid tear gas, and two school buses to transport prisoners! By the time I arrived there wasn't much sign of organized protest, though, and I think by then the city and the police were breathing a sigh of relief. The only fight was going to be whether the nomination went to Gerald Ford or Ronald Reagan. Everyone there knew the contest was tight. And for me the irony was that while Ford's policies had been more conservative than I'd usually support, Reagan was running against him as the *real* conservative.

When I got to the Ford suite I found the president there alone except for some of the Secret Service men. The president of the United States was padding around in his bare feet eating a bowl of spaghetti. He immediately offered me some spaghetti and we sat down to watch the opening gavel at Kemper Arena. I sat there twirling spaghetti around my fork and marveling at the fact that the man who sat across from me was the most powerful leader in the world, and would soon find out if he had a chance at holding office for another four years. I kept wondering what that must feel like, to have that kind of world power.

I ate some of the spaghetti and listened to some speeches and finally asked him point blank what it felt like to be the president of the United States. He smiled and shook his head.

"Let me tell you, I fog up the bathroom mirror every morning when I'm shaving thinking *I am the president of the United*

States. I was in Congress for years but nothing prepared me for the power and the responsibility that comes with the presidency. I wonder if anyone ever gets used to it."

Later we all went down to Kemper Arena and what happened then was amazing. I love Betty Ford, I'll say that right off. I don't know what other first ladies have been like, but in my mind you couldn't find one better than Betty. She's gracious, kind, funny, fun, intelligent, and simply one of the most likable people I've ever met in my life. Betty Ford is one of those people who make you feel like you've known her all your life and that you are a worthwhile human being. She does that even in meetings that last only a few moments. I think that's the quality that made her an important advocate for breast cancer research and alcohol and drug treatment. She believes she is no better and no worse than the next person down the line and because of that, the next person down the line benefits from her warmth and honesty.

So that night I found myself seated in the presidential box with two of the people I'd come to know and admire most in this world. The music was playing and people were dancing on the convention floor, holding up signs for both Ford and Reagan. It was a heady experience. And it got even more exciting because the band started playing "Tie a Yellow Ribbon Round the Ole Oak Tree" and the first lady asked me to dance. You bet! I jumped up and we started dancing around the presidential box. But what we didn't know was that about the time we started dancing, Nancy Reagan had arrived at the building and the television cameras had begun following her entrance. Unknown to Betty Ford and I, the cameras had also discovered our dance team and they were covering both Betty and Nancy on split screens. We realized what was going on when we heard Walter Cronkite's voice on the speakers saying, "Look at this! Mrs. Ford and Tony Orlando are upstaging Nancy Reagan's entrance! It's the Battle of the Wives!"

Later some reporters speculated that the whole thing was

staged to take attention away from Mrs. Reagan. And for a long time, I, too, wondered why in the world they would play "Tie a Yellow Ribbon" at the precise moment that Nancy Reagan was walking into the convention hall. Some time later I ran into one of the guys who'd been in charge of the events during the convention and I asked him if that dance moment had in any way been staged. He smiled in a sort of secretive manner and for a minute I was afraid it had been an elaborate plan.

"Don't tell me Betty Ford had anything to do with it!" I said, alarmed.

"No," he said, shaking his head. "It was Nancy Reagan. We asked Nancy for a list of her favorite songs and one of them was 'Yellow Ribbon.' "

Well, the incident was one hell of a coincidence, and if there was someone who made the call given Mrs. Reagan's song favorites, it wasn't me or by Betty Ford. That's not Betty's style and I certainly didn't come up with the idea. I couldn't have thought that fast given the excitement of being there in the middle of a nominating convention. In fact, my first reaction to seeing myself on the monitor dancing with the first lady was to say, "Mrs. Ford, do you know who's watching this?"

"I do." She smiled. "Three networks."

"Well." I laughed. "Actually, I was gonna say the old gang on West Twenty-first Street."

The real irony is that both Betty and I were heading for personal trainwrecks. Hers was powered by liquor and prescription drugs, mine by cocaine.

The rest of the convention is a blur in my memory, but I will say that you never feel as competitive and anxious about a "contest" as you do with something that will possibly determine who the next United States president will be. No Super Bowl or Kentucky Derby where you're betting on or pulling for a certain winner can compare. In the end, President Ford prevailed over Ronald Reagan 1,184–1,070. We had a feeling that the president would win when

Reagan lost a battle to insist that Ford name his running mate before the final presidential vote. Still, the race was tight.

The president named Kansas senator Bob Dole as his running mate and we were off to a race Gerald Ford would ultimately lose to Jimmy Carter.

But the night President Ford accepted the nomination his reelection seemed assured, and his speech made me even more proud I'd made the decision to support him. He gave a very straightforward, honest speech. He was proud to be the first president since Ike Eisenhower to have served when the nation was not at war. He knew that the country still faced economic problems and he vowed to turn those around if given the time.

He brought up the fact that people sometimes called him either the "accidental president" or the "unelected president." But he said he always saw his office as a duty to be done, not a prize to win. He admitted that since taking office during such a troubled time he had probably made mistakes, but he also said that on balance he believed that Americans had made "an incredible comeback" since August 1974. And certainly, he reminded people of his successes, including vetoing what he considered to be too many spendthrift bills passed by Congress.

Then he said something that made a lot of sense. He said that the president of the United States is not a magician who can wave a wand and make things right. Even so, he said, inflation was down, payrolls and profits were up. And with the prayers and support of the people, he wanted the opportunity to keep things going in that direction.

Without going into any criticism of President Carter—because I believe he also faced a tough road and he was a good man—I believe President Ford could have done what he promised that night. I also believe this: He took charge when our nation was unbelievably divided and sick to death of Washington and politicians. He restored some of the faith in public servants and I don't know if anyone else would have had the personality to do that.

Watching the concession speech that year was awful. You may remember that President Ford had a severe case of laryngitis and Mrs. Ford had to deliver the last part of the concession. Both were gracious during what I know was one of the toughest times in their political lives. Both President Ford and the first lady seemed absolutely genuine when they asked Americans to rally behind president-elect Carter.

Then I noticed something on the television screen that made the whole night even more personal. Susan, the Ford's daughter, was wearing a watch I'd recently given her. As tough and heartbreaking as the entertainment business can be, politics seemed far rougher that night. I sat listening to Betty speak, then, when the family walked off the stage and the cameras moved to the crowd, tears welled up in my eyes. I'd become so close to the Fords since that night I first met them at the White House, but even so I hadn't realized just how hard their loss would hit me. I was still sitting there staring at the television, wishing I'd been able to be there with them, when my phone rang.

"Tony," the very familiar voice said. "It's Betty."

I was stunned. It seemed like they'd only been off the television screen a few minutes.

"I just watched you on television! Where are you calling from?"

Betty explained that she was speaking from a phone one of the Secret Service men carried.

"I know you're feeling down now, Tony," she said. "It's been a hard fight. But we're okay. In fact, since we're out on the street now, I was just wondering if you needed someone to play a hooker on the show!" .

I was so taken aback I guess I half-choked out a laugh.

"Seriously, Tony," she went on. "I just thought I'd give you a little chuckle. I knew you'd take this hard. And I want you to come visit us as soon as we get back to Palm Springs. We'd love to see you, and life goes on you know."

• • •

Sure enough, not long before Christmas that year, I had a call from Betty inviting me to come to their place in Palm Springs. She told me to hook up with Cary Grant, who was also coming, so we could ride together. I'd never met Cary and the prospect of riding out to the Ford's place with him was exciting. I had no idea what he'd be like. As did most of his fans, I suppose I thought of him as the ultimate in suave. I wasn't to be disappointed. We agreed to meet at a certain place so I could drop off my car and catch a ride. He pulled up in a white stretch limousine, looking exactly like the movie star Cary Grant ought to look: distinguished, rich, elegant, royal.

When we rolled into Palm Springs he did something that caught me completely off guard and said much about both Cary Grant and the Fords.

"I think we should bring something to the party," he said to me.

I hadn't thought about bringing any wine or champagne or a housewarming gift. "Sure," I answered quickly, with no earthly idea what he had in mind.

To my astonishment Cary Grant instructed his driver to pull into a Kentucky Fried Chicken take-out line and pick up a bucket of chicken.

"Huh?" I blurted out. "Is this what we're taking to the party?"

"Gerry Ford loves Kentucky Fried Chicken. It's the best thing we could bring," Cary guaranteed.

I think the common, everyday touch did help because when we got there, despite Betty's assurances that life goes on, I could tell that President Ford was still shaken by the election loss. I know he felt he really hadn't had a chance to make the difference he had wanted to for the country.

On the other hand, he had Cary Grant delivering Kentucky Fried Chicken to the ranch!

Chapter 23

Cocaine-1 Tony-O

One of the problems with cocaine is that you don't realize when you've gone over the edge, when it's completely running the show. You've been able to appear "normal"—or maybe just a little overenergetic—for so long, that when you turn into an asshole, it slips by you. I realized just how big an ass I'd become after I appeared on the *Joe Franklin Show* in December of 1976.

I received a copy of the show in the mail one January afternoon in 1977 and popped it in the video player immediately, thinking it had been one of the best interviews I'd given during my trip to New York in December. I remembered being funny, witty, and charming. The tape I watched at home in Beverly Hills proved I'd been none of those things.

Watching the tape of myself acting like a cocky, arrogant jerk on the *Joe Franklin Show* made me sick to my stomach. I felt like I was seeing a stranger calling himself Tony Orlando, hogging the show, stepping on Joe's lines, unable to stick to one topic or finish a sentence.

Joe Franklin was a mainstay on WOR-TV in New York. Everybody from Liza Minnelli to Joe Lewis stopped in to visit him at channel nine, and they treated him with the same regard they would a network anchor. I liked him a lot. Yet there I was, drugged up and disrespecting him. I hoped none of my family had seen the show and been embarrassed around the old neighborhood.

I sat there wondering what had happened to the kid who followed Leo Cassivitis down Seventh Avenue through the garment district, the kid sipping chocolate egg creams at Mink's Diner, watching his father drinking strong black coffee and smoking a cigar with those rich clothiers in cashmere coats and Florida tans. I wanted the same respect my father had been accorded.

By then I wasn't just doing drugs, drugs were doing me. But like most addicts, I was the last one to admit I had a problem. Elaine confronted me with both drugs and women on a daily basis. She'd even talked to Telma, and with characteristic honesty, Telma didn't lie about our short-lived affair. Telma wasn't speaking to me by this time, so I felt I'd lost her as a friend forever.

But the worst was that I wasn't seeing just one woman at a time by then. I'd sunk so low that there were days at the Beverly Hills Hotel with five, six—even seven or eight—women at a time.

Cheating on my wife? I was cheating on everybody in my life—my mother, my grandparents, my uncles and aunts, my son, my fans, and myself. I was raised to be a straight arrow. Good people had raised me. I wasn't raised for sex orgies. I hadn't been brought up to sink so deep into that L.A. drug world that there was a stench about my life. It was a smell soap and water couldn't wash away.

I'd been doing cocaine for about a year and had known for months that I had to stop. My doctor, Ed Tanner, had tried to warn me about coke the last time I was in his office. I could still hear his words: "There's this guy I treat who's done so much cocaine that I don't even know if I can repair the damage to his nose."

There'd been plenty of warnings. A lot of people either knew for sure or suspected what was going on with me. Once, when

Cher had been on the set of our television show, after it was renamed *The Rainbow Hour,* she noticed all the rainbows I had on the set. She looked at me real close, and said, "Hmm. Are you on drugs?"

The show's director questioned me about cocaine. The drug dealer who supplied Freddie and I hung out on the set all the time. Telma and Joyce used to warn me about that guy. "Honey, stay as far away from that guy as you possibly can!"

But I wouldn't let anybody kick him off the set. Hell, it had been easier for them to get rid of my wife, Elaine, when she started bossing everyone around. When they banned her from the studio, I just shrugged it off, relieved, in a way. In fact, I didn't pay attention to anybody's warning, until I saw myself on that videotape.

I pulled the tape out of the player, feeling guilty and foolish. I'd already lost the television show. Bob Tamblyn had called and casually told me ratings were down and we weren't going to be picked up for the next season. In some ways it was a relief, but the way it was handled was terrible. I could foresee me losing everything else, too—my wife, my children, my record deal, and my self-respect. One thing you never hear anyone say about a junkie is "He's doing great! He's got his life together." That day, as had happened so many times in my life, I heard a voice in my mind saying, *You're not going about this right. You need to think this out, do something different.*

The WOR television appearance triggered a moment of sanity when my brain finally surfaced and told me cocaine was ruining my life as surely as it was ruining so many people I knew. I'd watched as Freddie Prinze lost weight and got crazier by the day. Every time he'd showed up at my house in the past few months, he had scared me with some new obsession. There were a lot of things about Freddie that worried me—his continuing gun fetish, his fixation with the Kennedy assassination, and the movie *Taxi Driver,* and more recently, talk of suicide.

The suicide talk came at a time when he should have been happiest. His son, Freddie Jr. had just been born, and Freddie worshipped that baby. That didn't affect the drug taking, just as my love for my son didn't stop me from doing cocaine. I remember Freddie telling me about one of the days he went to the hospital to see Freddie Jr. He stopped by the nursery, then went in search of medicinal cocaine. He found some, too, and snorted it in the men's room. Somebody'd *given* it to him. Right there in the hospital! God only knows how Freddie got away with the things he did, but he was the kind of guy who could talk his way in and out of anything. He'd just flash people that big innocent grin and they'd give him anything, do anything for him.

But Freddie had been in a lot of trouble in the past couple of months. He was in a lawsuit, had got busted for possession, and his wife, Kathy, had filed for divorce. Even before she filed for divorce Freddie questioned her loyalty to him. One day he showed up at my house, angry and depressed.

He sat down heavily in a chair and stared up at the ceiling. "Tony, I don't think she ever loved me. Not even the day we got married."

"I think she loved you then and she still does," I said.

"No. She never did. I don't know why, but she never did."

"Of course she loves you, Freddie," I'd said. "Everybody loves you."

But love him or not, after Kathy awakened one night to find her husband playing Russian roulette with a gun aimed at her head, she refused to take the chance that his gunplay might wind up hurting her or Freddie Jr. She slapped a restraining order on him.

I also worried about his mixing cocaine, quaaludes, and cognac. There had been a time when we accomplished things together. We wrote comedy sketches, scripts, worked on that film idea for a sort of Bob Hope and Bing Crosby road show project. The more drugs we did, the less credible the work we completed.

I wanted us both back on track. But I was in no shape to help Freddie. I had to be well to do that, and I was far from it.

So on the day I watched that footage of myself on WOR-TV, I decided to quit cocaine cold turkey. I went into the bedroom and pulled my stash out of the drawer. I rummaged through every drug hiding place I'd ever had—the garage, the closets, the bottom of my desk drawer. By the time I finished searching I was almost frantic, almost high on the idea of getting straight. I didn't find any more, so I walked into the bathroom and emptied the white powder into the toilet, flushing it out of my life. Then I went out back to the trash can and threw away the damn vial with its little spoon on a chain.

I left the WOR tape on top of the television to remind myself what drugs could do.

I didn't have any acute withdrawal symptoms, no cramps or thoughts of suicide, like some people I'd heard about. I slept well the first night, probably because the energy I'd expended that day hadn't been generated by drugs. The next day I talked to my manager about the upcoming tour, talked to my producer about recording sessions, spent time with my family, and congratulated myself on my strong will. I didn't tell my wife that I was quitting drugs. I'd let my actions speak for me.

As the week went by I started thinking that getting off drugs was easier than I'd thought it would be. I got down to seriously planning my next album and trying to keep a positive attitude. Every once in a while I'd pick up the WOR tape and remind myself that I was never going to embarrass myself or anyone else like that again.

I was at home on the afternoon of January twenty-seventh, trying to keep all negatives out of my head. I didn't want to think about missed opportunities or cancelled television shows. I wanted to flush self-pity down the toilet right along with the cocaine.

At some point that afternoon I noticed a note by the telephone in the kitchen. "Call Freddie."

I hadn't seen him in the week since I'd quit using. He'd been in Washington, D.C., for President Carter's inauguration on the nineteenth, then had flown directly to Vegas to do a show with Shirley MacLaine. I was actually relieved that he was out of town while I was pulling myself back together. Snorting coke together had become routine, and I had to break the habit before I saw him again.

I put the note back down next to the phone figuring he just needed some coke and wanted me to track down our drug dealer. Maybe I'd call in a day or so when I was positive I had the strength to say no to him.

The note didn't say where he'd called from, but I guessed he was probably at the second-floor apartment at the Beverly Comstock where he'd moved after Kathy had told him to get out. I decided to find out later who took the message, the housekeeper or the maid. It wasn't Elaine's handwriting. Maybe he'd given them more of a message than they'd written down. Then I lay down on the bed and watched television.

At some point I drifted off.

Chapter 24
Freddie

I was in a deep sleep when Elaine started shaking me.

"Tony, wake up." I looked at the clock and turned my back to her. I could hear rain spattering against the window.

"Wake up!"

Why was Elaine shouting at me before the sun was up? I shoved the pillow over my head but the next words I heard came through loud and clear, even from the next room. My six-year-old son Jon was crying, "Uncle Freddie's hurt himself."

Freddie . . .

"Tony, listen to me," Elaine said. "You're going to have to get to the Med Center at UCLA. I just heard it on the news. Freddie's shot himself and might not make it."

. . . *might not make it.*

I stared at the wall, couldn't function, couldn't think past the fact that he'd phoned me the previous afternoon and I'd hadn't called him back. I felt empty, like I was this big shell with no insides. I was scared, too, scared my best friend was going to die. He'd been talking about death for a long, long time yet he was a twenty-two-year-old who had every reason to live.

Jon was still crying in his room. After Freddie learned he was going to be a father he spent a lot of time playing with Jon, learn-

189

ing the ropes as a parent, I guess. The two had become great pals. I didn't know where I'd find the strength to crawl out of bed and go to my son and offer him any comfort. I tried several times to get up, but my knees were so weak I fell back on the bed. Plus, my hands were trembling so bad I doubted I could dress myself even if I could stand up. The words on that note kept popping into my head. *Call Freddie*. God, I wished I'd made that call. What had been going on? Then all of a sudden I thought of Kathy and the baby, Freddie Jr. What must she be going through? I knew she'd blame herself, especially since the divorce had turned ugly and she'd filed that restraining order against him.

Since I wasn't capable of walking across the room yet, Elaine turned on the television in the bedroom. Freddie's attempted suicide dominated the news. From all reports, Freddie's public was in shock. *Freddie Prinze shot himself*? That funny kid from *Chico and the Man*? It couldn't be true.

I could see that the UCLA parking lot was already swamped with reporters and television crews clamoring to get inside where I knew Freddie's mother, father, wife, and son were waiting, terrified. Seeing that circus outside the hospital made me realize that I had to pull myself together and be there for Freddie's family.

I sat on the edge of the bed for a few minutes before I could gather the strength to stand. Still shaking, I made it into my son's room and held him tight, feeling conflicted over staying with him or getting to the hospital as fast as I could.

"Don't cry, Jon," I said after a few minutes. "Daddy's got to go take care of Uncle Freddie." He nodded. Maybe he thought that's all it would take, that a daddy could fix things that easily.

I vaguely remember getting dressed and driving to the medical center, thinking about my son's fearful reaction to such a violent act. How was this going to affect Jon later, how would it affect Freddie's son? There seemed to be a hum going on around me. The normal traffic routine was going on, but the noise of the beeping horns racing engines condensed into a buzzing sound, an unreal sound.

At UCLA I stopped only long enough to ask a guard where I could find Freddie. I didn't even look for a parking lot, just parked illegally in back of the building and ran inside. The first person I saw was Freddie's father, Karl Pruetzel, who was on his way to the sixth-floor intensive care unit. We didn't say much as we rode up in the elevator to the sixth floor ICU. Karl seemed tired, confused, and alone.

As I rode up the elevator I thought about the last time Freddie'd been to a hospital. It was when Freddie Jr. was born, and Freddie had scored the cocaine. As I said, he could talk anyone into anything.

Looking goood!

He'd not only talked Richard Pryor into giving him a gun, Freddie had also talked his therapist into giving it back to him after the man had confiscated it. I never underestimated Freddie's charm.

When I stepped off the elevator at the sixth floor ICU and saw the crowd of anguished people, I felt an overwhelming sense of relief that I was no longer hooked on coke. Drugs had caused that anguish. Freddie'd had the gun, but drugs pulled the trigger. *If you're gonna do drugs you're gonna pay a price,* I thought. *Somewhere down the line.*

The place was starting to fill up with family and friends. Our friend Luis Rivera was there. He looked so much like Freddie and me that we could have been brothers. Isaac Ruiz, Mando on *Chico and the Man,* was there, crying and praying. I was glad to see Mando. The son of a preacher, Mando was very spiritual and I knew he'd be a great help to Freddie's mother, Maria. Freddie's secretary Carol was there. Jimmy Komack, the show's producer, was in the hallway, as were several young girls who said they were Freddie's girlfriends and others I didn't know.

Maria was in a waiting room trying to get a call through to the

Oral Roberts, prayer line. I looked at her and could see my mother in her face. Two deeply religious Puerto Rican women, so proud that their boys had made it in show business, had *done something.*

I hugged Maria, both of us trying to hold back tears. "What can I say? I love Freddie. We all do."

"I know, Tony," she said.

I tried to calm down Freddie's wife Kathy as best I could. Nobody had thought to call Kathy and her mother saw the news on television and phoned. Maria was being kind to her, though, including her in the family grief. Kathy loved her husband and no divorce or restraining order would ever make me believe any different. I hated the restraining order for Freddie's sake, but I understood why Kathy filed it. None of us had known what to do, how to help him.

In the hall people whispered about the events that surely led to this tragedy: Freddie's recent legal problems, his impending divorce, the lawsuit with his old manager, and his narcotics arrest. Someone told me Freddie had been taking quaaludes all day at the Beverly Comstock Hotel, calling attorneys about his legal problems, loading and unloading his gun, and scaring the hell out of his secretary, Carol. He'd spoken with his therapist, Dr. Kroger. He phoned Kathy and threatened to kill himself, as he'd done so many times before, then, just as his manager Dusty Snyder, walked into the room, Freddie pulled his pistol from under a pillow on the couch and shot himself.

I kept thinking that he'd also tried to call me. *Why the hell hadn't I called back?*

Since Kathy was still Freddie's legal wife the doctors approached her for permission to try and remove the bullet. "We can't promise he'll live," they said. "And even if he does, he'll probably be a vegetable. He'll have to be fed through tubes, to be diapered. That's probably as good as we can hope for."

Kathy looked numb as she signed those papers. It was around 11:30 A.M.

We waited there in intensive care, pacing the floor, praying, looking down the long hall filled with cubicles toward the room at the end of the hall where we knew Freddie lay somewhere between life and death. Time went out of whack as the minutes and hours ticked on while a team of UCLA's top surgeons operated. I couldn't have told you if I'd been there three hours, five hours, a day. We didn't know what to expect, if he'd live or what he'd be like if he did. At some point we moved out of the hall to the waiting room. Maria finally got the Oral Roberts prayer line on the phone, and they prayed with her for a long time. It seemed to bring her a little peace.

"Tony! Tony—"

I turned to see the local ABC news guy, Paul Moyers, standing there. I went out into the hall with him and closed the door to the waiting room. I wondered if he'd sneaked in the back door like I had done. "I'm sorry, Paul," I started. "I just can't let anyone from the press in there."

"It's okay, Tony," he said. "I just want to know how he is."

"Nobody knows, Paul," I admitted, starting to choke on the words. Paul was a good guy and respected our wishes. Another guy wasn't quite so cooperative. He walked onto the floor dressed like a doctor and tried to go to the door where they'd be bringing Freddie out of surgery. Luckily a nurse noticed his camera in time and kicked him out or Freddie's dying photo would probably have been all over the tabloids.

The next person I saw out in the hall angered me. It was our old drug dealer. *Damn him*, I thought. *I wonder if that's where Freddie got his last bag of quaaludes*. Seeing his piercing dark eyes and shifty manner reminded me once again that I was happy to finally be on the right track.

At 4:00 P.M., a doctor finally came out and said Freddie had made it through surgery better than they'd anticipated. I wasn't particularly reassured because I didn't know what that meant. I cornered another doctor and tried to get a straight answer. He shrugged. "All I can tell you is that the only thing keeping him going is that his body is in such good shape. He's very strong, and he's fighting to stay alive."

Yes, Freddie was strong all right and nobody knew it better than me. I listened to the doctor talk and automatically rubbed my back, remembering that day Freddie had nearly ruptured my kidney.

Yeah, the doctor was right. Freddie was big and strong and capable of putting up a fight. But he was also capable of wanting to know what it was like to be knocked unconscious just to experience oblivion. *Pull out, tough guy,* I thought. *Come back.*

I waited until Kathy and his parents had spent some time with him before I went in. There was a nurse who stood by the end of the bed through it all. I never knew her name, but she had a quiet reverence, like an angel standing guard over him.

He lay there, half his face blackened with gunpowder, blood seeping through a bandage that barely covered the gaping hole in his head. The index finger of his right hand was bent, frozen as though he still had the gun in his hand. All of a sudden I didn't want anyone to see it like that. Never mind the blackened face and bloody bandages. It was that trigger finger I wanted to hide from everyone.

How many times had I seen his hand that way? Freddie was always acting out suicide. *"Bang!"* He'd say with a grin, holding his finger against his head. *"Bang!"*

There in the hospital, I took Freddie's hand and straightened his trigger finger out. The guardian angel nurse watched me quietly, almost as though she knew what I was thinking, that I was trying to undo what had been done, to give him back some dignity. Finally, after standing there staring down at his bloody face for what might have been two hours or fifteen minutes, I was suddenly furious.

"Freddie, you son-of-a-bitch! Why'd you do it? That bullet didn't just hit you—it hit us all."

The nurse frowned at me and shook her head as if to say, *Don't do that, don't be angry*. I started sobbing so sorrowfully I felt like I wanted to cry forever. And I was also so angry I wanted to keep right on shouting, *Why'd you do it, man? Why?*

I don't know why I asked, because he'd told me why many times, in many ways. Freddie wanted to go out on top, when everyone loved him. Like James Dean. Tragically, larger than life, like JFK.

I took his hand and started talking to him again.

"You got what you wanted, man. You're all over the news. Half the press in California is out there waiting to see if you live or die. Somebody said there's more reporters here than when Bobby Kennedy got assassinated. They're all out there for you. Does that make you happy? Move your leg if you hear me. You think this is Camelot? It's the ICU, man. Can you hear me? You're gonna be the headline in tomorrow's *Times*. You got your wish. Come on, move your leg."

All of a sudden Freddie's leg moved and I jumped back like it was me who'd been shot. I looked up at the nurse. "Am I crazy or did his leg move? Can he hear me?"

"No," she said quietly. "It's an involuntary muscle contraction."

I wasn't so sure. "Freddie, if you can hear me move your leg again." This time nothing happened and I started to cry again.

Remember when you came over with all those guns strapped on your body, Freddie? I thought. *Remember that day you said you were DeNiro in* Taxi Driver? *I should have done something. I don't know how, but I should have stopped you then.*

All of a sudden Kathy came in the room again, begging her unconscious husband to hang on. I held her, wishing I knew what to say, having trouble comforting anyone else when I was so close to losing it myself.

"Don't die, Freddie! I'll take care of you!" she cried. "I'll do whatever it takes. Just don't die. I love you."

There in the hospital I prayed to God that Freddie could hear Kathy as she spoke.

I stepped back out in the hall and saw that the drug dealer was still hanging around. I wished he'd go away and leave us alone. I didn't want to look at his face, a face I'd seen too many times, smiling as he slipped me a vial of drugs in the men's room. I walked away from him.

The next hours are a blur to me. Because of the press waiting outside, we sent out for food and I remember eating a slice of pizza, having a few bites of a sandwich. People brought news about the public outpouring of grief and it helped a little. I slept some on a chair in the waiting room. Every so often I'd jerk awake and for a minute I'd think the whole thing was a dream.

By morning any real hope was gone. It was just a matter of time before that strong heart of Freddie's would give out. Around 7:00 A.M. Luis Rivera took Maria and Karl home to freshen up, and I decided to do the same. Exhausted, I slipped out the back door of the hospital, thankful my car hadn't been towed, and went back to Brentwood for a badly needed shower and shave. By the time I arrived Elaine had taken Jon to a friend's house and was ready to go back to the hospital with me.

Freddie hung on until around 1:00 P.M. on the twenty-ninth, thirty-three hours after the shooting. Then the doctors called us together and said it was over. We all went in together, and stood by his side, Maria, Karl, Kathy, Elaine, and I, watching as the doctor pulled the plug. Bile rose up in my throat as I saw Freddie's face turn from lightly tanned to ashen gray. He was one of the few close men friends I'd ever had outside of my own family members, and another New York Puerto Rican in a Hollywood whirl where neither one of us ever felt we quite fit in. I looked at his face and saw myself, just as earlier I'd looked at Maria and seen my own mother.

I stood there crying for a few minutes, and then bent over and kissed him on the lips. I don't know why I did that, kissed him right on the lips. Maybe it was the most intimate, personal gesture of love I could give my friend. His lips were already turning cold and hard.

From his deathbed, I went straight to the men's room, leaned over the sink basin and splashed some cold water on my face. I knew my soul was going to feel the shrapnel from the bullet that killed Freddie for a long time. When I finally pulled my head up I saw my drug dealer standing behind me in the mirror.

"What do you want?" I asked coldly.

"I thought you might need some blow."

A voice in my head said, *It's drugs that killed Freddie*.

I turned around and saw a vial of cocaine in his extended hand. I grabbed it angrily and shoved the tiny silver spoon down in the white powder. I pulled the spoon out and tossed its contents up in the air, hoping Freddie's spirit was within the sound of my voice.

"Here Freddie, you asshole!" I looked up and shouted, "You want some coke? Have some!"

I kept digging cocaine out of the vial and throwing it in the air in sort of a celebratory gesture, watching it settle on the men's room floor like a light snow fall. I got more manic by the spoonful.

"Have some more, you prick! Take your damn drugs!"

My dealer stood there watching me more with curiosity than dismay over the wasted coke.

"Okay, Freddie," I screamed, my face wet with tears. "Here's some more!"

The vial was almost empty when I stopped and stared down into it. *It's almost gone*. Then the moment of sanity I'd had the week before left as swiftly as it had appeared. The voice inside my head that had just said *It's drugs that killed Freddie* was silent.

"One more trip to the spoon, Freddie," I whispered, bringing the spoon up to my nose and inhaling deep.

That humming sound was back, the one I'd heard on the way to hospital. I scooped out the last of the cocaine and inhaled, then frantically looked at what I'd thrown on the floor. I might have been on my hands and knees snorting cocaine off the tile if the dealer hadn't pulled a full container from his pocket. It wasn't until I'd snorted it all that I felt good enough to go out and face people again.

"Thanks, man," I told my dealer. "I'm gonna need a lot more of that stuff to get me through the next few days. *A lot* more."

I'd just taken another big step on my way to a straitjacket.

Chapter 25

I Wind Up in the Cuckoo's Nest

The final blow came during a disastrous performance on July 22, 1977, at the Music Show in Cohasset, Massachusetts. I was doing coke and still half crazy over Freddie's death. I could still see him on that hospital bed, his fingers frozen as if he was holding the gun. I thought I was doing a show, but what I was doing was babbling about Freddie's suicide to the point where I became completely incoherent. Finally one woman yelled at me, "We didn't come to hear about Freddie Prinze!"

"Fuck you, lady!" I screamed. "Fuck you!"

Elaine finally led me off the stage promising to find me some help.

The tab came due for my hidden anger toward my father during that same trip. We were all staying at a hotel located just down the road from the Music Show. New Jerusalem Road ran from the venue, past the hotel, and on down to an abandoned house. One day, prior to my breakdown onstage, my drug dealer took me to that house. Oh, yeah—he was still in the picture. He was a manipulative, evil force and I was convinced I couldn't survive without him.

After I fell apart that day, I ran back to the abandoned house. There, in the rubble, I saw an old gas stove. On the stove was a

Catholic Infant of Prague, a baby Jesus statue with a crown. Below the stove was a headless bird, with a bloody knife beside it. I backed up, and when I put my hand down, I saw an old church Easter offering envelope. It said, "April third." That is my birthday.

I started praying and kept on until I finally stumbled down some stairs, to the basement of the house. There was a fisherman's net, with a giant pitchfork. Keep in mind, this is a fishing area, so it wasn't strange to find those two items in somebody's basement. But I didn't think about that. In my condition of complete psychosis, I saw this as a sign that I'd been to hell and was now looking to heaven, ready to be reborn. I ran back upstairs, and there stood Elaine and my father. But instead of seeing Elaine, I saw my mother.

Leo was trying his best to support me, to counsel me, to help me. Maybe it was this overdue emotional support that caused it, but I had what can only be called a combination religious rebirth in Jesus Christ, and an emotional rebirth as my earthly father's son. I may regret making this admission, because I know it sounds crazy as hell. But when people are on the edge, they do crazy shit.

What I did was this:

I said, "I have been reborn! You want to see just how much I've been reborn?" Then I stripped naked, and started rambling about my rebirth. I asked that they pray for me. The action was rooted in fear and panic. But underlying it all was anger, directed at myself and at my father. By the way, I could never call my father "Dad" but only Leo or Label or once in a great while, Father. I never felt comfortable calling anyone Dad. And even Papito, for all he meant to me, couldn't quite make up for that. Maybe I was asking God to give me another chance, while at the same time, sending Leo Cassivitis another message: *Look at me! I will start over anew. Please, let's don't blow it this time!*

It was a horrifying moment for Elaine and Leo. But if there is a time in a person's life when he can say "I met the Lord," that was mine. Because *in* that moment, I could feel my heavenly Father reach out to me, and I knew it was going to be okay. I could let loose of whatever pent up emotions I had regarding Leo, and we really *could* start anew.

My reentry into the world started that moment. In retrospect, thank God it was my father Leo who was with me through those terrible days—days when I thought I was going crazy and might never make it back to reality. I knew that mental illness ran in the Cassivitis family. Dad had been through depressions. He had one brother who ended up in a mental hospital and had had a frontal lobotomy. I think that's one reason he stood by me. And I got much needed strength from him.

Months later, after I'd been in and out of a psych ward, I took my shrink and went back to that house on New Jerusalem Road. It was there that I figured out something about my drug dealer and that headless bird: He was into voodoo. Nobody had let that slip the whole time he was hanging out with me, but as it turned out, he was. He even begged me to give him the ornate knife that I had found next to the bird. *Of course* he wanted it; it was his knife. I also learned that both dead birds and the Infant of Prague are sometimes part of voodoo rituals. I just didn't know it back then.

The shrink and I went into a little store where she asked the storekeeper for information about the house in question. I had a ball cap and sunglasses on, and he didn't recognize me.

"People around here won't go near it," he said. "The woman who lived there is buried in the front yard." He shook his head, and added, "Tony Orlando went inside that house once and I heard he was never the same afterwards."

But getting into therapy and confronting that old house was still a long way off. And finding religion just after my public breakdown in Cohasset didn't make me sane. Every person close to me insisted I check myself in somewhere for professional help. We were still all at the hotel on New Jerusalem Road—Elaine, my parents, my business manager, Gary Gotterer, my manager, Dick Broder, and my publicist, Frank Lieberman and his wife Karen. The Liebermans were very, very stabilizing influences on me, I might add. We gathered in a circle, and one by one, they agreed that I needed help. There was another reason, besides the peer pressure, that I checked in. I saw a television program where the producer, Josh Logan, was talking about manic depression. It seemed to fit my symptoms perfectly. Of course, what we now know, is that cocaine psychosis can put you in a manic-depressive state. Unfortunately, back then mental hospitals were not really geared for druggies. We've come a long way in drug treatment since the seventies.

In the end I checked myself into Payne Whitney's general psych ward; it wasn't the country club chic most stars anticipate when they check into rehab. The only personal property I took was a little cross that Mamma had given me.

The enormity of committing myself didn't hit until those big steel doors swung shut with a sickening *clang*. I walked down a long hall and into the main recreation area, expecting—I don't know what. A bunch of sick people, maybe. Sick? Man, that word doesn't begin to describe it. The room was filled with cra- zies. There were guys trying to strangle each other. Guys acting like they were playing tennis with imaginary rackets. One old woman was wandering around muttering to herself and pulling her skirt up over her head.

Worse yet, somebody yelled my name. *My* name! *God help me*, I thought. *Tony Orlando's not just another crazy to this bunch. He's been here every Wednesday night on the television screen.*

The first thing I figured out was that someone keeps close tabs on you in a mental hospital. *Close tabs*. There was one nurse who literally was there with a pen and paper every time I turned around. If I got agitated and surly, there she was, writing

down the words: *agitated and surly*. The second thing I figured out was that a mental hospital could be just like prison—there is no such thing as privacy even from the other "inmates."

The first time I went into the bathroom I almost died because the toilets were just lined up, with no stalls. It was one thing to take a leak in a rest room where there was just a line of urinals, but a bowel movement with an audience was another story. Guys in the army used to tell me about places where they ran into those kinds of facilities and I remembered thinking I'd be disgusted by the whole thing. Well, there I was and yes, I was disgusted. Within an hour of checking in, I felt a serious need relieve myself. I went in the restroom and sat down, thanki God there wasn't anyone else in there at the time so I could ta my dump in private. I had barely dropped my drawers whe guy called "the Turk" and his pals came in. They stood ard shucking and jiving:

"Hey, Tony Orlando! You a *big TV star?*"

"Hey, man, do TV stars fart when they take a shit?"

"Yeah, man. You wanna fart for the Turk?"

I didn't know what the hell was getting ready to happ visions of prison attacks started flooding through my thought *Oh my God. I did this to myself. I'm in here for two hours at the least and there is no way to get out! Tl is like maximum security except for one thing—the can follow you even into the men's room!*

I took that dump pretty fast, mainly because those g the shit out of me. So I wiped my ass, pulled up my p as is humanly possible, breathed a little sigh of nobody'd jumped me and then tried to act noncha washed my hands. I started for the door, thinking free. That's when the Turk grabbed me. He grabb arm, wheeled me around and landed a punch in m

One by one the others joined in and frankly, jus of me in the men's room of Payne Whitney.

I guess they figured they needed to make their getaway then, because all of a sudden they shot out of the door and left me lying there on the floor. I lay there thinking, well at least I didn't get raped like in some prison horror story. I decided right then that I had to get the hell out of there and the only way I knew to do that was to call Elaine.

I could have cried with relief when she answered the phone.

"Elaine, come get me! This place is a nightmare."

"Can't do it, Tony. You have to stay seventy-two hours."

"I checked myself in, for God's sake! I wasn't committed!"

"Doesn't make any difference. You've got to do the whole seventy-two hours."

"Elaine, I just got beat up. These guys beat the crap out of me!" Silence on the line.

"What's the matter? Don't you believe me?"

"Are you medicated?"

"Medicated or not, I know that I just had to take a shit in front of a bunch of thugs, and they ended up kicking hell out of me!"

"I don't see that I can do anything. You have to stay seventy-two hours." Dead phone.

When I turned around, there was "Nurse Rachet" taking notes. She knew full well that those guys had beat me up, because she just wrote it in that notebook: "On such and such a day at such and such a time, T.O. involved in a fight."

I saw her writing it down and went nuts. I started yelling, "I got in a fight? I just got the crap knocked out of me! What's the matter with you?"

The nurse yelled for some orderlies and when I tried to jerk away from them they slapped me right in a straitjacket and poured some green medicine down my throat. If this all sounds like the drugged up hallucinations of a madman, so be it. But I swear to you that this experience was straight out of *One Flew Over the Cuckoo's Nest*.

It was dark when I woke up, still tied up in that damn strait-

jacket. And I heard someone calling my name. "Tony . . . Tony . . ." Then I *did* think I was hallucinating. I saw that the door to my room was open and there was that same crazy old woman holding up her skirt. Maybe it was a hallucination or maybe just a nightmare, I don't know, because the next time I opened my eyes she was gone.

I thought about a lot of things as I lay there waiting for a nurse or an orderly or someone to come let me out of the jacket. I thought about Mamita and Papito and Uncle Orlando and wondered what they would think of this. What would Papito have thought about that conversation we'd had so long ago? The one where he told me to make my mark, never to follow the crowd.

I sure as hell didn't want to follow that crowd, the one that was led by the Turk.

I hadn't seen the last of him, either.

The next day, I was on the pay phone in the ward when the Turk came up and grabbed the receiver. All of a sudden he spied my ring, the ring my *father* had given me! The Turk grabbed my hand and jerked the ring off my finger. He'd already beat the crap out of me once and I was gonna be as polite as possible.

"Come on, man," I said. "My dad gave me that—"

Just then a little skinny cat eases over and the Turk walks off with my ring in his hand.

"Is the Turk bothering you?" he asked.

"He just stole my dad's ring," I answered, hoping the Turk would just beat us both up and not kill us.

"You want it back?"

"Yeah, but I ain't messing with the Turk, I'll tell you that right now," I said quickly.

Then the little guy lit up with a smile like a big flashbulb and introduces himself.

"I'm Shaun Cassidy, Tony. I think you knew my father. He burned up."

Well, I was pretty sure he wasn't Shaun Cassidy, but who was

I to argue about it? I was in the nut house. So I said "Yes, I knew Jack Cassidy and it was a hell of a bad deal when he got killed."

"You were always nice to my dad," Shaun said. Then he got this evil look in his eye and walked over to the Turk.

"Okay Turk, give Tony back his fucking ring," he said, grabbing the Turk's collar. *Jesus,* I thought, *Shaun Cassidy's dead meat!* But then I couldn't believe my eyes. The Turk handed him the ring and walked off. Nobody did a thing, not the Turk and not his gang of crazies.

"Don't be messing with me and Tony," Shaun called out to them, with this deranged grin on his face. It was obvious that the bad asses in there thought Shaun Cassidy was crazier than they were. They weren't messing with him.

I done found me a bodyguard, I thought. *Thank you, Jesus.*

The worst thing I saw while I was there didn't directly involve me. It involved a young girl named Caroline. She had the darkest circles under her eyes I have ever seen. She looked like Mia Farrow at the end of *Rosemary's Baby*. She seemed scared as hell and was as jumpy as a rabbit. I'd chalk it up to drugs, except that it seemed like she was deathly afraid of men. She shrunk back any time a man approached. So I don't know what actually had happened to her, or why she was there.

At some point, I heard a scuffle, and turned to see her fighting with a couple of huge male guards. When she didn't submit to them, one grabbed her by the hair until they got her hauled off into a room, where, presumably, she got strapped into a straitjacket. Like the beating I took from the Turk and his pals, this was real. It wasn't some drug-induced hallucination. My reaction, however, was subject to question.

I grabbed the phone again, and dialed the weather.

"Geraldo!" I yelled. "I've got a helluva story for you! You're gonna win the Pulitzer! You gotta do a story on Payne Whitney! People are getting beaten up in here. They're dragging little girls around by their hair! Remember that thing you did about how they were mistreating retarded kids? This is bigger!"

Nurse Rachet came along and hung up the phone.

In the end, I shut up and did my time. There's really nothing else you can do unless you want to be locked up for good.

Let's get real. I needed help. I needed to get off drugs and I needed therapy. But a general ward of a mental institution is a horrific place, and I didn't see one person getting help by being there. Even considering the medication they gave me, and the paranoia I felt when those doors swung shut, I saw a lot of bad shit in there. And those seventy-two hours didn't do jack for my mental health.

The only time I felt good about anything was right before I left. Caroline was sitting in a corner, and I walked over and gave her Mamma's little cross. She didn't shrink back, just held out her hand and let me drop the cross into it.

Through my business manager, Gary Gotterer, Frank Sinatra offered to put me up at his suite at the Waldorf Towers when I left Payne Whitney. It was August 15, 1977. I picked up a copy of the *New York Times* and read an article about a new book coming out by Elvis Presley's bodyguards. *My God,* I thought. *He's on drugs!* Maybe other people who'd been around Elvis had figured out about the drugs, but I hadn't. I hated the fact that Elvis's reputation was under question, but I knew those guys, and I knew they wouldn't just make stuff up. I thought they were sending him a wake-up call.

I'm sure that the intensity of my reaction was due to Freddie's death and to my own meltdown. Drugs had been behind both events, and I thought I had to contact Elvis, to reach out or help in some way. I called Frank Lieberman, who was able to get Elvis's home phone number. I called off and on throughout the night, but no one ever answered. The next day, I went for a walk for the first time since I got out of the hospital. I went down to a cathedral and lit a candle for Elvis. Then I lit one for Priscilla and one for Lisa Marie. When I got back to the Waldorf Towers, Elaine met me at the door.

"You better sit down, Tony."

"What's happened?"

"They found Elvis dead this morning."

I know they said Elvis died of a heart attack at the time, but I always knew even if it *was* a heart attack, it was brought on by the drugs. It was the first time I'd seriously thought that drugs could kill by bringing on a heart attack. I'd worried that they might make someone suicidal, and, of course, I knew people died from overdoses. But the heart attack idea just hadn't crossed my mind. It seemed like dope was trying to kill everyone it could, and through any means possible.

I remember standing in the living room, looking out over the New York skyline, listening to Judy Garland sing "Somewhere Over the Rainbow" from a *Judy, Judy, Judy* album I found in Frank's record collection. There was a real rainbow straddling the city. Now I know that Cher once equated my rainbow television set with drugs, but rainbows really had become a symbol of life to me over the years, and I came to a moment of clarity. I'd been thinking of Freddie. I realized that I'd also been thinking that maybe suicide wasn't the worst way to dump all your problems. That scared me a lot worse than the Turk and his crowd. I thought, *Freddie is dead. But you are alive, and you can still save yourself.*

Chapter 26

Balancing Act

I was holed up in New York, seeing almost no one, when the phone rang. My father came to tell me who it was, using the same incredulous tone people always did as he said, "Muhammad Ali is on the phone for you."

I went to the telephone, and said, "Hey, Champ. How you doing?" I was as surprised as anyone at the call, because in a few days he was fighting Ernie Shavers at Madison Square Garden. He had a lot better things to do than phone old friends.

Ali didn't mince any words, he wasn't in a sparring mode.

"What are *you* doing, man? You gotta get outta the house. You gotta get up and outta that house every day, or you're gonna be in worse shape than you are now! In fact, you are getting outta the house. You're coming to the fight."

I promised to be there.

It took every ounce of energy I had to get to that fight, but it's hard to go back on your word to a man like Ali. I went to his dressing room before the fight, and it was packed with his entourage and a few guests. Ali seemed oblivious to the crowd. For one thing, he was sitting there completely naked, throwing punches.

"Search, destroy, search, destroy."

I stood to one side with John Travolta, but I didn't say any-thing because I knew he was trying to get his mind right for the fight. When he broke a sweat, he looked up.

"Tony, man. It's good to see you. Hang on. I'll be right back."

He went back to shower and dress for the fight. When he came back out, he smiled and said, "See, this is what you should be doing. Get out of that house."

Ali won the fight in a tough fifteen-round decision, and we talked again. But the striking thing to me was that he shared a moment of encouragement *before* the fight. Even as he was fac-ing the battle, he stopped to be concerned about a friend. And it would be due to friends like Ali that I'd ultimately win my own battle, the one I was fighting with despair.

I might add that Ernie Shavers showed me that night just how tough an opponent he could be, and I never forgot it. Ken Nor-ton stopped by my dressing room in March 1979, the night before he fought Ernie. It was late, and I said, "Kenny, you better go to bed. Don't underestimate Shavers. Ali told me he hit him so hard that Ali felt he'd been knocked clear back to his ances-tors!" Ken didn't seem worried.

The next night, Ernie came out blasting. He hurt Ken bad enough that Ernie won with a TKO in the first round. Ken later told me that when his head cleared, the first thing he heard were my words ringing in his ears.

Betty Ford is another person who stood steadfastly beside me. It was her idea that I go on the *Mike Douglas Show* and talk about my crack-up. Betty thought that because of my reputation as an all-around good guy, it was important that I talk to the public about what had hap-pened. If people saw that the guy next door could fall apart, they could also see that he could try to pull himself back together.

That was one of the most difficult things I ever did. The audi-ence I most feared was my family. I'd let them all down in pri-vate, and now I was going to admit it in public.

I went on the show anyway, because Betty Ford is usually right about what's right. I talked about depression, about cocaine, and about Freddie's death. In the end, I said, "There are two ways to quit drugs—my way or Freddie's way. Please quit my way, not my friend Freddie's."

Not long after I got back to L.A., I had an invitation from Johnny Cash to appear on a show he was taping at his farm in Tennessee. You'd have to be a fool to turn down an invitation from Johnny Cash, no matter what shape you're in, so I went. And, it was a soothing experience, because John has that same, spiritual, supportive quality as Muhammad Ali.

In fact, he normalized me somewhat for the first time since I'd got out of Payne Whitney.

He took me on a long horse-and-buggy ride around his property. Given his western image, I was surprised to hear him say that he didn't like to ride horses. He was at ease driving the buggy, but never liked to climb into the saddle.

Johnny lightened me up with a little joke. He pulled up next to a bush with some fruit on it.

"Now you're a city boy, right? You don't know much about the country."

"No."

"Well, you ain't country until you've had a persimmon."

Unknown to me, a persimmon is inedible until it's ripe. It's an explosion of sour. I took a bite and thought my face was imploding.

"Now, you're country." He laughed.

Johnny put his western hat on me, took a photo, and sent me a huge signed, blowup of the shot. I think it was his way of saying, "cowboy up."

The emotional road back was an easier path than the career road. NBC gave me a shot at a comeback with a one-hour special. It went well, and I went back out on the road. Still, nothing really popped. I didn't have a record out. I felt like a question still hung in the air: *Is Tony still strung out?*

Then one day, about two years after my breakdown, Norman Brokaw came backstage at an Atlantic City show. You'll remember that Norman is the guy David Geffen had said he admired for his loyalty to the William Morris Agency. It didn't take Norman long to see that I was straight.

"Tony, you have to do Broadway, and I've got just the vehicle for you. *Barnum*."

I knew about the show. The great Jim Dale was starring in it, and I knew that he'd be a tough act to follow, if I even got the gig. I went down to the St. James Theater and watched Jim in the role. I was scared to death that I wouldn't get the part, that people would think that I was a burned-out druggie and a has-been. But once I saw what was involved, I knew why they'd take a chance on me. The role required whoever played P.T. Barnum to walk a tightrope. Nobody else *wanted* it.

"That tightrope is precisely why you have to take this part," Norman said. "If you can walk that wire, you'll show the world you're straight. That you're reliable."

I agreed, knowing that all it would take to finish me off in the eyes of the media was for me to fall off that wire on opening night.

I had a couple of weeks to rehearse, so I went to the Big Apple Circus in New York, and used the facility's practice wire, strung only about three feet above the ground. I tried and tried, and every time, I fell. I tried using a pole like I'd seen high-wire artists do, and I tried holding my arms straight out in an attempt to find my balance. Nothing worked.

I was gathering a crowd of kids who were getting a charge out of my flops. I went over and sagged down on a bench, wondering what the hell I was gonna do. Then, this one little black kid who'd been watching me hopped up on the platform.

"I bet I can do it," he said.

He stood there, looking straight ahead, then started walking. When he teetered just a little, he threw his hands straight up in the air, like he was reaching for the stars. And he walked the length of the wire.

"Try that," he said. "Reach high."

I did, and even though I wobbled, I got almost halfway before I fell. The next time I tried, I made it a little farther, and the third time, I walked the wire as easily as the kid had done.

On opening night I was sweating bullets. I'd looked out through the curtain and seen so many of my friends who were there to offer encouragement. If I flopped, it would not only be in front of the media, who might or might not believe in me. It would be in front of people who did. People like Johnny Cash and June Carter, Catherine Thomas, Gregory Hines, and the president and Mrs. Ford. That would be far worse than failing in front of the press.

Then it was time. I stepped up on the platform and looked straight ahead. I didn't reach out to either side for balance, and I didn't need the pole for a crutch. I put my hands straight up in the air, and literally skated across that tightrope. The applause was deafening. I looked out in the audience and saw Johnny Cash with that big grin on his face, his teeth shining white in the darkened theater. But no one in that audience could have known what that tightrope really meant to me. Finally, I knew I had my legs back. Like my little friend at the Big Apple Circus had told me, all you've got to do is *reach high*.

I played the role for two weeks, and the resulting press was unbelievable. *People* magazine did a story. All the television talk shows wanted me to appear. Norman was right—that tightrope had turned the tide.

But while the Broadway experience was at a high, Elaine and I were at an all-time low. At least with the television show, there were producers who told her to leave when she started raising hell about something. But when I got back on the road, there wasn't a buffer. One time at the Blue Room in New Orleans's Roosevelt Hotel, I was getting ready to go onstage, trying to get the show started, and Elaine was yelling that she was leaving me. I kept saying, "Not now, *please*!" That happened over and over. She had one hell of a temper. Well, figure this—she worked with Jerry Lee Lewis all that time and he never messed with her! That's one tough woman. Too much for me, that's for damn sure!

We slept in separate bedrooms, barely spoke, had almost no meaningful communication. Since she was always calling for a divorce, you'd think I'd have given it to her on a platter. But I saw divorce as such failure. I couldn't see that the real failure was that we were putting Jon through our bullshit.

At least I was straight. And I'd need to stay that way, because a very important person in my life was about to need me in full control of my faculties.

Chapter 27
Murray's Final Sign-Off

Murray the K did so much for me when I was starting out on the entertainment road that it was one of my greatest honors when he asked me to travel his own last mile with him.

Murray battled lymphatic cancer for eight years before it finally got the upper hand. The last year before his death he came to see me at the Las Vegas Riviera, and I was stunned to see how good he looked, even though I knew he'd been sick. He looked just like the same old Murray. But he admitted that it was starting to get him down. It took a lot for Murray to admit that.

When I got back to Los Angeles, he called me and asked me to come over to his house. He told me that he'd decided he had to stop his chemotherapy and asked me if I'd take him to the doctor. I knew then that Murray saw the end in sight, and that while he wasn't quite giving up, he also had come to terms with the inevitability of death. He must have been thinking along those lines when he came to Vegas and told me about the pain. He said he was going to need to take care of some things, and I understood that he was reaching out for some help. When I got to his house I looked around at all the stuff stacked up—tapes, mementos everywhere.

"Murray, have you seen anyone about a will?"

"No," he admitted. "I haven't done anything."

"Okay, I'll track down a lawyer. You've got a lifetime of your own history here. You've got to think about your family, about where your things are going to go."

We went to see the doctor, who questioned whether Murray understood the consequences of his decision.

"Yes," Murray said. "Tony's getting me a lawyer. I'm gonna get my house in order."

After that, Murray's physical condition deteriorated at an astonishing rate. Without really knowing why, Murray had picked the perfect person to travel that road with him. Rhonda had taught me that no task is demeaning when it involves helping someone you care for. No bedsore could make me cringe, no messed bed could cause me to run from the room. As Murray got worse, I naturally slipped into Rhonda mode. I came every day, cleaned him up, helped him get something to eat. I had nurses check on him as well, but only at the very end, when he required twenty-four-hour care, would he allow a full-time nurse to be hired.

One day I told him that the lawyer was coming to finalize his affairs. When I came to help him get ready, I found that he'd mustered up the strength to put on his suit and hairpiece. That just killed me. Murray could barely help feed himself, but he was still that snappy dresser at heart. And that's how Murray handed out his final possessions. He sat in his chair, dressed in his best suit, hairpiece firmly in place, holding a gold-tipped cane.

Murray was very adamant about his wishes. "This armchair will go to my ex-wife, Jackie. And that other chair to my ex-wife Jackie."

"Uh, Murray," I said. "We got a little problem. *All* your ex-wives are named Jackie!"

"Oh yeah," Murray said. "So this armchair goes to my *first* ex-wife Jackie . . ."

He ran down a list of things, telling the lawyer which family members got his tapes and other memorabilia, and then said, "Tony, I want you to have my desk, and the little ivory monkey holding up the world—the one that George Harrison gave me."

I started to protest, and he held his hand up like the music aristocrat he was. "And that big television. You have that."

"Murray! Stop!" I said.

"No! It's important to me," he said. So I said okay, I'd take the desk, the monkey, and the big television.

And so a show business legend disposed of his earthly goods. He wasn't some rich music executive or star with houses and cars to will to his family, but Murray took pride in every bequest.

The sicker he got, the more I worried about him feeling like people had forgotten him. Damn! It wasn't fair that this guy, who'd done so much for so many, was going to die with just me paying attention. Very few people had actually come to the house to see him. Little Anthony had been there, and Dionne Warwick. And you could see how Murray appreciated being remembered.

So I got to thinking about the upcoming American Music Awards, wondering if Dick Clark might do some sort of a tribute, or at least a mention of Murray and his career. I decided to make a phone call to Dick. As usual, Dick was a champ. He had an immediate idea: when Smokey Robinson came on the stage, he'd have Smokey pay tribute to Murray. That's the greatest thing about Dick Clark. You may not have had a hit in twenty years, but he'll still come to your party.

Not only did Dick arrange for Smokey to talk about Murray, he wanted to come visit him. That was a potentially dicey situation. Murray respected Dick, but underneath it all, I knew that Murray also had just a tinge of jealousy about Dick's overwhelming success. Music had been far less kind to Murray the K. Still, it tickled Murray that Dick was coming to his house.

It was something else when he was getting ready for Dick's visit. By that time Murray was wasted down to practically nothing. He was to the point that if the nurse was gone, I had to help him hold his penis to use the bedpan. But he was as determined to look sharp for Dick Clark as he'd been for the lawyer. I bathed him, helped him get his hairpiece set, and dressed him in that three-piece suit. When Dick came in the house, it crossed my mind that there had been three deejays that really had the power to make stars, and two of them were in the room. The other, of course, was Alan Freed.

"You look great, Murray," Dick said.

"You're full of shit, Dick," Murray shot back. "I look like hell."

Dick sat down. "No, considering what you've been through, you look fantastic."

Then Dick said something that I believe meant more to Murray than anything anyone had ever done for him. "You know you're the one who started it all, Murray. Just look what you've done for broadcast radio. Look at all the people you made famous."

Murray looked at Dick's face, which held no pity, only respect. "Thank you Dick. I don't think you can know how much I appreciate that."

I had to look away because I was starting to tear up.

The two of them talked a long time about the music business, about the singers they'd worked with, and experiences they'd had. The greatest thing was that it was never about a healthy legend feeling sorry for a sick one. Dick saw to it that the conversation remained that of two peers reminiscing.

Only after a lengthy talk did Dick finally say he had to get to rehearsal.

"I love you Murray," Dick said, as he was leaving.

"I love you, too, Dick," Murray said.

It is a moment that lives in my mind and heart to this day.

There's another part to the story that isn't so nice that has to do with my marriage, which was rapidly disintegrating. By this time Elaine was so unhappy that she found any reason to get mad. The time I spent with Murray was a particular bone of contention. I tried to explain that there were nights when he couldn't sleep and needed company. But she wasn't buying it. She'd say, "Don't give me that 'he's dying' shit. You just don't want to be at home." Well, maybe she was right by that time.

Murray had this guy named Al renting a room from him, but I never thought that Al paid enough attention to Murray. Don't get me wrong, Al seemed like an okay guy. But I didn't think he ever appreciated what a legend Murray was, let alone cared about him enough to make any regular effort to look in on him. He certainly wasn't going to clean a bedsore or change a dirty sheet. So once, when I had to play a show in Reno, I begged Elaine to go check on Murray.

After that time, she never seemed to mind looking in on Murray. I thought it was Al who interested her, not Murray the K. But then, I wasn't an innocent in the fidelity department, either. That's how we lived out the last months of our marriage, about as uncommitted as it gets.

I stayed with Murray on the night of the American Music Awards. I didn't have an exact time for Smokey's appearance, and I kept worrying about Murray's pain shot. If he was in intense pain, he might not pay attention to what Smokey was saying. But on the other hand, when he got a pain shot, he turned on his left side for the shot, which was away from the television. If Smokey didn't get on right after the shot, Murray might drift off and miss the *whole* thing.

Sure enough, just as the nurse turned him over, Smokey was announced.

"Murray!" I said. "Listen!"

"Give me my fucking shot!" Murray shouted.

"Hold the shot a minute!" I insisted. *"Murray, listen to Smokey!"*

"There's somebody out there watching that we in this room love," Smokey said. "He's not feeling too well these days, and I want to extend a thank you from me and everyone at Motown Records. Thank you Murray the K, from everyone in the whole record industry. Get well soon."

The audience burst into wild applause.

"Listen Murray! The whole industry is applauding you!"

Murray raised up a little and looked at me. "It's about time," he said. "Now give me my fucking pain shot!"

The day Murray died, Brooks Arthur was there with us. The two men had talked about every artist from George Harrison to Paul Simon. Murray told Brooks he was failing fast. He'd drift in and out of sleep. I'd get worried and shake him a little to see that he was still okay. At one point I put some cracked ice on his lips. That's when I saw something dark seeping from his mouth. I knew Murray couldn't do it any longer and I prayed to God that He keep him from any more pain.

I never heard him take another breath. Maybe he was already dead. I called the nurse, who checked him and called the coroner.

They came and loaded him into the body bag, which resembled a garbage bag in my mind. Then they shoveled him into the back of a station wagon. It wasn't even a hearse. I kept thinking about all the people whose lives he'd touched: Diana Ross, Smokey Robinson, Johnny Mathis, Jackie Wilson, the Beatles. It killed me to see Murray carted off like that, like he was just so much chopped liver. In the end, when it's all said and done, maybe it doesn't matter. Maybe all that matters is that Murray is remembered by the people he helped, and that, in spite of the final ride in the station wagon, his life is what really counted.

"What are you going to do now?" Brooks asked.

I didn't have the numbers for his family right there. The lawyer had all that. So I decided to let the lawyer tell the family. I decided to call his old radio station, WINS in New York. I didn't leave my name because I didn't want anyone thinking I was trying to horn in on a legend's death. But I at least passed along the information. Somehow it seemed right that radio knew first.

The next thing I knew, Murray's old renter, Al, was living at my house with his girlfriend. And the next thing that happened was that the girlfriend called me on the road and said Elaine had thrown her out of the house. Of course she did.

The marriage was dead anyway, but it still pissed me off that for all those years I'd been hearing I was the bad guy to the point I'd started believing I was worthless. I'll take every bit of the blame for our separation in 1977, when I was doing coke. I wasn't faithful to her then. Hell, I wasn't faithful to anybody back then. But when I straightened out, I tried to be a good husband and a good father to both Jon and Kenny.

I came off the road and had a talk with Al. I told him I knew all about him and my wife, and was moving out. Al protested at first, saying that Elaine was too old for him, that he wouldn't even consider making a move on her.

"Sure, sure," I said. "And I got a bridge to sell you."

I told him that as far as I was concerned, he could have her. I just had one request: "Do not play daddy to my son Jon. Don't try to take my place, because no matter what happens with the marriage, I'm always gonna be Jon's father. Don't be taking him to ball games, or trying to be his new dad. I'm gonna take him to the games and I'm gonna stay in his life."

I did not want to ever take the chance that Jon would feel a distance between us, that he would start to think that I wanted him out of my life.

My secretary, Robin Howington, got me through the divorce. Robin was—is—one of the best friends I ever had, male or female. And it was strictly platonic. She got me through a lot of bad times. Let's face it, in some ways, I was still a kid. I'd gone from living with my mother to living with Elaine. I hadn't gone through the growth period of leaving home to go to college, to get an apartment, to take care of my world. I didn't know how to handle my money, pay the bills, keep things together. I was ridiculously immature when it came to things like that. Without Elaine, I was almost afraid to live alone. Robin stayed with me and kept things together.

I'm really proud of all Robin has done over the years. She's married now, with two kids. She produces the shows on Animal Planet, and her talent came as no surprise to me. For one thing, a producer has to juggle a lot of responsibilities, personalities, egos, events, problems—you name it, a producer has to handle it. Robin had to step in and handle my life after Elaine and I divorced.

I moved a couple of times, first to a rented condo on Balboa, in Encina, and then to a rented house on Mulholland Drive. When the house in Brentwood sold, I took my half of the money and bought a house in Hidden Hills. In the end, Elaine got 10 percent of my gross income for life, unless she remarries. One bad part to the divorce was that I ultimately lost touch with my stepson, Kenny.

I still find the whole concept of "visitation" rights disgusting when it comes to children of divorced parents. To tell you which days you can see your child is to build a wall. But my son, Jon, and I remained close—our relationship never faltered. What happened between Elaine and I didn't happen between Jon and I.

Back in the years following the divorce, Jon and I shared a passion for baseball that went a long way in keeping us close. I had the greatest seats at the L.A. Dodgers games. From the time Jon was six years old I had the dugout box and kept it for eighteen years. Jon was practically raised in the Dodgers' dugout. Tommy Lasorda became a very good friend, and he became part of our father-son relationship, as well. One time after a game, Tommy took us up into the empty stands, where we could still get a hot dog. He put his arm around Jon and said, "When my brothers and I got into a fight, our father would make us each take the end of a rope. Then he'd have us pull in opposite directions until we were exhausted. Then he'd say, 'Now, both of you pull together and see how easy life can be.' "

That story had a great impact on both Jon and I. We've always tried to pull together.

Baseball is still a big part of the relationship between my son and I. Jon will call me on the phone and his first line will be, "Did you hear that no one signed Barry Bonds and he went back to the Giants?" Or he'll say, "Did you hear that the Dodgers got Nomo again?"

I mentioned earlier that I love sports figures, and it's more than just boxers, like Papito had been. I *love* baseball and the people who play it. There are many reasons I love the sport. First, I didn't go to high school or college where you get to play sports. But also, those players have to commit themselves, not just one-on-one, but as a team. They've got to have a dream, like an entertainer has dreams. And again, like performers, that dream has to turn to a challenge and from that to a drive, a goal, and a commitment.

Most of all, those baseball players have to have a team player attitude. Like Tommy said, they have to be pulling from the same end of the rope.

Chapter 28

Some Hits, Some Misses, but Still Swingin' . . .

I see stories everywhere. And I have a great respect for the story-tellers of the world, not just for their talent, but for their importance to our culture. Once, when I was playing Las Vegas, Alex Haley stopped by my dressing room. We were talking, and I confessed that I'd always wished I had a formal education. His answer was interesting. "When I ask a scholar something, they go to their history books. But when I questioned old men in Africa, they had memories of three generations. The history was in their stories."

One story I read in the *Los Angeles Times* ended up becoming a good and positive part of my life. It was the story of a Chicano police officer, who believed if he could walk three hundred miles, he could make a miracle and save his young daughter's life. Norman Brokaw helped me negotiate the story rights with the fellow, and we started pitching the idea to the networks. Not a bite. The script was so dramatic, with so much human passion, that I couldn't believe no network wanted it.

Finally, after getting turned down all over town, I started wondering if it had anything to do with the ethnicity of the story. I approached Ricardo Montalban, a client of Norman Brokaw's son, David. Ricardo is a fellow that fans probably see as a famous movie star, a handsome screen idol, but he is much more than that. Ricardo is an activist for Hispanics in the entertainment field, having founded Nosotros, Spanish for "we." Part of Nosotros's goal is to improve film and television opportunities for people of Spanish-speaking origin. He became interested in my project, and got the deal done.

I signed up Edward James Olmos, the great Latino actor, and realized right away that I needed his help with my own acting. I ended up paying him to be my drama coach, and the film was better for it. My mamma will tell you that seeing that film was one of her personal highlights of my career. She *loved* telling people, "My son is in a movie."

Thanks to Edward James Olmos, I did a good job in that movie, and it convinced me I could do some acting, if given the chance. That chance arrived with Bill Cosby.

At the time, in the mid-eighties, Cosby was at a peak—he seemingly couldn't do anything wrong. We'd been friends for many years, and one day he called me up and said, "It's your turn."

He wanted me to come on his show and do an episode that could be spun off into a series for me.

All I could say was, "Wow!"

The show happened to fall right during the writers' strike, so it ended up that Bill had to write the whole thing himself. He asked me if there was any situation I could picture myself in, a situation where I could interact with a lot of different characters. But he didn't want me to play an entertainer of any sort. I thought about it, and we talked, finally coming up with the idea of centering the show on the Hudson Guild in Chelsea, which had been a community center when I was growing up. Chelsea was a true microcosm of the city, with every ethnic group imaginable, plus a large community of writers, artists, and theater people. Bill said we'd cast me as a youth director at the community center. Bill even went down to the community center, drew some designs, and built a set identical to the lobby of the Hudson Guild.

I'd gained some confidence as a result of *Three Hundred Miles for Stephanie,* but I knew I had a lot to prove to make the jump back to network television, especially as an actor instead of a variety show host. The concept for that episode of Bill's show was based on me, the youth counselor, working with a boy who wouldn't speak, and trying to get emotions out of him. It was a killer concept, if I could pull it off.

Bill's creativity is fast moving—he changes on a dime, and usually for the betterment of the script. But you better be quick on your feet. He's kind of like a jazz musician—he vamps. If you ain't able to vamp with him, you better not play in that quartet.

The dress rehearsal was phenomenal, so much so that Marcy Carcy, the producer came running backstage to congratulate me. But when it came to the actual show, Bill changed the script. It was a change for the better, but I'm sorry to say that I wasn't quick enough, I shouldn't have been in that quartet. Or maybe I blew my load too early. Maybe Jackie Gleason was right on the money when he refused to rehearse, maybe some people lose something the second time up to bat. Or maybe it was because someone told me that Carol Burnette was in the audience. Whatever the reason, I was so uptight that I started forgetting the new material. Bill had to feed me the lines.

When the show wrapped, I overheard Warren Littlefield, the head of NBC, tell Bill to get me some acting lessons. Worse yet, *Life* magazine had been following us around taking notes.

Bill said I'd done fine, and even took clips of the show on the *Tonight Show,* and bragged about me. Joan Rivers was hosting, and she bragged, too. But after they showed the clip, I heard only a smattering of applause from the studio audience.

The network turned down a spin-off, and it's no wonder. I've watched it several times over the years, and even with the mellowing effect of time, my performance stunk, then and now.

I went down to a house in Palm Desert with my tail between my legs. I'd go out and do my dates, but I didn't show up *anywhere* in Hollywood or New York. I really felt like I'd let Bill down, like I'd had the chance to play with the big cat and couldn't keep up. I also felt I'd let Norman Brokaw down, because he represented both me *and* Bill. Bill must have known how I was feeling—he knew that I'd overheard Warren Little-field's comment—so he called me up one day and said, "You can act. I saw *Three Hundred Miles for Stephanie*. I know you can act. You did some incredible work in that."

I still hid out in Palm Desert, feeling really down. But as it turned out, it was the darkness before Dawn.

Sherwin Bach, who managed Anita Baker and the Tijuana Brass, and had discovered the Carpenters, was managing me at the time. Sherwin came down to my condo at the Lakes Country Club in Palm Desert. He took one look around in disgust.

"You gotta get outta here," he said. "This isn't the real world. It's like some fairy-tale land—all this damn golf. Not only that, but even though we've got some bookings to finish out this year, we don't have *one* booking for next year. Why don't you call Telma and Joyce and see if you can put together a reunion tour?"

Well, I'd always wanted to do more shows with Telma and Joyce, but the girls had both been heavily involved in other career moves since my 1977 breakdown. Telma was starring in *Give Me a Break,* and Joyce had been on the road with Smoky Robinson, and was doing a lot of session work. I figured I'd give it a shot, anyway. With the writers' strike still going on, Telma had a window of opportunity, so the idea might just fly.

It did. When I called, Telma didn't hesitate.

"Honey, I'm ready! Let's go!"

Joyce was just as enthusiastic.

We decided to start the tour with the solo dates I already had on the books. To my surprise, nobody wanted to book all three of us! It was the money, of course. My next date was at the

Trump Plaza in Atlantic City, and it had already been promoted as a Tony Orlando show. The casino felt that revising the promotional materials and ads was a big—and unwarranted—expense.

We went anyway, and kicked butt.

Our first booking as the actual Together Again Tour was at the Desert Inn in Las Vegas. It felt so good to be back with those girls. There was such a good feeling, no old tensions, no false steps—just pure joy in stepping out again. We stayed on that reunion tour until one night in Lake Tahoe, when Telma got word that she had the chance to audition for *Family Matters*. She was apologetic about it, saying she would pay for her own ticket back to audition, but that it was an opportunity she couldn't turn down. Joyce and I understood. There were no apologies needed.

I'm usually against phony groups, where one guy puts together new people and it's passed off as the original. But when the idea of having Pam Vincent come on the road presented itself, it seemed right. As I said earlier, Joyce's sister had been on every record Dawn had made. The only thing she hadn't done was go with us on tour. She loved the idea, and so the tour continued. We might still be out there doing "Candida" if I hadn't wanted to open a theater in Branson, Missouri, in the early nineties. As much as Joyce and Pam liked doing the shows, they weren't up for moving to the Ozarks, and playing two shows a day. I went ahead with the move, but I missed hell out of working with the girls.

I was sitting in my suite at the Golden Nugget just the other day, in February 2002, and decided to call and check on how Joyce was doing. She'd lost her daughter to sickle-cell anemia about a year ago, and had been on my mind a lot. While we were talking, I said, "You know, we had something magical back then."

Joyce said, "We sure did."

Who knows, we may be out singing together again one of these days.

Chapter 29

Finding Cinderella . . .

One thing I learned when we were on the road, especially when we played festivals or theme-park shows, where you are fairly accessible, is that some fans become like family. I've always appreciated fans asking for autographs and will never understand artists who resent it or see it as an intrusion. I'm solidly in the corner of whoever first said, "I'll be worried when nobody *wants* an autograph." These are the people who pay your salary—your employers, as it were.

Entertainers don't work for the record companies, movie studios, television executives, casino owners, or club promoters. We work for the public. Those other entities are just middlemen. The minute an entertainer loses sight of that, he's in a lot of trouble. You also have to be alert to intermediaries stepping in between you and your fan base. Usually the person works for a concert venue, or maybe it's one of your road crew—people who think they're protecting you.

One time in 1972 we played Disneyland, at the stage that rises up out of the ground next to the Yellow Brick Road. I was helping the crew pack up equipment after the last show, when I heard a woman yell, "Dawn! Could we have an autograph?"

That, of course, was when we were still performing as just Dawn, pre-Tony Orlando and Dawn.

Just as I turned around, a park patrolman walked up to a small group of people. "You'll have to leave," he said abruptly. "We're trying to break down the set."

"Wait a minute, officer," I shouted. "It's okay."

I rushed over and asked who wanted the autograph signed.

"It's for my daughter, Francine," one woman said, pointing to the dark-haired girl standing beside her. She introduced herself as Rose Amormino, there at the park with her fourteen-year-old daughter and her son. I signed "Dear Francine, God bless you. Thanks for asking! Tony Orlando (I'm Dawn . . .)."

We stood there talking for a while, and when I finally left, I felt like I'd spent the time with friends who'd be around a long while. I'd felt an immediate kinship with this family, maybe because they were Italian. I've always related immediately to ethnic people, to families that reminded me of my own. It turned out that I was right about the Amorminos. They were loyal fans and—more important—good friends throughout the years. Rose and Mamma became fast friends.

They came to many shows, including to most of the tapings of our television show. I started looking forward to seeing them in the audience, they became a touchstone of sorts. That was especially true after I went through the drug days, the crazy episode. They kept right on coming to my solo shows after the Tony and Dawn days. If I played Las Vegas, I could count on seeing them on opening night, and I always made a concentrated effort to thank them for keeping the faith. I'd kid Francine through the years.

"Hey, Frannie, how old are you now?"

"Eighteen."

"You going to college? You didn't leave school did you?"

"No, I'm in college."

"You're sure getting to be a pretty girl," I'd say. "You got any boyfriends?"

That always embarrassed her.

Once, around 1988, Frannie invited me to come to dinner at their home. She said, "You know, we've known each other for almost twenty years—we'd love to have you come visit our home. You've never met my dad." We set a tentative date, but, fool that I was, I didn't write it down and in the flurry of a new tour, I forgot.

Several months later, my tour manager called me in Las Vegas. "Tony, what's the matter with you? I saw Rose Amormino. You stood them up for dinner! The whole neighborhood had tied yellow ribbons around their trees. They were really excited and proud that you were coming."

The worst was yet to come. I learned that Frannie's father, the man she'd wanted me to meet, had died in the meantime.

I felt about as lowdown as you could feel. I immediately called them and apologized. True to their nature, they acted like it was no big deal. But it *had* been a big deal, and I knew it. They'd looked foolish to their neighbors, and for that, I'd never forgive myself. These people had been too good to me over the years to deserve that.

"Look, as soon as I get back to Los Angeles, I want to take you out to dinner and apologize in person," I told Frannie.

I didn't screw up. I was there, and on time.

I'd known Frannie had a schoolgirl crush on me for a long time, but that's what I saw it as—a kid thing. So, after we talked a while, I did as I always had, and kidded her.

"So Frannie, when are you going to get married?"

This time Frannie did not hesitate with the answer? "When I find somebody who measures up to you."

"Frannie, people will start worrying about you, coming to see Tony Orlando shows instead of having boyfriends and all that."

"Well, I'm in love with you, anyway."

I still thought she was confusing me with a face on an album cover, a guy on a stage—not the real person. And if she did that, she was never going to find anyone who deserved her. Nobody can compete with an image.

"We've never even been on a date, Frannie. We've never been alone. You can't possibly know what I'm like enough to be in love with me."

"You're wrong," she said, evenly. "I know a lot about you. I know you have a good heart, and I know you are a good man. And I know I love you."

That night was like the old song, "The first time ever I saw your face." But in this case, it was more like I was seeing her clearly for the first time since she'd grown up. All those years, even as she was becoming a beautiful young lady, I never thought of Frannie as anything but that little girl standing by the Yellow Brick Road in Disneyland. Now, Frannie was an adult woman.

I worried that maybe she was letting a poster on her wall stand in the way of a relationship with some nice guy. And sitting there looking at her I realized that any guy would be lucky as hell to have her. She had a kind, sensible, serene quality, an inner strength that more than matched her dark, Italian beauty. But even though I'd been divorced since 1983, I didn't see how I could be that person. I was fourteen years older than she was, divorced, loaded up with financial responsibilities and leading a hectic life that hadn't done my first marriage any good. Frannie deserved more than that.

We sat at dinner and talked for six hours. I was struck at her maturity, her clarity, her wisdom. Well, except for that one little chink in her sensible nature—she was in love with me.

I asked her out again, and as time went by, I was struck by the honesty and maturity of her feelings toward me. I began to feel an adult love for her. The age thing bothered me because people would say, "Gee, your daughter looks just like you!" Frannie still looked like a teenager.

Six months later I asked her to marry me. As it turned out, her father had predicted it from the time Elaine and I divorced and I didn't immediately remarry.

Frannie and I wed on April 29, 1990.

It seemed to me that because of the years that had gone by, Frannie and I had something very special, almost like a fairy-tale ending to a long relationship. I was pretty broke at the time, so I took out a second mortgage on my house in Hidden Hills, and threw an extravaganza. The wedding took place in Northridge, California, at a Greek Orthodox Church. I even rented a horse and carriage to take us to the church.

Leo—Father—stood beside me as best man. We were where we should have been all along, father and son, side by side.

Our daughter, Jenny Rose, was born on August 14, 1991. What a difference twenty years had made for fathers and childbirth! In 1970 Elaine and I didn't know we were having a son. In 1991, Frannie and I knew we were having a daughter. In 1970, I pictured myself smoking a cigarette with the guys while the birth took place. In 1991, I was able to go in the delivery room with a video camera.

In my enthusiasm, I overlooked two things.

First, I was not prepared for how invasive a cesarean section is. There was a barrier between Frannie's upper torso and the operation, of course. So I filmed her smiling face asking about the baby, then started to zoom in on the actual delivery. It looked like a lake of blood. Scared me to death. Still, there is nothing like being a part of the birth. All fathers should be there. You change. I think it makes for a better marriage, and yes, for better parenting.

Second, until my daughter was actually born, I had no idea how much I'd been worried about us having a baby girl. In the dark recesses of my mind, I equated a baby girl with my sister, and the terrible health problems she'd faced. I was so paranoid about Jenny in those first couple of days, that once, when I stood looking at her in the bassinet, I thought I saw her have a seizure. It was just a little baby spasm, but in my mind, it was the beginning of something going terribly wrong. I reported it. That was a bad thing, because they immediately put her in the ICU and did some spinal taps. So my fears actually put her in jeopardy, or at least made her go through an unnecessary invasive procedure. I was in a panic, and that got Frannie in a panic. My mother was furious with me. "What's the matter with you? That baby's fine!" she said.

It got worse, when a doctor came and told us that Jenny's organs were reversed! My God! We were freaking! I kept telling Mamma, "I told you something was wrong!"

Our own doctor got wind of the conversation, and called us back. "This is ridiculous. There's not one thing wrong except that an intern flipped her X rays." Like Mamma had said, the baby was fine.

Once everything had been sorted out, we took Jenny Rose home to Hidden Hills. The house was a ranch-style that overlooked the valley. There was a white fence all around it. When I came up the driveway, there stood my mother-in-law, Rose, my mother, Ruth, and my father, Leo. They were all cheering. When I saw my mother and father standing together, celebrating the birth of their second grandchild, I felt like life had come full circle.

Jon was twenty-one years old, and had never even held a baby before. When Frannie handed Jenny to him, Jon nearly froze. "I'm afraid to move!" he admitted. It was the beginning of a great bond between a brother and sister. To this day, those two are very close. Jenny Rose adores her brother and Jon adores his sister. They talk either by phone or e-mail almost daily. Jon loves to take Jenny to movies and arcades, loves to hang out with her and hear about her school, her friends. Jenny thinks Jon hung the moon. It's a joy for me to see, because I was determined not to fall into that trap I've seen so often in the entertainment field—

and everywhere—the "first kids" syndrome. Too often, men who remarry and have a child later in life, act like that's the beginning of the world for them, as if the first kids are secondary. It's probably just that they realize they have a second chance to make good as a parent. But their actions end up giving their older children second billing. All of your children should get top billing.

Chapter 30

Tar Beach to Ozark Mountain Boy

Just as Mamma had become spellbound with the desert back in 1975, I fell hopelessly in love with the Ozarks in 1991. I didn't know much about the entertainment complex at Branson, Missouri, when I was booked for a gig at the Roy Clark Theater. But from the minute I set foot on Ozarks ground in that fall of 1991, I knew I wanted to live there, to raise Jenny Rose in that beautiful place. The landscape around Branson was like a picture postcard. Everywhere you looked you saw a scene that drew you in. The only drawback I could see was that those Ozark Mountains had bugs right out of *Jurassic Park*. But bugs bedamned, by the time I finished the gig, I knew what I had to do.

Jenny Rose was just an infant, and I knew it would take some convincing to get Frannie in the mood to make a major move. I started my campaign with phone calls—"Frannie, you have *got* to see this place!" "Frannie, this would be the perfect place to raise a child!" "Frannie! You're gonna love it!" Then, just for good measure, I made a lengthy videotape of fall in the Ozarks.

I needn't have worried. Frannie fell in love with Branson before the videotape finished playing. It's a place that retains a small-town atmosphere yet serves up show business in a big way. You'll not find a more state-of-the-art place than theaters

like mine was, like Andy Williams's. You could hold the
Kennedy Awards in Andy's theater and I believe it would feel
appropriate. You could do the same with the Grand Palace. We
moved to Missouri in 1993.

Just as I'd been hesitant to buy a house when I first moved to
California to do the television show, I decided to take a condo
on the lake when we first moved to Branson. When we did buy,
it was a house on a hill, overlooking the town—modest, but sitting on four beautiful acres.

Frannie and I had talked it over at length, and she agreed with
my feelings about huge homes being divisive to a family. Back in
that ten-thousand-square-foot house on Bristol, in Brentwood,
you could have gone days without running into another person.
Jon's room location could have had another zip code from the
master bedroom. When I moved out of that house, I told myself
I'd never again have a house that separates you from your own
world. I wanted to be able to see every room in the house—to
look down the hall and be able to see the doors to my children's
rooms—to be able to call out to them from any room, and
they'd hear my voice. I just don't think that those large houses
are healthy for family life unless you are a family of about thirty
people.

Aside from the size, they are just a reason to hire more people
for upkeep, more reasons to try and keep up with the Joneses,
to find the right wallpaper, the right decorator to come in and
do it, the more reasons to waste time on things you don't need.
Things that have nothing to do with being a happy family.

My house now is certainly big enough—about 3,700 to 4,000
square feet. But it's a two-story house, and I can stand in the hall
and see Jenny's room, our bedroom, the kitchen, the dining
room entrance, the entryway. I can stand in the kitchen and call,
"Jenny!" and she'll stick her head out of her door and say,
"Yeah, Dad?"

I've loved living in that house. I've loved living in Branson.

• • •

Opening night at the Tony Orlando Yellow Ribbon Theater was a crapshoot. First, we were terrified that it wasn't going to be finished on time. They were rolling carpet almost up to the time the doors opened. So we'd been rehearsing our show, a two-and-a-half-hour Broadway-style revue with an intermission, at the College of the Ozarks. We worked around the clock, and I guess my system started to wear down, because two days before we opened I landed in the hospital with pneumonia. Everybody freaked except me. I had a feeling that with some antibiotics and a day's bed rest I'd be fine. It worked, and I hit the stage right on time.

I was freaked out, but not over the last minute carpet rolling or my own health. I was having butterflies in my stomach for my son Jon. That opening night was his first appearance as a comic. I knew he could do it, but that made no difference to my stomach. I wanted him to shine. And he did. He did only five minutes that night, but over the next year, he took the stage over three hundred times. For me, it not only meant pride for my son, but happiness that he was with me in Branson.

Jon picked a career that's even tougher than singing. He's a standup comic, and a damn good one. He's played casinos, comedy clubs and many other venues all over the country, to rave reviews I might add. As I write this, he's readying for a stint in Atlantic City, opening for the great Dionne Warwick. What a business! You'll remember that I got my first success as a publisher by pitching the theme from *Valley of the Dolls* to Dionne. Life is circular—although there's no connection to Jon's getting that gig and his being my son. I helped open a few doors over the years, but he's done the rest on his own. Most show business kids will tell you that one or two open doors is about all they can expect. After that, they're on their own, and in fact, they are often judged by higher standards. Jon's doing it, and I find that the pride of doing something well yourself is far surpassed by seeing your child do well.

Going to Branson in 1993 became another part of the "sixteen factor" in my life. I had my first record deal when I was sixteen, "Halfway to Paradise" went to number sixteen on the charts. The very first road trip I took, I stayed in room 1616 at the Pittsburgh Hilton. The record deal, the first hit, the first tour—all of that happened in 1961, which is two sixteens backed up to each other if you flip the number nine. Then, when you add 16 to 1961, you get 1977, when I had the low point. Add 16 to 1977, and you get 1993, when I made one of the most positive choices I've ever made, the move to Branson. The number sixteen had popped up all through my life in many other instances, so it makes me wonder what might happen in 2009, which is what you get if you add 16 to 1993.

I performed at the Yellow Ribbon Theater from 1993 to 1997. The way it usually works in Branson, is that someone else actually owns the theater, and they pay a salary to the performer. That's how my deal was set up. Most years I played up to four-hundred shows a year, and while it's a hard schedule, I came to love the city even more than when I first discovered it. One thing that worried me was the number of name acts that had left the town: Loretta Lynn, Johnny Cash, Willie Nelson, Ray Stevens. I believed in Branson as both an entertainment center, and a great hometown with values I appreciated. I hated to see it lose any luster.

In 1996, the representative of one of my old friends, Wayne Newton, approached me. He said that since Wayne was involved in a lawsuit with the theater that bore his name, maybe the two of us could work out a deal where Wayne played some dates at the Yellow Ribbon Theater. I did not want Branson to lose Wayne in addition to the other name acts then missing in action. Additionally, I was thrilled to work with him. We'd been friends for over forty years and I loved the man.

Wayne and I talked, and I told him to pick the dates he wanted to play. I figured that the theater could draw around six-

hundred people a night in walk-up traffic. He could rent the theater on those days and take home the gate. When he came in, I
offered to share my dressing room, because it was the only one
with a kitchen and living room. To put Wayne Newton in lesser
accommodations would have been disrespectful, as far as I was
concerned.

The shows went great and we had a ball—for one year.

In 1997, the Yellow Ribbon Theater owners filed for bank-
ruptcy, and another theater group approached me about a headlining spot. I asked the people to also include Wayne, with the
same deal we'd had at the Yellow Ribbon. Wayne accepted. But
for some reason, the warmth was gone. Problems started right
away. Wayne didn't want me to use the stairway from his set, he
sent little notes about problems instead of talking to me.

Finally, just before we were to sign the deal at the Talk of the
TOWN (standing for Tony Orlando/Wayne Newton), I called
him and asked him if there was a problem. We talked things
over, and went for it. But we never signed the papers, and things
never were the same.

Bottom line is this: Wayne didn't make as much money at the
theater as he'd anticipated. For one thing, the walk-up traffic
wasn't as strong as it had been at the Yellow Ribbon. He said and
did things that really hurt and disappointed me as I saw a forty-
year friendship go down the drain.

Ultimately there was a lawsuit which was settled out of court.

The situation with Wayne, just like the one with Barry
Manilow all those years ago, left me angry and sad. Friends are
important to me. Those are the only two times I've ever felt like
one of those friends has turned on me. Trust me, it's not a good
feeling. I've often wished that I could put Bobby Darin's old
advice to better use in my life. Mashed potato problems aren't
important enough to cry over. The problem is, I'm the kind of
guy who does.

In the past few years I've just concentrated on my road show, playing a lot of casino dates, as well as dates in Branson theaters, including the Osmonds' facility.

In 1998, just before my father died, he made a phone call that meant the world to me. He was at his home in Coral Gables, Florida, with his third wife, Abby, who was such a wonderful companion to him. He hadn't been sick, so I don't know what prompted him to call me that particular day. Frannie and I had taken Jenny Rose and a little friend of hers to Sea World. When he called our hotel room, Dad sounded in perfect health.

"Tony, I want to thank you for everything you have done for me," he said. "There is so much I would have missed if not for you. I got to meet so many people, to ride in limousines, to go to big events—seen places I never would have seen. I've met presidents because of you. I shared the pew with you when Pearl Bailey died."

I said, "Label, that is the sweetest thing—to hear you say that to me!"

"In case anything ever happens to me, it's important that you know how I feel, Tony."

He talked on and on. At last, he said, "Keep a light heart."

That night Frannie and I went to dinner. When we returned, Rose called and gave us the news. Father had suffered a massive heart attack and died.

I delivered a eulogy at his funeral, and I told the story about Leo hooking that magnificent marlin at Cabo San Lucas. I said, "It's time to cut the line." I never cried over my father's death. Not until this year, as I wrote about that last phone call. Then, the tears finally came.

In spite of, or maybe because of, the one-two punch of a lawsuit with an old friend and the loss of my father, looking to a new millennium seemed to open up a new chapter of creativity in my life. Part of what kick-started this new phase was a return to Broadway, orchestrated by yet another Brokaw, Norman's son David. I not only returned, to the Broadway stage in 1999, but the show marked a return to my early days, to the brilliant material offered up by the Brill Building. *Smokey Joe's Cafe* featured Lieber and Stoller songs, great material like "I, Who Have Nothing," made famous by the great Ben E. King. I'd come full circle.

The best thing about *Smokey Joe's Cafe* is that it has no book, no play, it is just a succession of songs. One singer after the next pays tribute to that legendary writing team, done in a skillful way, a Broadway revue–style show. The most incredible cast of singers I ever heard in my life surrounded me. I knew I couldn't go out there and crack a joke or do anything that would distract from singing those songs. I couldn't follow Sammy Davis's old advice: "They never listen to a moving target."

I think if you asked any of the performers who played that role—people like Lou Rawls, Pam Tillis, Rick Springfield—they'd tell you that the cast was formidable.

I had to deliver vocally. I couldn't be an entertainer. All I could do was go out there and be a singer. I believe that the birth of me as a singer happened there on the stage of *Smokey Joe's*. I always felt I was a good entertainer, but never had confidence in myself as a singer. But after you stand onstage with a cast like that show has, going toe-to-toe vocally, you change. For me, the change was complete when one of the cast said, "Hey, man, you fit like a glove."

That confidence shows up in my stage show now.

I also began to write and record songs as never before. I'd been looking back to my childhood, and the people who taught me values, ethics. The two who most stood out were Papito and Mamita. I wanted to do something that would pay tribute to them.

"Papito Plays the Trumpet" was inspired by a photograph of Papito playing trumpet at the Coconut Grove. There he was, the man who'd raised me, putting food on the table by working two jobs during the day, then going to the Coconut Grove to play music at night. With all the talk about immigrants, and what they do or don't do for America, I think of my grandfather. I think of how hard he worked, how much he loved this country. He first showed it by enlisting to fight for the U.S. Then, when he did come to New York, he gave this country, and his family, everything he possibly could. That is what built America—immigrants throughout history, working hard for their country and their families. That's the story of my Papito. But the back story is Papito, trumpet player.

Papito played in a Latin American band
He played so well that all the musicians called him the man
He worked so hard just to keep food on the stove
While playing first trumpet at the Coconut Grove
He plays his music with passion every night
He hits the high notes so high that they sailed out of sight
After each gig he packs up and goes home alone
Back to Mamita who's there to welcome him home
She loved him, Papito

I wrote a song called "Caribbean Jewel" about Mamita and her beloved Puerto Rico. When I sing it onstage, I dedicate it to Papito and Mamita's daughter, my mamma. It's a song celebrating a true island paradise. Mamita was proud of her native land, and equally proud that she was a descendant of the explorer, Ponce de Leon.

Mamita passed away in 1987, in New Jersey. This time, I did make it in time to see her alive. It was one of the things I'd most feared in my life—losing Mamita. But in that Joan of Arc spirit, she helped me through even in her final moments.

The day before she died, Mamita looked like she was getting better, she almost had a glow about her. I took her hand and said,

"You have fought so courageously." Mamita had a way of looking at you so that you felt like her eyes looked straight through to your soul. "If you were held up in an alley tomorrow, and some guy was getting ready to kill you, would you fight for your life?"

"Of course," I said.

"When you fight for your life, it pleases God very much," she went on. "It compliments His work."

I've thought about that many, many times since, and she is so right. It is telling God that what He created on earth is *worth* fighting for. Since that time, when I've visited terminally ill people, I've shared that piece of wisdom from Mamita. The last thing I said, as she slipped away, was "Good-bye, Joan of Arc."

As I continued to write and record, I wrote about that trip Mamma and I took on the El Capitan, where I believe my imagination first opened up. Ironically, Frannie and I took that same train years later, and it brought all those memories flooding back. It was fate, I suppose, that I ultimately shared what might have been the first really intense life experience—that train ride across the desert, with Frannie, with whom I have had the first truly beautiful, loving marriage bond. The woman who taught me what a real marriage partnership is all about.

I wanted to include "Harmonizing Nights," which is a look back at my doo-wop days. And as I continued to work on the project, I realized I was putting together an autobiographical album—maybe the album I'd always wanted to make, eclectic, with choice musical breaks, soulful and personal.

I've got the perfect band for it, too, a band that allows my recording and my live show to do it all—doo-wop, Ben E. King, seventies pop.

The story of the Lefty Brothers Band starts in the steel mill town of Sterling, Illinois, with a couple of brothers named Kerry and Tracy Cole. Kerry is a vocalist and keyboardist; Tracy is a vocalist and lead guitarist. Kerry was playing in a club in Springfield, Missouri, close to Branson, in 1981, when Tracy graduated high school and joined the band. In the early nineties, one of the guys then playing in my band was going over to Springfield to hear Kerry and Tracy on a regular basis. He asked Kerry to come hear our show. Kerry was less than enthusiastic. He had the idea that I'd be doing a succession of novelty tunes, some seventies pop thing that didn't hold much interest to him. But he came, anyway. And later told me he'd been shocked at the music. He sure hadn't expected doo-wop or blues alongside "Knock Three Times."

Kerry ended up singing backup with us, and when, a few years back, I put together a new band, he suggested the Lefty Brothers. This time it was me who went out to hear them. Well, they blew me away. I like to tell people that I listened to them and wondered what they *couldn't* play. There was this one old cowboy wearing a belt buckle as big as a toaster who was hollering for a country song—and not just any country song— something by Willie.

I though, "Oh, boy . . ."

Then Kerry started singing "Always on My Mind," and I thought the Red-Headed Stranger was backstage vocalizing. Kerry sang all around the beat, just like Willie.

The guys called themselves a bar band, but here's how I saw them: an incredibly diverse, all-around top back-up band. So now, my backup is the Lefty Brothers comprised of the Cole brothers, Pete Generous on drums, and Jim Shelton on bass. Of course, my brother David had been playing keyboards with me for quite a few years, and he's still with me. Having the two keyboardists offers me the opportunity to have one doing straight keys, while the other is on strings or organ. It fattens the sound considerably.

What I loved about hiring these guys, other than the obvious benefits to my show, was that they'd spent twenty years playing music, and had even been named the top club band in the Midwest—yet they hadn't been on any big tours. I loved introducing them to Atlantic City, Las Vegas, Reno, to events like the Jerry Lewis telethon. The guys will tell you that their biggest thrill was a Fourth of July celebration in Boise, Idaho, with fireworks, hot-air ballooning and 200,000 people in the audience. It was a pretty big thrill for me, as well.

The band has become like family to me, as all bands should to an entertainer.

Chapter 31

Paradise

My life was scripted by some of the best. In the beginning there was Mamita, Papito, Mamma, Leo, and, strangely enough, my stepfather, Louis. Even though we had such a rocky relationship, when he died, I learned more from him than I had throughout his life. For one thing, I learned that we have to look deeper into each other, to attempt to understand what motivates a person's actions. I'd love to have Louis sitting in a chair across from me now, to tell him how I appreciated his protecting Mamma even while he was dying with cancer.

Rhonda was my angel on earth who now resides in Heaven. I can see her clear-eyed, laughing, dancing, singing. She now has all that she was denied down here. But what she did have here was unconditional love. And unconditional love is what Rhonda gave me. Bless you, my little sister.

During our eighteen-year marriage, Elaine played a major life-changing role. And who knows, maybe I misread my first wife like I did my stepfather. Like all divorces, there's blame to go around, and I'll shoulder my share. Without that marriage, I wouldn't have Jon. That alone makes it good.

Jon is so many things to me: son, great friend, fellow sports nut, a comic who always makes me laugh.

And, of course, now I add Frannie and Jenny Rose to the list of people who write my life. Their chapters are among the best. If I learned anything from Mamita and Papito, it's that your family is what counts. If I have given mine even half as much as they've given me, then that would be considerable.

The only decision I ever made that has never had one downside, not even one tiny negative, was my decision to ask Frannie to marry me. Francine and I don't fight, we don't argue. Even if we have a momentary difference, it can be measured in seconds, then you can measure the time to expel it in hours. We talk about it, and usually laugh about it. Frannie stays upbeat, she's not someone who has mood swings. You never come home wondering what her mood is gonna be. It's gonna be positive. That's just the way she looks at the world.

Frannie combines a streetwise, East L.A. Italian background, with an almost childlike, happy attitude—all wrapped up in a very old soul. I will admit that it took me a few years in the marriage to see just how deep her mind is. It was her delight in life, her lightness, even aside from her physical beauty, that first attracted me. And because of that funny, childlike quality, her own family thought of her as a kid well into adulthood. I sometimes avoided talking business with her because of that very reason, which was stupid on my part because she has a first-rate mind. It was, in fact, a way of disrespecting her as a woman. Luckily, I soon saw the error of my thinking, and started asking her advice on every move I made. She's got tremendous instincts.

One of the most beautiful things about Frannie is the sound of her laughter. After eleven years of marriage, my greatest joy is listening to my wife and daughter laughing in the hour before Jenny goes to bed. They read and tell jokes and share secrets. It's a giddy hour. That's medicine for me. Maybe that sounds hokey. But that's okay.

Part of the beauty of the marriage is that we have the same

kind of families. Frannie's Greek and Italian family loves each other and they make no bones about it. There was also a disciplined household, and a value system that my family shared. Two of Frannie's brothers are Los Angeles police officers, and they are wonderful, compassionate people, too—the kind of officers that make you proud. I never met Frannie's father, due to my own screw up about the missed dinner, but everyone says he had an incredible sense of humor that lives on. I've heard every joke he ever told, several times, and I've laughed with each telling. That humor was passed on to Frannie, and now to my daughter.

Jenny is a gem. She's much like her mother, with a maturity beyond her years. Her role models, aside from Frannie, include those Olson twins, who are more into self-confidence building than in hawking belly-button decorations. She loves school, dancing, skating—laughing.

My mother-in-law, Rose is still living, and she's still just as sharp as ever. I gotta tell this one on her. When we were going through the mess with Wayne Newton, nobody was madder about it than eighty-three-year old Rose Amormino. The idea of a friend messing with her son-in-law insulted her Italian code of loyalty. One day when Frannie and Rose were driving Jenny and a friend to town, they passed the theater and saw the marquee announcing Wayne's show. Rose stuck her head out of the car window and put her hands to her face. Her middle fingers were extended downward, and the outer fingers straight ahead.

"What was she doing?" Jenny's friend asked.

Before Jenny could answer, Rose turned around and said, "That was an old Italian curse from an old Italian!"

The next day, Jenny's friend and her mother were driving along the same road, and the marquee read: "WAYNE NEWTON CANCELLED DUE TO ILLNESS."

Jenny's friend said, "Wow! I think Jenny's grandma is a witch!"

You can't help but love Rose Amormino. Talk about having the mother-in-law you dreamed of!

The other thing I love is Frannie's relationship with my son Jon. Like Rose is the ultimate mother-in-law, Frannie is the ultimate stepmother. I've never seen Frannie and Jon disagree, or be disagreeable. Frannie goes out of her way for Jon, and Jon goes out of the way for Frannie, while never disrespecting Elaine. In fact, Francine has built a bridge between Elaine and I. After all, no matter what happened to our marriage, Elaine and I will always share our son, Jon. And during times when Jon needed something, it was Frannie who was the connecting component.

When you consider that Frannie is the person who has paid the price of my divorce financially, her willingness to be the peacemaker is astonishing. As you get older in a youth-oriented business, and your career downsizes, you have to reach deeper into your pocket—into the whole family's pocket. In some second marriages, that becomes a very large issue, but Frannie will not allow it to be so in ours.

I do believe ours is a Cinderella story come true. I don't know if Frannie got the prince, but I sure got the princess.

So in the end, what is left in my life is my family, Frannie, Jon, Jenny. There is no tar on this beach. My career may always be halfway to paradise, but in my personal life, I'm already there.

... to be continued

Index

810 94
Music Bio